ỹ good success

ing

King James Runs to Shore in Confusion for
being afraid of the English Fleet

King William Doth Grant his Gracious Pardon
to Prendergras for the first discovery of ỹ Plott

Brigadeer Rookwood, Major Lowick and
Captain Cranborn these were Tryd at ỹ Kings Bench

Charnock, King, and Keys, were ỹ First, thô
Sir William Perkins, and Sir John Frend, &
Then Rookwood, Lowick, Cranburn died at Tyburn

The Triumphs of Providence

It is not to be doubted but there ever have been, and will be, in the World, so long as it is stocked with the Race of Human Kind, not only Individuals, but Combinations of many Men, as also Parties of large Extent and Denominations, perpetually intent upon Projects, which may be called Plots, to advance their real or supposed peculiar Interests. And it is found that, when the Principle, by which they move, is false, then their method of proceeding will be base and treacherous.

ROGER NORTH. *Examen*

The Triumphs of Providence

THE ASSASSINATION PLOT, 1696

JANE GARRETT

CAMBRIDGE UNIVERSITY PRESS

CAMBRIDGE

LONDON   NEW YORK   NEW ROCHELLE

MELBOURNE   SYDNEY

Published by the Press Syndicate of the University of Cambridge
The Pitt Building, Trumpington Street, Cambridge CB2 1RP
32 East 57th Street, New York, NY 10022, USA
296 Beaconsfield Parade, Middle Park, Melbourne 3206, Australia

© Cambridge University Press 1980

First published 1980

Text set in 10/12 pt Linotron 202 Sabon, printed and bound
in Great Britain at The Pitman Press, Bath

British Library Cataloguing in Publication Data
Garrett, Jane
The triumphs of providence.
1. William III, *King of England*
2. Jacobites
I. Title
364.1'524'0924   DA461.5   80–49950
ISBN 0 521 23346 1

Contents

Contents

Plates

between pages 84 and 85

Endpapers; 'The Triumphs of Providence over Hell, France & Rome, In the Defeating and Discovering of the late Hellish and Barbarous

PLOTT, for Assassinating his Royall Majesty KING WILLIAM III', taken
from a print of 1696 (reproduced by permission of the British
Museum)

The top centre panel shows an imaginary papal procession for the
success of the plot. The pope is borne on men's shoulders, with the
devil whispering in his ear. The centre panel, surmounted by LIMP –
Louis, Iacobus [James], Mary and the Prince of Wales – shows Louis
XIV vomiting up the spoils of war, with a physician in attendance. In
the background are James, his family and advisers. Inset above an ape
administers a clyster. At the sides are a four-headed Jesuit and a
triple-headed courtier. The lower centre panel depicts the scene of the
intended murder. The would-be assassins wait for their victim, while
William in his coach is protected by the 'Eye of Providence [which]
sees All'. The side panels show real and imaginary scenes of the
intended invasion and the conspirators' progress towards Tyburn.

Acknowledgements

It is more than five years since I embarked, as an untried beginner, on this attempt to unravel the tangled web of an early Jacobite conspiracy. If I have succeeded in disentangling at least the main threads, it is very largely due to the help given me by so many people without whose knowledge, interest and encouragement this book could never have been written. I wish there were space to thank them all by name. There are however some to whom a personal acknowledgement, albeit an inadequate one, must be made.

My first thanks are to Robert Latham for his wise advice, constructive criticism and patient reading of the typescript in its early stages. Next is Paul Hopkins to whose unstinting help with sources and material I owe more than I can say. Grant Longman supplied me with much information about Jacobitism in Hertfordshire, and Mrs K. Judges was most helpful on the topography of Richmond and Turnham Green. Ronald Blythe and Brian Lee have given me a great deal of practical advice on the making of a book. And for their interest and encouragement at the very start of this venture I am grateful to Lionel Munby and the tutors of the University of Cambridge Board of Extra-Mural Studies. They set me going.

I would like to thank the Librarian and staff of Cambridge University Library, of Duke Humphrey's Library at Oxford and of Nottingham University Library for allowing me access to printed and manuscript sources. Also the staff of the Public Record Office, and of the County Record Offices of London, Warwickshire, Hertfordshire and Berkshire. Acknowledgements to all those who have helped with the illustrations are given elsewhere, but I would like to say a collective thank you to them here, and to the several persons who took so much trouble to help me find appropriate pictures.

I am greatly indebted to William Davies and his colleagues at the Cambridge University Press for their helpfulness and for their amendments and suggestions, which have so much improved this book. Last and best thanks are for my husband, who has been an ever-present help in more ways than can be enumerated here. The least I can do now is to dedicate the book to him.

J. G.

Cambridge
1980

Note on spelling and dates

No spelling has been modernised. Surnames, except when they have been mis-spelt in quotations, are spelt as signed by the persons themselves. An exception is Sir John Friend, who was not very literate and alternated between 'Friend' and 'Freind'. In his case I have used the more usual 'Friend'.

Dates in the text are in the old style, that is, ten days behind the modern calendar; I have however taken the year as beginning on 1 January and not 25 March as was the practice in the seventeenth century.

PART 1

The fifth column

1
The genesis of Jacobitism

THE LAST QUARTER of the seventeenth century could well be described as the Age of Plots. Conspiracies punctuate the history of the period with almost monotonous regularity, creating at times an atmosphere of tension and unease that occasionally rose to fever pitch. Nearly all these plots either were or were alleged to be directed against the life of the reigning monarch, and none came near success. The conspirators, however, seem never to have been discouraged by repeated failure, nor by the reflection that the previous record for king-killers had been a poor one; if one excepts the judicial murder of Charles I, no reigning king is actually known to have been murdered since William Rufus in A.D. 1100. And even that murder has never been fully proven, for to this day it is uncertain whether the arrow that killed him was shot by accident or design. Of the long line of Rufus's successors, none was so assiduously or so ineffectually plotted against as William III. For most of his twelve years' reign there can hardly have been a moment when the adherents of the exiled James II were not discussing plans for the removal of the foreign usurper and the restoration of their 'rightful King'. The Assassination Plot of 1696 was the last and most serious of a series of such conspiracies; its object was to murder William and, with the help of the French, to restore James to the throne from which he had been ousted in 1688. Like its predecessors the plot failed, and for two reasons. Firstly, there were too many accomplices, with the inevitable result that some of them betrayed their fellows. But the second and more important reason for its failure was that James's supporters the Jacobites were a minority party. The majority of Englishmen, though they might grumble at Dutch William, preferred his rule to that of a papist king who, they were convinced, had scant respect for their hard-won civil and religious rights. They did not want James back.

Viewed from this distance in time, the Jacobite cause seems doomed to failure, but it cannot have seemed so to James's devoted adherents. With unquenchable optimism they risked life and fortune in the hope of re-establishing a regime that to most Englishmen had become as unpopular as it was out-dated. 'King James is a 'coming', the Jacobites repeatedly assured each other; but, unhappily for them, King James never got nearer home than Calais, and the end result of each attempt to bring him back was a fresh crop of executions at Tyburn. Nine of his followers died there in 1696 all, to the very last, declaring their devotion to the cause of their 'rightful king'. What made so many risk so much for what, with hindsight, seems a hopeless cause? It was in an attempt to find an answer to this question by tracing the history of the plot and of the lives of those who took part in it that this account came to be written. And because one part of the answer must lie in the circumstances that shaped the lives and coloured the outlook of the Jacobite conspirators, a brief outline of the events leading up to the Revolution of 1688 and the rise of the Jacobite party needs to be given here.

The effect of early impressions upon a person's later behaviour is important and should not be overlooked. Most of those involved in the earliest Jacobite plots, including that of 1696, were boys or very young men at the time of the Restoration in 1660. Most too came from families that had been royalist during the civil wars and who had in consequence suffered some eclipse of fortune during the interregnum. Thus they grew up in an atmosphere of deprivation and hostility to Cromwell's rule, and so the impact of the Restoration upon the minds of these young persons must have been a profound one. Gone, suddenly, were the austerities, the glooms and factions of the parliamentary regime and no one, not even a young child, could have failed to be impressed by the general rejoicing, the clamour of bells, the bonfires and the colourful processions that greeted Charles II on his return to his kingdom. Nor could the most unobservant be unaware of the changes that followed: the reappearance of forbidden sports and pastimes; the bright clothes of the nobility and gentry; the anglican liturgy that replaced the bleak service in church on Sundays. Thus for those youths nurtured in the doctrine of divine right the Restoration must have left an impression of happiness and freedom that would remain with them all their lives.

All too soon the euphoric atmosphere of the Restoration began to dissipate and 'Good King Charles' must have wished for more golden days, for economic difficulties were to beset him for most of his reign. The reluctance of parliament to grant him adequate supplies drove him to seek surreptitious subsidies from Louis XIV. They were small in relation to the total royal revenue but they were later to loom large in terms of their political significance, for the growing power of France was already threatening the peace of Europe, and to protestant England it represented a threat of domination by a power both catholic and absolute. Hence Charles's close association with the French king was regarded with disquiet by his government; had it been known at the time that Louis, in return for a handsome subsidy, had stipulated that Charles declare himself a catholic, 'as soon as might be convenient', that disquiet might have escalated into rebellion. But Charles, whatever his private leanings towards Rome, knew well enough that such a step could cost him this throne; the convenient time for his conversion did not come until he was on his death-bed and soon to be beyond the reach of outcry from his protestant subjects.

The bitter dissensions that divided protestant and catholic were already old by the late seventeenth century, but still the very word 'papist' could spark off ancient terrors and hysterias in the mind of a protestant Englishman. The fear and suspicion with which catholics were regarded was out of all proportion both to their numbers and to their political influence. Recent estimates have put them between 4.0 and 1.9 per cent of the total population of England,[1] and moreover since the reign of Elizabeth they had suffered under severe penal laws designed to render them politically harmless. Their small numbers and lack of political and religious freedom were, however, partly offset by the fact that they were most numerous among the landed gentry.

It was the hostility aroused by the catholic tendencies of the Stuart family that ultimately caused the downfall of the dynasty. Charles himself was strongly (and rightly) suspected of catholic leanings while his Queen, Catherine of Braganza, was a devout catholic. She had no children and so Charles's brother James Duke of York was heir presumptive to the throne, and after him his eldest daughter Mary. Mary and her sister Anne were the only surviving children of James's first wife Ann Hyde, who was herself a catholic convert; great care, however, was taken to see that the two princesses were brought up in the protestant faith. Ann Hyde died of cancer in 1671 and two years later James married again. His bride was the fifteen-year-old Mary Beatrice of Modena, a devout and beautiful girl whose heart had been set upon becoming a nun. The marriage was very unpopular as it had been hoped that a protestant bride would be chosen and, since Mary Beatrice was young and healthy, there was every likelihood that she would produce an heir. Its unpopularity, and that of James, was greatly increased by his public announcement in the same year that he had joined the Church of Rome. As this would inevitably mean that any children of the marriage would be reared in their parents' faith, the country was now faced with the unpalatable prospect of a continuing catholic dynasty. James's marriage and conversion caused a great outburst of anti-catholic demonstrations by the London mob. This was the era of the elaborate and often horrific pope-burning processions that were held on such occasions for popular rejoicing as the fifth of November. The climax of these pageants was the burning of a huge effigy of the pope, its belly often filled with live cats, 'who squawled most hideously as they felt the fire: the common people saying all the while that it was the language of the Pope and the Devil in a dialogue betwixt them'.[2]

Anti-catholic feeling culminated in 1678 with the discovery of the so-called Popish Plot, the alleged object of which was to assassinate Charles and place James on the throne. The plot set off a wave of mass hysteria that has few parallels in history, and in the slaughter that followed at least forty people were condemned to death on the flimsiest of evidence. In almost every case the only crime of these unfortunates was to be catholic. The furore over the Popish Plot lasted for three years and during it parliament, with a powerful Whig majority, brought in two Exclusion Bills that were designed to ensure a protestant succession by excluding catholic James. Charles, supported by a minority of loyalists, resisted both Bills with every means in his power; they were eventually defeated, and the succession was saved, but by the narrowest of margins. The battle over the exclusion divided the country into two camps: the Whigs, who contended that it was justifiable to set aside a ruler if he could not or would not support the religion and liberties of his subjects, and the Tories, who held that James's right of succession was divinely ordained and therefore inalienable. In a sense, the Jacobite party could be said to have its origins in the exclusion crisis, for it was from among the Tory supporters of James that the Jacobites were recruited after the Revolution. The Tory party indeed were later to suffer heavily because of their association in the popular mind with Jacobitism; but although almost all Jacobites were by origin Tories, this imputation was unjustified, for the Tory party as a whole remained loyal to the Revolution settlement.

In 1681 after the exposure of the principal informer, Titus Oates, for the lying perjuror that he was, the alarms of the Popish Plot died away, while the failure of the Whigs to alter the succession resulted in a swing of power to the Tories, who were to remain the dominant party for some time. Disquiet over the succession was also somewhat allayed by the failure of James's wife, Mary Beatrice, to produce an heir. After eight years of marriage she had had several miscarriages and still-births, but only one living child, a daughter who died at the age of three. The possibility that protestant Princess Mary would eventually inherit the throne began to seem less remote, and this comfortable prospect did much to reconcile the English to the idea of catholic James succeeding his brother. Tory dominance was enhanced in June 1683 by the discovery of the Rye House Plot, allegedly a conspiracy to murder Charles and James and place the Duke of Monmouth, Charles's eldest illegitimate son, on the throne. As in the Popish Plot, much of the evidence for this conspiracy was fabricated, and the king and the duke seem never to have been in any real danger. Its discovery, however, resulted in an upsurge of loyalty to the ruling house that effectively drowned the suspicions and animosities of the preceding few years. Then too this was a time of relative peace at home and abroad, which brought with it lighter taxation and a more prosperous foreign trade. It was the golden evening of Good King Charles's hitherto less-than-golden day, and for the remaining eighteen months of his reign an atmosphere of peace and amity prevailed between Charles and his subjects. He was acclaimed as 'the Father of his people', a title which caused him some amusement for, as he said, he had in fact fathered a good many of them. He died on 6 February 1685 and James was duly proclaimed king.

The popularity that had surrounded the throne during the last years of his brother's life was still at its height, and James succeeded in an atmosphere of enthusiastic loyalty. His first and only parliament, almost exclusively Tory, voted him an income considerably larger than any that Charles had enjoyed, and in return he graciously promised to support his subjects' liberties and to protect the Church of England. His position was further strengthened by the swift crushing of the Monmouth rebellion later that year. The defeat of a pretender who was both illegitimate and a self-styled champion of the protestant faith must have convinced James that his people acknowledged his own inalienable right to the throne, and must also have given him the impression that they were becoming less rabidly opposed to his religion.

James was an exceedingly obstinate man who clung to his faith with all the ardour of a convert. He was not, at any rate in his earlier days, as stupid as his later detractors have made out, and was far from being the blood-boltered and tyrannical idiot depicted by Macaulay. He was solemn, hard-working and abstemious in all but his addiction to women. His mistresses, however, were fewer and less glamorous than those of his brother, who once said that they were all so ugly that he thought the Jesuits must have imposed them on James as a penance. James seldom made a joke; like most bigots, he lacked a sense of humour and he also lacked the affability that had endeared Charles to his people; he tended to stand on his dignity. He was by nature authoritarian; he was totally incapable of seeing any point of view but his own; and he had no conception of the depth and vigour of the opposition that his championship of the catholic cause aroused in the majority of his subjects. It was his lack of imagination as much as his fervent attachment to his religion that was to cost him his throne.

It was not long before James began to revive the doubts and fears that had been hushed at his accession. Very early in his reign it became apparent that he was working towards complete religious and political freedom for his co-religionists and, it began to be feared, for the ultimate re-conversion of England. Catholic chapels, schools and seminaries began to appear in London and elsewhere; James himself was ostentatious in the practice of his religion. He also made full use of his royal prerogative to appoint catholics to high office and to infiltrate catholic officers into the army and the navy. He packed the legal profession with as many catholics and their sympathisers as possible. Predictably, he rapidly lost the popularity that he had enjoyed at his accession. The Tory parliament that had voted him such generous subsidies was soon antagonised, and James silenced its protests by proroguing it for the rest of his short reign. He lost the support of the Church of England when he set up the Ecclesiastical Commission, which was in effect an instrument for enforcing royal supremacy over the Church, and which was presided over by that ungodly man Judge Jeffreys. In May 1688, both Church and people were further antagonised by the imprisonment in the Tower of seven bishops for protesting against James's Declaration of Indulgence, designed to establish freedom of worship for both catholics and dissenters; the Declaration was received with almost universal hostility, for it was seen as a direct threat to the supremacy of the Church in matters spiritual. The bishops were tried for seditious libel in June and were acquitted amidst tumultuous popular rejoicing. The Church had successfully defied the king, and the people saw this, rightly, as a victory against royal absolutism.

In the same month, to the joy of all catholics and the consternation of all protestants, Queen Mary Beatrice gave birth to a healthy son. While James and his party rejoiced at the arrival of a catholic heir, the opposition attempted to nullify their hopes by putting about a story that the baby had been smuggled into the palace in a warming-pan. There was no real evidence to support this unlikely tale, but for obvious reasons it was widely believed at the time; the queen's previous obstetric history did in fact lend it some plausibility, but she later proved its falsehood by giving birth to a daughter, the Princess Louise Marie on 28 June 1692. This child, incidentally, grew to be a great comfort to both her parents, who used to call her 'La Consolatrice'.

With the birth of a Prince of Wales the growing revolt against James came to a head. Something had to be done if the religious and civil liberties of Englishmen were to be protected from the arbitrary rule of a succession of catholic kings. In July 1688 seven leading Englishmen wrote secretly to Prince William of Orange, inviting him to come to England to rid the country of 'popery and tyranny'. He accepted the invitation, but not before he had made sure it was endorsed by a majority of the most powerful and responsible men in the country. William of Orange landed at Torbay on 5 November. Most of the aristocracy, including the already powerful Marlborough and Princess Anne, promptly deserted James and flocked to join the 'protestant liberator'. By Christmas William was in effective control of the kingdom and James, who had sent his wife and baby son before him, had fled to France. Thus, almost overnight and with scarcely a drop of blood shed, the Glorious Revolution had become an accomplished fact.

James, with his family and a small entourage of loyalists, took refuge with his cousin Louis XIV. The personal ties between the two kings originated during James's years of exile at the French Court and had always been close; Louis from the outset treated the fugitives with great kindness and generosity, welcoming them with every mark of respect and at once establishing them in the palace of Saint-Germain-en-Laye, his own birthplace; he also granted James a handsome pension and subsidised the little Court that had followed him into exile. This generosity was not entirely disinterested for, quite apart from their personal ties, Louis had strong political motives for taking James under his protection: James represented a powerful weapon with which to harass the arch-enemy William of Orange, and he did not fail to make use of him as and when an opportunity arose. It goes without saying that Louis hoped to see James restored, but he was too wise a man and too able a strategist to back a forlorn hope; hence his policy was to give financial amd military support to the Jacobites whenever there seemed to be some chance of restoration. As soon as these hopes faded Louis would cut his losses and withdraw. Win or lose, this paid off for the French, for although James never regained his throne, the threat of a French expedition to England was always sufficient to divert large English forces from the war on the continent. So long, then, as the Stuart Court remained at Saint-Germain under French protection it posed a threat to the peace of England.

William of Orange was the son of James's eldest sister Mary and thus was James's nephew. He was also his son-in-law, having married James's eldest daughter the Princess Mary in 1677. Had it not been for the birth of the Prince of Wales, there was a strong likelihood that William, through his wife, would eventually have become the ruler of England. But whatever his private ambitions may have been, William had not in the first place been invited to the country to assume the crown. James's precipitate flight, which incidentally had probably been engineered by William, took the country by surprise and left it without a king; and since the king was head of the government, there was an imminent threat of administrative chaos. William himself knew exactly what he wanted: to become the effective ruler of England so that he could use her power and resources to help him defeat his life-long enemies, the French. But the nation that he had 'liberated' was deeply divided on the question of how, and by whom, the throne left vacant by James should be filled. As soon as James was out of the country William summoned a Convention – in effect a parliament without royal sanction – to discuss and settle this issue. William, in his own way, had almost as authoritarian a concept of kingship as had his uncle James, the difference being that William used his powers more intelligently and for less unpopular ends. He soon made it clear to the Convention that he was not prepared to be a cipher in the government of England, nor would he consent, as he put it, 'to be his wife's gentleman usher'. If the English would not accept him as ruler in fact and name, he would return to Holland forthwith and wash his hands of the whole affair. Stimulated perhaps by this threat, the Convention finally arrived at an acceptable solution: James was declared to have abdicated. William and Mary were to be offered the crown jointly, with the supreme power resting firmly in William's hands. With the offer of the throne, parliament presented the Bill of Rights. The Bill did not seek to destroy the regal power, but merely to ensure that no monarch in the future could misuse it by illegal infringement of the 'ancient rights and liberties of the subject'. Although it is nowhere stated that the Bill of Rights was a contract between ruler and ruled, this in effect is what it amounted to. William, on behalf of his wife and himself, accepted the contract along with the crown.

William and Mary were crowned on 11 April 1689. Since no one could claim that they had inherited the crown by divine right, the oath of allegiance had to be re-phrased. James and his predecessors were sovereigns *de jure,* but for the new rulers the phrase *de facto* was substituted. The oath was a test of loyalty to the new regime, and no one who refused to sign it could hold public office. It was subscribed by all the Whigs and most of the Tories, but many of the latter signed it with private reservations; as they saw it, a ruler *de facto* need only be obeyed for as long as he could hold the throne he had usurped and no further allegiance would be due to him if he were replaced by James or his son. A number of more die-hard Tories refused the oath and lost their employment in consequence. Most of the clergy took the oath to the new sovereigns, but five of the bishops, headed by Sancroft, Archbishop of Canterbury, refused to do so; they were followed by about five hundred of the lesser clergy and an unknown number of sympathisers. The Church, these non-jurors maintained, had solemnly ratified King James's divine right to the throne at his coronation; to deny this divine right by owning allegiance to his *de facto* supplanter would be to deny the authority of the Church, which, under God, had conferred it. In defence of that authority these same bishops had successfully defied James in 1688. They stood firm for it now, although it meant the loss of their sees and their livelihoods. A wholesale ejection of the non-juring clergy was the inevitable result of their non-compliance; from henceforth they had to live as best they could on the charity of sympathisers, and ministering to small schismatic congregations where King James could be prayed for in secret. Naturally these gatherings were regarded as nests of sedition, and sporadic attempts were made to suppress them. Most of the non-jurors were in fact harmless and pious folk, but there was a militant minority among them who became active in King James's cause.

It is scarcely surprising that loyalty to the new sovereigns was far from universal. Events had moved so fast that there had been little time to adjust to the new state of affairs and, moreover, while the adherents of William and Mary hailed the Glorious Revolution as the dawn of a new era of civil and religious liberty, there were many who saw it otherwise – as the substitution of a native and rightful king for a foreign tyrant. And the very ease and suddenness with which the wheel of fortune had revolved led men to think that it might just as easily turn again; if that happened a returning James would undoubtedly deal harshly with those who had helped to send him into exile. There was thus good reason for insuring against this possibility by secretly keeping open some lines of communication with the Court at Saint-Germain; even some of William's most enthusiastic supporters were not above this, although they were careful not to commit themselves. Among others, Lord Halifax, 'The Trimmer', who was generally supposed to have trimmed his sails to the wind from Holland, was

11

hedging his bets by 1689 and made no secret of this to his friend Sir John Reresby when he said to him, 'Come, Sir John, we have wives and children. We must consider them and not venture too far.'[3]

There was a good deal of disenchantment with William at this time, for which he himself was partly responsible. William was a small sickly man with chronic asthma who sadly lacked the Stuart charm and glamour. He was by nature seclusive, and what Burnet calls his 'disgustingly cold manner' repelled even his well-wishers, as did his poor command of English and his general 'foreign-ness'. It was also thought, and not without reason, that he had accepted the crown only as a means of furthering his wars with the French, and that he had little real interest in or love for his new kingdom. Much resentment was also caused by the favours that he heaped upon the Dutch friends and advisers who had accompanied him to England. William did not really trust the English; after all, they had beheaded one king and exiled another within less than half a century. Small wonder then that he relied heavily on the Dutchmen whom he knew and trusted and with whom he had worked for many years. He gave further offence by appointing a number of Tories to high office in pursuance of his policy of keeping a balance of power between the two parties. Disaffection, then, was by no means confined to believers in the sacredness of divine right and in the consequent atmosphere of doubt and distrust it is not surprising that plans for the restoration of James began to proliferate soon after that unlucky monarch had set foot in France.

2
King James's men

W ILLIAM AND MARY could congratulate themselves on the blood-
less nature of the Revolution in England. But William and Mary, when
they became rulers of England, also claimed the crowns of Scotland
and Ireland. In neither of these countries was the Revolution settlement to be achieved without bitter fighting. In Scotland the Lowland
presbyterians declared for the new monarchs, and they were proclaimed King and Queen of Scotland at Edinburgh in March 1689. One
of the principal effects of the Scottish settlement was to dispossess the
unpopular episcopalian church and to restore presbyterian supremacy.
The dispossessed bishops and clergy not unnaturally became non-
jurors, and many were active workers for King James. The Highland
clans had refused to acknowledge the usurpers and were in full revolt
by the spring of 1689, but in July they were decisively defeated at
Dunkeld. The chieftains accepted the situation with William's offer of
indemnity, although most remained loyal at heart to James. It was an
enduring loyalty; for so long as there was a viable Stuart cause the
Highlands were a refuge for its partisans and a source of danger to the
established regime in the south.

The Irish rebellion was a much more prolonged and hard-fought
affair than the flare-up in Scotland. Both James and Louis saw Ireland
as a stepping-stone to England, and for Louis the campaign was a
means of diverting his opponents' forces from the war already in
progress on the continent. In 1688 Louis despatched an army to the
middle Rhine against the federation of small states known as the
League of Augsberg, formed to combat the encroachment of the
French upon the Spanish Netherlands and adjacent territories. In
December 1688 Louis declared war on the Dutch and threatened to
invade the United Provinces, and in May 1689 William, with the
sanction of both Houses of Parliament, formally declared war on
France. The War of the League of Augsberg, which was to last for
eight years, was under way. To the oppressed catholic Irish this
seemed a heaven-sent opportunity to rid themselves of their English

13

overlords, and in the spring of 1689 the Irish rose against their protestant landlords, dispossessed them of their estates, set up a parliament in Dublin and sent pressing messages to James to come and rule over them. Louis sent James to Ireland with a strong French force and a hastily mustered contingent of the Jacobite soldiers who had followed their master into exile. The campaign at first went well for the rebels, but James and his army were decisively defeated at the Battle of the Boyne on 1 July 1690. He fled with his entourage from the battlefield and immediately took ship for France.

Peace in Ireland was not fully restored until October 1691. James's beaten army was disbanded; the surviving French, English and Irish soldiers were treated with remarkable leniency by their conquerors. Those who wished were allowed to return to France and the great majority, about 11,000 men, did so. A further 1000 took advantage of the amnesty offered them and went over to King William. About 2000 Irish were allowed to return to their homes.[1] Thus ended James's first and most serious bid to regain his kingdom. The English government may well have regretted their gentlemanly behaviour towards the soldiers who had fought for him in Ireland; most of those who returned to France were formed into James's Irish Regiment, subsidised by French money and in effect part of the French army.

James's personal guard at Saint-Germain was largely composed of refugee catholic officers and men who had fought for him in Ireland. Many were to be employed as spies and agents, travelling secretly between France and England, fomenting sedition and gathering recruits for a rebel army. These men incurred much danger and hardship in the course of their missions, for captured Jacobite agents were liable to long imprisonment, if not hanging. However, it was not very difficult to escape the vigilance of the authorities as the smuggling fraternity offered safe if expensive sea passages and, once landed, King James's men could always find shelter among their friends and sympathisers. How easily and often the agents came and went is shown by a report on a Mr Marshall, captured on the coast of Kent in 1692, and who had been 'sent with orders from King James foure times in less than a yeare into Essex, Suffolk, Norfolk, Huntingdonshire and Cambridgeshire'.[2] How many more agents, more fortunate than Marshall, there were in England at any one time it is not possible to say, but it was in great measure due to them that the spirit of rebellion was kept alive in the years from 1689 to 1696.

The failure of the Irish campaign had put an end to hopes of bringing back James by way of Ireland, but this did not deter a number of quite highly placed persons in London from making in December

1690 an ill-conceived and abortive plan for his return. Inevitably, the Preston Plot was discovered and its instigator, Lord Preston, together with the Queen's half-brother, Lord Clarendon, was sent to the Tower. The non-juring Bishop of Ely, who had seriously compromised himself and his fellow non-jurors, had to fly the country. Only a comparatively obscure young man called Ashton, who had been caught carrying the lords' correspondence with James, was executed for his part in the affair. The chief result of these machinations was to put the government more on the alert; there were more frequent raids on the non-jurors' meeting-places and the taverns where James's lay supporters were known to foregather. Narcissus Luttrell, whose *Brief Relation of State Affairs* provides an invaluable record of day-to-day events of the time, records several such incidents in the weeks immediately following the discovery of the plot. There were some arrests after these raids, but no very severe action was taken against the offenders most of whom in fact were usually released for want of evidence. Except at times of national crisis, neither the government nor the public seems to have regarded the Jacobite gatherings with great alarm, treating them rather as noisy nuisances than as a real threat to the peace of the realm. Probably most Englishmen, and especially the ordinary working men, did not greatly care whether their rulers were *de facto* or *de jure*. A protestant king and queen, a stable government and peace at home were advantages far out-weighing a sentimental attachment to a dynasty that had not on the whole proved particularly trustworthy.

The minority that adhered to James justified their attempts to oust the usurpers on religious and political grounds, but underlying these motives was a strong feeling of personal loyalty to their 'rightful King'. Stuart kings were not remote figures to their subjects. Charles II was noted (and sometimes criticised) for being affable and accessible to all sorts and conditions of men. And although James lacked his brother's easy manners and was more careful of his kingly dignity, he too lived and moved among his people as a familiar figure. Stuart kings, then, were 'familiar' in an older and more literal sense: they were part of the 'family' as the word was understood in those days. And just as the head of a household, however extensive, was regarded in a paternalis-tic light by all its members so too the monarch, 'the Father of his people', was accorded a similar loyalty and obedience.

James II, whatever his shortcomings as a ruler, could inspire loyalty and affection not only in his immediate entourage but also in his more humble followers who had little personal contact with him. The sporadic outbursts of enthusiasm with which his supporters were wont to celebrate the royal birthdays were emotional demonstrations and since they usually ended in uproar and arrests, did no good to their cause. Nevertheless, the more unthinking would mark such occasions with too much drinking of loyal toasts, and if possible with a bonfire in the street outside the tavern. There was affection as well as loyalty in these demonstrations, and it is particularly noticeable among the rank and file of James's ex-soldiers. Many of them had drifted back to London, where they hung about the Jacobite taverns and met agents and old comrades-in-arms from Saint-Germain. The first question asked of the newcomers would be, 'how doth the King and Queen and the Prince of Wales?' After her birth in 1692 the baby Princess would be solicitously enquired after as well. It is clear that these rough soldiers felt a personal concern for the welfare of their 'true king and master' and his family. Although the Jacobite party was riddled with unscrupulous, ambitious and venal men, the best and most disinterested of them were motivated by simple devotion to James and his cause.

As well as being a minority party, the Jacobites suffered from the disadvantage of being divided almost from the first by difference of opinion as to the terms of a restoration. Those who were for an unconditional return of James came to be called the Non-Compounders. As their name implies, they held that to impose conditions on a king was tantamount to a denial of the doctrine of divine right and royal infallibility upon which their political faith was based: the king could do no wrong and must be trusted to rule in the best interests of his people. The chief spokesman of the Non-Compounders was Lord Melfort, a Scottish peer who had turned catholic in 1688 for political reasons. He had a great and unfortunate influence over James, whose authoritarianism he encouraged to the great detriment of his cause. The Court at Saint-Germain was almost exclusively catholic and non-compounding; in England it was the more aggressive among the protestants, including many of the non-jurors, who were Non-Compounders and who were most active in conspiring against King William and his government.

The party called Compounders comprised the more moderate and predominantly protestant Jacobites and formed the great majority of James's supporters in England. They were for a restoration conditional on a firm guarantee that James would respect the religious and civil rights of his subjects, and that he would agree to certain limitations of the royal prerogative. Only under these conditions, the Compounders argued, would a restoration of James be acceptable to the English. Their protestant leader was Lord Middleton, one of the wisest and most distinguished of the moderates. Middleton remained in England for some time after the Revolution, acting as a rallying-point for the compounding party, but in 1693 he joined the Court at Saint-Germain, eventually replacing Melfort as Secretary of State. Middleton directed his energies towards counteracting the influence of Melfort and the Non-Compounders who surrounded James, and to persuading his king that the only hope of restoration lay in agreeing to the limitations of royal power proposed by the Compounders. In this, although labouring under the disadvantage of being almost the only protestant in an almost exclusively catholic court, he was partly successful. It was thanks to Middleton that the Declarations issued in the king's name became far more conciliatory in tone, but by that time James's credit was already too much damaged for Middleton's efforts to have any real effect on the course of events.

In the late winter of 1691–2 William was planning to divert the French forces from Flanders by mounting an invasion of Normandy and the Channel ports. Simultaneously, King Louis was making preparations for an armed expedition to England with the object of restoring James to the throne. The reports of widespread disaffection that for some time had been pouring into Saint-Germain had led Louis and his advisers to believe that James had only to land in England for there to be a mass desertion from William – the Revolution of 1688 was in fact to be repeated, but in reverse. These hopes were much encouraged by the reports of Jacobite agents sent secretly to England to recruit and organise support for a rising that was timed to coincide with the landing of James and a French army. Prominent among these agents was Colonel John Parker, one of the most active and daring of the many Jacobite agitators who were flitting busily between England and France, carrying coded letters and stirring up trouble in London and the provinces.

Parker's history is typical of many of James's faithful soldiers. He came of a family that had been settled in Ireland for several genera-tions, and was a professional soldier. He began his career as an Ensign under the Duke of Monmouth and by 1685 had risen to the rank of Major. In that year he fought against his old commander in the Monmouth rebellion and was promoted to a colonelcy. After the Revolution he followed James to Saint-Germain, and early in 1689 was sent to Limerick to raise a regiment for his king. Parker was a brave and competent commander; his regiment was decimated at the Battle of the Boyne and Parker himself was badly wounded, but he and his men fought throughout with great courage.[3] After the Boyne he escaped to France like many other officers of James's beaten army and took service for a while in the French army. He left this service in 1691 and joined the expatriates at Saint-Germain who were devoting themselves to planning a restoration. Parker soon became one of the most notorious of James's agents and a much-wanted man in England but, although he was several times captured, he always managed to escape before he could be brought to trial. A proclamation offering £400 for his arrest was issued in 1694 and describes him as:

Aged about 40 years; a fair man, somewhat long visaged, with a sharp chin and a high thin nose, and is a little marked with the small-pox; his hair is brown, but he generally wears a fair periwig; his size is rather less than middle stature, with soft speech and a smiling countenance. He goes a little lameish with some wound he has received, as he pretends[4].

This intrepid little man limps and smiles his way through most of the plots and conspiracies of the period, to the government as elusive as a will o' the wisp, but solid as a rock in his devotion to his royal master.

Landing in Kent on one of his clandestine missions in February 1692, Parker was captured by the King's Messengers, along with several companions. However, he managed to escape and made his way to London without the undesirable company of his captors. With astonishing confidence, he took little trouble to conceal himself and appears to have been undetected for some while, during which time he interviewed a number of important persons suspected of disloyalty to the government. However, his stay in London came to an abrupt end when, as Luttrell reports, 'Colonel Parker . . . was seen publickly bowling at the mint in Southwark; notice of which being sent to the secretaries' office, a messenger with 6 files of musketeers was sent to secure him, but came too late, he being gone.'[5]

Parker arrived unmolested in Lancashire, his real destination. The northern counties, especially Lancashire and Yorkshire, had a high proportion of catholics and non-juring Tory squires, and were thus a happy hunting-ground for Jacobite agitators. During the early months of 1692 Parker was extremely busy in Lancashire, raising and equipping a secret army from among the gentry. He claimed to have a regiment of at least 600 men ready at a moment's notice to march to meet King James whenever he landed in England. 'Waft yourselves ouer & we will throw ourselues at your feete with the 2 Idols Liberty and Property', he wrote to James's Secretary of State, Lord Melfort. Later in the letter, however, this grandiloquence is tempered and he complains of the lukewarm attitude of some of those he approached. They were 'shy of laying out money' and would not act unless they had something more substantial than a promise of thanks for their pains.[6] Furthermore, Parker found to his indignation that most of the local catholic clergy, headed by their bishop, were actively opposed to a rising and discouraged many of their flock from taking part in it. The bishop pointed out, with truth, that 'if things should chance to miscarry . . . it might in all probability be the occasion of the Rewin of the Catholicks of England'.[7] Clearly the Jacobites in Lancashire were neither so numerous nor so zealous as Parker had hoped.

While Parker and others were busy in the provinces attempts were being made in London to enlist a number of influential persons suspected of disenchantment with the Revolution. Marlborough almost certainly promised support, and in fact was already in correspondence with Saint-Germain. His disaffection sprang from thwarted ambition; he felt that his very considerable services to William, particularly after the Battle of the Boyne, had not been adequately rewarded. Among others, the Secretary of State, Lord Shrewsbury, was approached, but he ever afterwards denied that he had had any seditious intent. The Jacobites' prime target was Admiral of the Fleet Lord Russell, whose loyalty to William had latterly been in some doubt, like that of much of the Navy with whom James, when Admiral of the Fleet, had always been popular. High hopes were entertained of Russell, for if he were won over there would be no opposition from the fleet to a French landing, and James's chances of success would be immeasurably increased. No doubt a good many vague promises were given; after all, the possibility of a Stuart restoration was still not as remote as it was to seem later, and many a politician must have seen the wisdom of keeping at least one toe in the other camp. So long, that is, as they could do so without compromising themselves.

Both Louis and James seem to have been convinced that there would be sufficient support in England for the venture to be worth making. In May 1692 a French army under Marshal Bellefonds began to assemble on the Channel coast, while a substantial naval force gathered at La Hogue. James was to be in titular command and with his Irish regiment was despatched to Boulogne to await embarkation for England. Jacobite hopes ran high, while the rest of the country was in a corresponding state of alarm. But these hopes soon received a severe set-back. On 19 May the English fleet under Russell won a resounding victory over the French at La Hogue. This put an end to any prospect of an invasion for some time to come, for the French losses in men-of-war were heavy enough to rule out the feasibility of a descent upon England. And incidentally the conduct of Russell and the navy at La Hogue effectually laid to rest any doubts about their loyalty to William and Mary. The news of the victory caused a good many

Jacobites up and down the country to lose heart and transfer their allegiance, as Humphrey Prideaux, Dean of Norwich and a firm Whig, gleefully relates:

Till this happy turn our Jacobites were come to that height of confidence to talke openly that all was now their own, and some of them suspended payment of ye taxes; and at ye bishops visitation at Norwich . . . the Jacobite clergy would not own his jurisdiction and refused to appear; but on Sunday night ye news coming of ye victory, they all came the next day and made their submission, and I hope now they will have ye witt to carry themselves better.[8]

As the fear of invasion from France was lifted, so also was the danger of insurrection at home. The French army was switched to other theatres of war while James, who had waited at Boulogne for the signal to embark for home, returned sadly to his prayers at Saint-Germain. He had ceased for the time being to be a useful pawn in Louis's war game. The general relief at this turn of affairs provoked an upsurge of popularity for William such as he had not enjoyed for some time. On his return from the summer's continental campaign he and Mary made a triumphant progress to London. The crowds turned out for them when they reached the capital on the evening of 20 October, and, 'There were extraordinary luminaries in all the windows in the public streets, which their majesties took notice of, and a great crowd of people followed their coach to Kensington with Huzza's; some of them in their return broke the windows of such as had not putt out the lights.'[9]

Whatever the Jacobites might say about general disaffection, this reception left little doubt as to where the crowd's loyalties lay. With time, the Revolution was becoming established and accepted; the majority viewed with alarm the prospect of a return of a papist king backed by an army of 'French dragoons and Irish raparees'.[10] It is noteworthy too that after 1692 there was a decline in the political and social importance of the persons who conspired against William and his government; whatever secret regrets some of them might have had for the Stuarts, the top politicians had by then too much to lose by compromising themselves through surreptitious dalliance with Saint-Germain. Their wavering loyalties settled round William and Mary, and for the rest of the reign such grandees as Russell and Shrewsbury gave no sign of disaffection.

The Jacobite party, however, was still a focus for the discontents and dissatisfactions of those who for one reason and another still hoped for a reversal of the Revolution. But the defeat at La Hogue and the consequent abandonment of plans for the rising at home had had a discouraging effect, and for over a year afterwards they were relatively inactive, biding their time until things looked more propitious.

It was not until October 1693 that fresh attempts were made to persuade King Louis and his ministers that the time had come to make another move. Without the backing of a substantial French army it seemed to the English Jacobites that the restoration would have little chance of success; it was therefore imperative to persuade Louis that there would be sufficient support for James in England to make another venture worth while. A report on the situation in England was accordingly prepared by Melfort in October 1693. It is a most encouraging document, calculated to give the impression that almost the entire nation was eagerly awaiting the return of their absent king. It begins with a long list of persons influential in William's government, such as Lords Danby, Russell and Carmarthen, all of whom are said to be secretly disaffected. The Jacobite peers, Ailesbury, Montgomery and several others, are naturally included, together with all the non-juring clergy and a great many more who had signed the oath. The catholic community is for King James to a man; an army of 3000–4000 Horse is ready to march to meet him on his landing, while disaffection in the army and navy is said to be so rife that it was confidently expected that the majority of the soldiers and sailors would desert William at a moment's notice. Furthermore a number of the larger ports, such as Exeter, Hull, Bristol and Tilbury, are only waiting for news of his landing to open their gates to King James. Louis is even assured that the expedition would cost him nothing, for the loyal merchants of England would pay his troops out of their own pockets. In short, the report conveys the impression that if Louis would kindly lend James 30,000 soldiers to see him home, the whole of England (with the trifling exception perhaps of King William, Queen Mary and Bishop Burnet) would instantly acclaim him and set him on the throne. Honesty, however, compelled Melfort to add, 'it is true, there are not convincing proofs of all this', because the need for secrecy made it impossible to produce documentary evidence.[11] It is scarcely surprising that Louis and his ministers were not sufficiently convinced by Melfort's report to act upon it; James was kindly but firmly told that the 30,000 men were needed elsewhere at present.

Such set-backs never discouraged the Jacobites for long; there was always the hope that the situation abroad might change and cause Louis to reconsider his decision. It was therefore important that the small army raised by Parker in the north should be kept in being and not allowed to melt away. In addition it was deemed necessary to make further preparations against King James's return by raising more men in London and the rest of the country. Accordingly, the indefatigable Parker arrived in London in November 1693 with a Royal Commission to levy men for a rising in and around London. Inevitably, there was also in his mind a plan to engineer the disappearance of William, but this was so secret that there was no word of it in his instructions. The elimination of William was always seen by the more extreme Jacobites as essential to the success of the restoration, and plans for it run like a dark undercurrent through all their military preparations. But Parker's primary task on this visit was to raise an army. He brought with him a number of blank commissions for the officers whom he was empowered to appoint, and set about distributing them with his customary discretion and efficiency.

One of Parker's most useful contacts in London was Brice Blair. Aged about 52 and a Scottish presbyterian by birth, Blair had turned catholic in King James's time. He was an experienced soldier, having fought in James's army in Holland before the Revolution and afterwards in Parker's Irish regiment, where he served as an Ensign. After the Boyne, Blair, like so many of James's ex-soldiers, had drifted back to London; here, unemployed and down-at-heel, he hung about the coffee houses and taverns, subsisting mainly on the charity of the better-off Jacobites. He seems to have been acquainted with most of them and was often employed to run errands or arrange clandestine meetings; this made him a valuable recruiting agent to Parker, who was soon making full use of him.

Money was needed if men were to be armed and paid, and King James's resources were barely sufficient to maintain his own bodyguard, while most of Parker's recruits were quite unable to finance themselves. Colonel Parker was therefore on the look-out for men who would subsidise as well as take part in a rising. He instructed Blair to find him some 'rich citizens who would be hearty in King James's service'. Blair soon introduced him to Sir John Friend, one of his richer tavern acquaintances. He had first met Sir John in 1692, and since then they had dined together on several occasions at Sir John's expense, and since the latter was known for his loyalty to King James they must have discussed the possibility of a restoration. Sir John Friend was then fifty-eight years old, a staunch protestant and a person of some substance. He was of plebeian origin, and had inherited a large brewery in the Minories. Under the Stuarts he had risen to a position of moderate distinction, becoming Colonel of Artillery in 1685, and later that year was appointed to the lucrative post of Commissioner for the Excise. He was much in favour with King James, who had knighted him in 1685 and had given him a contract to supply beer for the army. But Sir John's beer was of such poor quality that it caused a minor mutiny among the troops to whom it was issued, who thought it was a deliberate attempt to poison them. He refused to take the oath of allegiance to William and Mary after the Revolution, and consequently lost his colonelcy of Artillery and his post in the Excise. He must have owed these positions to his wealth rather than to his brains, for Burnet says that 'his purse was more considered than his head',[12] and he had little education. So far as is known, Sir John took little or no part in Jacobite activities prior to 1693, but he was still a rich man and his purse was always open for the relief of the less fortunate among James's supporters.

This rich and simple-minded merchant – intensely loyal to King James – was just the kind of man Parker had been looking for. He offered at once to make him Colonel of the regiment to be raised in London, a position which Sir John accepted with enthusiasm. King James sent him a cordial letter and a Commission signed with his own hand, a document which Sir John displayed to Blair with simple pride. At the same time he appointed Blair his Lieutenant-Colonel and set him to work to recruit men, giving him £100 to spend on treating prospective recruits to drinks. How much of this bounty was actually spent for this purpose is open to doubt; a good deal of it probably went straight into Blair's pocket, for he was penniless and was constantly nagging his patron for more money. One consequence of his appointment was that Sir John was flattered by being introduced to the higher ranks of Jacobite society, meeting with aristocrats such as the Earl of Ailesbury and his friend Lord Montgomery, whose father, Lord Powis, was Chamberlain to King James at Saint-Germain. Neither of these lords seems to have been actively involved in the projected rising at this stage, but clearly they were both prepared to give discreet encouragement to such enthusiasts as Sir John by their notice, for Blair states that he 'verily believed he did not know these persons previously'.[13] But it cannot have been the lure of social advancement that led Sir John to accept a Colonel's commission, because his devotion to the Jacobite cause was beyond question. Nevertheless, a very natural desire to regain his pre-revolutionary status, and even perhaps to brew more bad beer for the army, must have influenced him to some extent. He was not so devoted nor so simple as to expect no reward from a monarch whom he had helped to restore to his throne.

3
A quartet of conspirators

Parker now turned his attention to appointing captains and other ranks. Some of King James's commissions were distributed among the ex-soldiers in the taverns; there was no shortage of candidates; Parker well knew that 'of such there are many to be found starving at London'. Captain's commissions were also given to several of the more fortunate of the ex-officers who were living discreetly and quite comfortably on their country estates. These men, experienced soldiers who had fought for James before the Revolution and afterwards in the Irish war, were to form the backbone of the fighting force. There were in addition a number of appointments of persons with little or no military experience, but whose known loyalty or influence would make them useful recruits. In this category were included four men who were later to play key parts in the Assassination Plot: Cardell Goodman, Robert Charnock, George Porter and Sir William Parkyns. All four will figure prominently, and it is therefore appropriate to give here some details of their origins and histories. Conspiracies are apt to draw together a strange assortment of people, and this one was no exception; few individuals could be more different than these, but each in his own way was very much a man of his time.

Cardell Goodman, or 'Scum' Goodman as his enemies called him, had never been a soldier; he was an amiable rogue whose history reads like the synopsis of an opera by John Gay. Goodman was born in Southampton in 1653, the son of a royalist parson who had been ejected from his living by the Cromwellian government in 1651. At the age of 13, Goodman was entered as a pensioner at St John's College, Cambridge, taking his B.A. in 1670–1.[1] He was expelled soon afterwards for taking part in a riot, in the course of which he and several others defaced the portrait of the Duke of Monmouth, then Chancellor of the University.[2] Goodman went to London where according to his biographer Theophilus Lucas he obtained a place as Page of the Backstairs to Charles II. Three years later his father died, leaving Goodman a legacy of £2000. Within two years he had squandered his inheritance and had become one of the most notorious rakes in London. Not surprisingly, he so neglected his duties as Page of the Backstairs that he was dismissed, and thus at twenty-four was thrown upon the world with nothing but his looks, his wits and a sumptuous wardrobe. He finally obtained employment as an actor and after a while his evident talent earned him a considerable reputation, but little money: actors at that time were miserably paid.

Goodman was a companionable and genial man. In later life he had an engaging way of telling stories, usually discreditable, of the shifts he had been put to by poverty in his early days as an actor. Once, while still splendidly dressed but penniless and hungry, he swaggered into a tavern and was served by a respectful cook with a prodigious meal of roast mutton. When the landlord found that his grand customer had no money he booted him out with a sharp kick in his elegant breeches. He did not mind the kick, said Goodman – it was fair payment for twenty pennyworth of meat. The grand clothes wore out or had to be sold, and Goodman was reduced to sharing a wretched lodging and a bed with a fellow-actor. They even had to share the one good shirt, which they took it in turns to wear. This arrangement came to an abrupt end when Goodman, for the furtherance of some amorous exploit, appropriated the shirt out of turn. His companion objected so vigorously that the ensuing quarrel developed into a duel, fought out then and there in the room. Neither party was seriously hurt, and Goodman omits to mention which of them won the contest.

Even the most popular actors had to subsist on a pittance totally inadequate for a person of Goodman's extravagant habits; at the height of his fame he is said not to have earned more than 40 shillings a week. To supplement this paltry income he was, as he put it, 'compelled to take the air and borrow what money the first man he met had about him';[3] that is, he took to highway robbery. At about this time he became involved with a gang of clippers and coiners, and consequently was arrested in 1681. However, he managed to suborn the witnesses for the prosecution, and got off scot-free.[4] He had a talent for evading the worst consequences of his misdeeds.

Goodman's most famous performance was that of Alexander in *The Rival Queens,* a tragedy by Nathaniel Lee. It was in this part, in 1682–3, that he caught the wayward fancy of Barbara Palmer, Duchess of Cleveland, the ageing but still beautiful ex-mistress of Charles II. He became one of the last of her many lovers; she took him into her household and made him her Master of Horse, a responsible and well-paid position. This relieved Goodman of the necessity of earning a living on the stage, and of having to supplement his income by 'taking the air'. He kept up his interest in the theatre, however, and would occasionally appear in benefit performances. By now he had become rather a grand personage in the theatre, and although his enemies had given him the soubriquet 'Scum', his fellow-actors at least accorded him the respect due to his talent. The young Colley Cibber, then at the outset of his stage career, says that he was reduced to tears of gratitude by a few words of praise from the great Mr Goodman.[5] The Duchess liked to see her lover on the stage and always attended his performances. On one such occasion, when Goodman was playing Alexander in a benefit performance for young actors, the Duchess was late. Though Queen Catherine was in her box and had commanded the actors to begin, Goodman refused to allow the curtain to be raised until Her Grace of Cleveland had arrived. When remonstrated with for this piece of *lèse-majesté* he 'swore several great oaths that if the Pit and Boxes were lin'd with Queens he would not act until his Duchess was come'.[6] Fortunately Her Grace arrived just in time to save Her Majesty from the humiliation of having to wait upon the convenience of her husband's ex-mistress. The curtain went up and Goodman went on to give one of his best performances.

The affair between a great lady and an actor of dubious reputation caused a good deal of scandal and was a source of considerable annoyance to King Charles: it is possible that he, or those about him, attempted to get rid of the Duchess's latest lover. In September 1684 Goodman was arrested and committed to Newgate on a charge of robbery. The charge was in respect of highway robberies committed some years previously and Goodman, as he admitted long afterwards, was certainly guilty. But there was insufficient evidence for a conviction. The jury brought in a verdict of 'ignoramus' and Goodman was released.[7] But he was not at liberty for long. One month later, on 21 October, he was re-arrested, this time on a more serious charge of having suborned an Italian adventurer, Alexander Amedei, to poison two of the Duchess of Cleveland's sons by Charles II, the young dukes of Grafton and Northumberland.[8] However, it soon became apparent that the charge had been trumped up by Goodman's enemies with the connivance of Amedei and that once again there was insufficient evidence to warrant a conviction. Goodman, however, was found guilty of a 'misdemeanour', fined £1000 and ordered to find sureties for his good behaviour for the rest of his life.[9] He then applied for a royal pardon, which Charles, probably due to the intercession of the

Duchess, was in process of granting just before his death. Later in
1685 King James, mainly it was said because of his admiration for
Goodman's acting, granted him a free pardon 'of all robberies and
felonies, wilful murder excepted, and of all trespasses and misdemeanours committed before October 20th. of that year'.[10] This
suggests that there were further charges pending against Goodman but
if so the slate was now wiped clean. It was gratitude to King James
that led him to become a Jacobite after the Revolution. The royal
pardon, he said, 'was doing him so particular an honour that no man
could wonder if his acknowledgement had carried him a little farther
than ordinary into the interest of that Prince'.[11]

Goodman left the stage in 1688 and took to gaming, often acting as
croupier at the Duchess of Cleveland's gaming-table. Her amours,
never discreetly conducted, were much celebrated by the lampoonists,
more especially after the Revolution when she had lost the protection
both of her royal lover and King James. 'The Duchess of C[leveland]'s
Memoirs', a ballad in execrable verse, appeared in 1707, in which her
notorious association with Goodman was duly recorded:

> Poor Rowley being dead and gone,
> I howl'd and had remorse Sir.
> To comfort me Scum Goodman came,
> Whom I made Master Horser.[12]

By the time Parker appeared in London in 1693 Goodman, now a
middle-aged roué who lived mainly by gaming, was well known in
Jacobite circles, where he was still spoken of with respect as 'Mr
Goodman the Player'. It may have been his connection with the
Duchess that prompted Parker to offer him a commission, for
naturally she was no friend of King William, and so might be prevailed
upon to support the rising with money and influence. Apart from
gratitude to King James, it is hard to see what other qualifications
Goodman had for leading a troop of Horse in a rebellion; he had no
military experience, and certainly could not have afforded to arm or
maintain his men. Parker, however, must have thought it worth while
to enlist him; and Goodman, no doubt in the hope of future reward,
accepted the commission. He does not seem to have done any active
recruiting, but he soon became one of the inner ring of the conspiracy
and attended a number of meetings where the rising was planned. He
was also present on several occasions when the removal of King
William was discussed, but took little or no part in the final
arrangements of 1696. Nevertheless, he played a considerable if not

27

leading role in the whole conspiracy and after its discovery an even more important part in the case of Sir John Fenwick.

The second player in this oddly assorted quartet was Robert Charnock, sometime Vice-President of Magdalen College, Oxford. Born about 1663, he was the son of Robert Charnock, a Warwickshire gentleman. Some members of the Charnock family had migrated to Bedfordshire, and were friends and 'most good neighbours' of the Earl of Ailesbury. Robert junior, who seems to have been something of a social climber, evidently tried to take advantage of this connection to ingratiate himself with the earl who, however, was most unfavourably impressed. 'I never could endure the sight of him', Ailesbury says in his memoirs, 'and he heavily complained of my coldness and reservedness towards him . . . he had, as I was told, a good share of understanding and wit, and moderate good learning . . . but he was naturally of a dark, close temper, and misfortune had made that humour worse'.[13]

Charnock's misfortunes came later in life, but he had his hour of fame, or rather notoriety. He had a good education, being admitted to Magdalen College as a Demy (Scholar), and took his B.A. in 1684. His undergraduate career seems to have been uneventful, except for one incident early in 1684 when he came under censure for unruly behaviour, which was duly recorded in the College Register:

March 12 1683/4. Mr Clerke, commoner, complain'd of Sir Chernock [sic], demy, for abusing him at Woods his rackettcourt, calling him foole, Welsh ambassador (an expression for an owle) and otherwise vilifying him both facto et verbo, which was witnessed by a gentleman commoner of Merton Coll., by name Mr. Kater, and young Mr. Wood of the rackettcourt'.[14]

For this unbecoming conduct Charnock was punished by being 'putt out of commons for a week, being the first tyme that such a complaint had been brought against him'. Two years later, in 1686, Charnock joined the Catholic Church.[15] Ailesbury thought this conversion was politically motivated 'to ingratiate himself and get preferment'. He may have been right, for there was no surer way to win favours from King James and Charnock soon benefited from it: early in 1687 he became a Fellow of the college by royal mandate. James had already appointed a number of catholic Fellows to both universities by mandate, because the law forbade the appointment of persons not members of the Church of England. Such appointments were unpopular but hitherto had aroused no strong protests, no doubt because they were sporadic and not numerous enough to cause alarm.

In May 1687 the President of Magdalen died. His death gave James the opportunity to embark on one of his most unpopular projects, the conversion of the college into a catholic seminary.[16] As a first step he commanded the Fellows to elect as their new President Anthony Farmer, a catholic and a member, but not a Fellow, of Magdalen. All the Fellows except Charnock explained in the most respectful terms that they could not comply with His Majesty's command without violating their statutes. These laid down that a President must be elected from among themselves, and that he must be a man of 'good reputation and godly life'. Farmer, they submitted, was ineligible on both these grounds. The Fellows, hoping to forestall any further royal interference, at once proceeded to elect as their President Dr John Hough, a man suitable in all respects for the office. Enraged at this disobedience, James sent the Ecclesiastical Commission to Oxford to deal with the recalcitrant Fellows and to see that his command was enforced.

The Commission, escorted by three troops of Horse, descended upon Oxford on 28 May 1687 and summoned the Fellows to account for their conduct. They politely but firmly refused to depose Dr Hough in favour of Farmer and produced irrefutable evidence that the latter was a most unsuitable person to hold so responsible an office, or indeed any office at all. The evidence is entertaining reading, but it must have caused the Commission a good deal of embarrassment. Farmer, it appeared, had begun his university career at Trinity College, Cambridge, and had been expelled for misbehaving himself in a dancing-school. He next spent a period as an usher in an unlicensed school kept by a non-conformist – this was a legal offence. When the school was closed by the authorities, Farmer went to Oxford and was admitted to Magdalen Hall, but his 'troublesome and unpeaceable humour' soon caused the college authorities to ask him to leave. A fellow-student deposed that Farmer on several occasions had attempted to draw him and others into 'debaucheries, taverns and bawdy houses', and furthermore that he had taken money from them, 'publicly to expose unto them a naked woman, which he did'. In addition to this disgraceful behaviour Farmer, although reputed to be a catholic, had boasted to another student that he only pretended to be a papist, and that he kept company with other papists purely for his own advancement.

Perhaps through the influence of Charnock, Farmer next got himself admitted to Magdalen College. It may also be due to Charnock's influence that he was not soon expelled again for unruly behaviour. The college porter deposed that Mr Farmer often came in very late and so far gone in drink that 'he could scarcely go or speak'. He was notorious for his habit of drinking and gaming till all hours in the taverns. On one occasion he and one of his disreputable companions uprooted the town stocks at Abingdon and threw them into the pond called Mad Hall's Pool. Finally, the wife of the landlord of the 'Lobster' at Abingdon contributed a nice example of what was considered unacceptable behaviour in a seventeenth-century tavern – or a modern one for that matter:

> Mrs. Mortimer is ready to assert, that when Mr. Anthony Farmer returned to the Lobster about eleven at night, he came much concerned in drink, and was for kissing the said Mrs. Mortimer, which, he being a stranger, she permitted him to do; but in the doing of it, he, the said Mr. Anthony Farmer, put his tongue in her mouth, which was such a rudeness, that she immediately went out of his company, and would not come nigh him anymore.

A note at the end of these depositions says that there was further evidence of things 'too dreadful to be written or spoken of'.

How such a scallywag as Farmer came to be put forward for the Presidency of an Oxford college is hard to understand. It can only be supposed that there was a shortage of catholic candidates and that James knew nothing of his antecedents; he must have been shocked to learn of them, for he had a strong sense of propriety. Farmer's name was hastily dropped and he disappeared into obscurity. But James was not to be deterred. In June he sent a fresh command to the Fellows to depose Dr Hough and elect the aged and allegedly crypto-catholic Samuel Parker, Bishop of Oxford. When all the Fellows, with the exception of Charnock, refused this command the Ecclesiastical Commission returned to Oxford and installed the bishop by force. The recalcitrant Fellows refused to acknowledge the election, and as a punishment for their obduracy were summarily expelled from the college and debarred from holding any clerical office in the future. However, so much sympathy was aroused for their plight that the consequences of this harsh decree were much softened; all found temporary shelter in remote benefices or in the homes of sympathisers. A number of demies were expelled at the same time, and they too found shelter and support. Public anger and alarm at the treatment of the Fellows had by now spread far beyond the university. As Burnet says, 'The nation, as well as the University, looked on all this proceeding with a just indignation. It was thought an open piece of robbery and burglary.'

The vacant fellowships were filled by catholics, many of them priests, while a number of catholic young men were admitted in place of the expelled demies. Charnock now reached the apogee of his career. He became Vice-President and since Bishop Parker was too old and ill to carry out his presidential duties, was in virtual control of the college. His high-handed exercise of his authority went far to exacerbate the resentment caused by the take-over. He had the chapel refitted for catholic services, thus excluding the remaining protestant demies from worshipping there. For protesting against this and for refusing to recognise his authority Charnock caused their names to be struck off the commons list and forbade them access to the buttery – in effect starving them out. Some of the bolder demies disputed his right to do this, but Charnock told them brusquely, 'learn to behave yourselves more reverently, or you shall dispute it through a grate'. These few survivors were soon expelled, and by April 1688 Magdalen College had become a catholic seminary.

Bishop Parker died in March 1688 and was succeeded by Bonaventura Gifford, titular Bishop of Madura. Gifford was a learned and saintly man, and it may safely be inferred that he found his Vice-President something of an embarrassment, for he got rid of him as quickly and as kindly as he could. One of his first acts was to grant Charnock leave of absence for a year *ad consulendum sanitatem in partibus transmarinis.* No doubt Gifford felt that the health of the college, rather than that of Charnock, would benefit by the latter's residence abroad. He departed to France in July and never returned to Oxford. Gifford too was soon to leave Magdalen. Rumours of William of Orange's plans for a descent on England had already reached James by September 1688, and he at last realised that he must placate his angry subjects or face open rebellion. Among the unpopular decrees that he now hastily reversed was that for the expulsion of the Fellows of Magdalen. On 28 October they returned to Oxford, escorted by three hundred gentlemen on horseback and a great crowd of cheering townsfolk. Their restoration was celebrated by a 'splendid entertainment in the President's lodgings, while in the evening the bells expressed the people's satisfaction. Bonefires in the town added pomp to the occasion.' The catholics were given fourteen days' notice to move out of the college. Most left Oxford immediately, but seven of them, poor and homeless, remained in the town for some time. The restored Fellows were kindly and charitable persons; they sent these persons 'two dishes of meat daily during their stay by way of a present'.

Charnock meanwhile must have regained his health, for he joined Parker's Irish regiment in the spring of 1689 and served in Ireland, first as Lieutenant and later as Captain.[17] After the Boyne he left King James's army and, according to Ailesbury, made his way to Spain. By

1692 he had drifted back to London, 'a poor grumbling Jacobite and younger brother, and most poor, picking his teeth at Will's Coffee House... he hunted for bread'.[18] Ailesbury's statement that Charnock married a Spanish widow cannot be correct, and he was mistaken when he said that the lady soon left him. Charnock certainly had a wife at the time of his arrest in 1696, but she was a shadowy person about whom very little is known. There is no mention of her in the printed depositions or in the report of Charnock's trial in *State Trials*, and she was not living with him at the time of the Assassination Plot. The only references to Charnock's marriage that have so far come to light are in the unpublished depositions taken by Sir William Trumbull, the Second Secretary of State, in early March 1696. Thomas Higgins, arrested on suspicion and questioned about his acquaintance with Charnock, deposed that he had recently seen him at his lodgings, 'going on with a plot about a lady' ('recently' must be taken to mean some weeks or months previously). Thomas Bertram, interrogated some days later, said that Charnock had recently married a fortune.[19] From this it would seem that Charnock's matrimonial plot was more successful than his political one, for he must have married this lady shortly before the discovery of the conspiracy and his own arrest; but who she was and when the marriage took place is not known. Like so many seventeenth-century wives, Mrs Charnock played a very subsidiary part in her husband's life, except at the end of it. She is recorded as having an official permit to visit him in prison, and she interceded unavailingly for his life. Her fortune did Charnock no good, and she was a widow within a few weeks of her marriage.

George Porter was one of the chief promoters, and finally the most deadly betrayer, of the Assassination Plot. Among the disappointed, dishonest or deluded men who drank and grumbled and plotted in the Jacobite taverns, George Porter was the arch-villain. No one had anything good to say of him, not even the Whig politicians whose ends he served. Burnet describes him as, 'a man of pleasure' and 'a vicious man, engaged in many ill things'.[20] Ailesbury calls him 'a vile wretch as to morals and way of living'.[21] Porter was not approved of either by some of his fellow-conspirators, one of whom gives some indication of his appearance, saying that 'he had as much fat in his brains as he had in his body'. No more precise description of Porter has so far come to light. He came of a good family, several of whom had held office under Charles II and James II. His uncle, Colonel James Porter, had been Vice-Chamberlain to James before the Revolution and afterwards had followed his master to Saint-Germain, where he held the same office. James Porter was a catholic and so was his nephew George, nominally at least.

In an age when the slightest quarrel was apt to end in a duel and even the death of one of the protagonists, Porter was almost pathologically aggressive. This uncontrolled aggression got him into serious trouble in 1684, when he was arrested for the murder of Sir James Hacket. It happened that this gentleman had taken his children to the theatre on the afternoon of 11 October. The theatre was full, and a crowd had collected in the street to see the more notable theatre-goers. After the play Sir James tried to make way for his children through the jostling throng by flourishing his cane. Porter had also been in the audience and was just in front of Sir James who, in flourishing his cane, accidentally struck him on the shoulder. Porter turned round to see who had struck him and received a light blow in the face. Whereupon he drew his sword and ran the unfortunate gentleman through the thigh with such violence that 'the weapon appeared both ways, likewise cutting his fingers as he struggled to draw it forth'. Porter pulled out the sword and some of the horrified bystanders tried to take it from him. Standing over the prostrate body of his victim and flourishing his dripping sword, Porter declared that anyone who tried to disarm him would be served in the same way as Sir James. The Watch was summoned and Porter was eventually disarmed and committed to Newgate. Sir James Hacket was carried home in a coach by his distracted children; he died of his wound six weeks later. Porter was tried for murder, but the charge was later reduced to manslaughter. He pleaded guilty but escaped the penalty, a heavy fine and burning in the hand. This was probably due to the influence of his uncle, for he was granted a royal pardon and so got off scot-free.[22] Ailesbury rightly thought the pardon quite unmerited, and adds a postscript to the story, showing Porter to be a coward as well as a murderer:

this pardoned wretch rode at Foubert's academy, and my cousin John Brice . . . nephew to the deceased, riding there also, affronted him on all occasions, even switching him; but the valiant assassinator bore it all very patiently, and I was credibly informed that he, a few years later, Murthered an upholsterer at the Mews Gate: all I can say of the matter, is that he was capable of it![23]

The earl's animus against Porter was no doubt largely due to the fact that he had to pay the latter an annuity of £200 during both their lifetimes. The sale of annuities was popular and often profitable in those days of limited investment opportunity and uncertain tenure of life, and in 1688 Porter bought an annuity from Ailesbury through a mutual acquaintance. The deal went ahead in spite of Ailesbury's intense dislike of Porter; he was at that time very short of money and besides thought he would be the gainer, as in his opinion Porter was, 'one that I would not give a year's purchase for his life, so eaten up is he with a certain disease, and that spits blood, and always in quarrels and ill places'. But Porter's constitution proved stronger than might have been supposed. To Ailesbury's extreme annoyance he lived until the summer of 1728.[24]

Porter had had some military experience, serving as a Captain in Colonel Slingsby's regiment of Horse for a short period before 1688.[25] He left the army after the Revolution, and took no part in the Irish campaign, preferring to stay in London and conspire in the taverns with the other malcontents. In May 1692 a proclamation was put out for his arrest as a dangerous Jacobite, and he fled to France.[26] When the alarms occasioned by the threatened French invasion had died down he felt it safe to return to London, and was soon to be seen again in his old haunts. His annuity of £200 must have been totally insufficient for his needs, for he lived as an idle man-about-town, kept at least two servants and was so heavily in debt by 1695 that he was continually changing his lodgings in order to evade his creditors. It is difficult to believe that Porter would have joined the Jacobite movement for any altruistic motive; he was the sort of man who would take part in any subversive activity for what he could get out of it. He accepted a Captain's commission from Parker, but took little or no part in raising a troop; he did however lay by a small store of arms. Surprisingly, he seems to have been able to inspire some confidence in his associates, for he soon became a leading figure in the Assassination Plot and was even supposed by some to have been the contriver of the whole scheme.

Sir William Parkyns, both in his history and his character, contrasts strangely with the dissolute Goodman, the embittered and impoverished Charnock and the even more disreputable Porter. A staunch protestant and family man, Sir William was 'bred to the law and the gown' and up to about 1693 had led the peaceful life of a Chancery lawyer and man of property. There were early connections between him and Charnock however; they came from the same county; Charnock had been a schoolfellow of Sir William's nephew Matthew Smith, son of his eldest sister Anna; and Charnock's sister had married George Heywood, a tenant farmer on the Parkyns's family estate. Charnock, then, had probably known Sir William since boyhood, and it may have been this link that led to his drawing Colonel Parker's attention to him as a likely man for King James's service in 1693.

A quartet of conspirators

William Parkyns came from an ancient and respected Warwickshire family, which like so many others had risen to gentry status by the purchase of monastic lands after the Dissolution. They held the manor of Marston Jabbett, a hamlet near Coventry, and for the previous two generations had been entitled to a coat of arms. Sir William's father, also called William, was a legal man, for some years a Master in Chancery and a Justice of the Peace for Warwickshire, and was thus a person of some importance in the county.[27] The family were royalist by tradition (a Colonel Parkyns had fallen fighting for King Charles at Naseby), but since William Parkyns senior remained in undisturbed possession of his estate during the interregnum he cannot have been a very active supporter of the king. William, his son and heir, was born in 1649, the eldest of a family of seven.[28]

Little is known of William junior's early life and education, but it seems he was destined to follow his father's profession. He was entered as a Pensioner of Trinity College, Cambridge, at the age of sixteen (the identification is not absolutely certain), but left without taking a degree.[29] He presumably studied law at Cambridge, for in 1671 he became a member of the Inner Temple and was called to the Bar a year later at the age of twenty-three.[30] The Inner Temple was one of the Inns of Chancery, whose members practised in the Chancery Court. Originally a Court of Equity, by the end of the seventeenth century the Chancery had fallen into some disrepute. Celia Fiennes, writing in 1691, says of it, 'this formerely was the best Court to relieve the subject, but now it is as corrupt as any and as dilatory'.[31] A Chancery practice tended to be looked down upon by lawyers in the other courts as a soft option, 'the Chancery', as John Evelyn remarks, 'requiring so little skill in deep law learning, so the practiser can talke eloquently, & that Court so profitable, few care to study the Law to any purpose'.[32] Whether or not William Parkyns studied the law to any purpose he seems to have found it profitable, for by 1675 he was able to purchase the office of one of the Six Clerks of Chancery. This was a lucrative post, and the price was correspondingly high; it is not known how much William paid for it, but it cannot have been less than several thousand pounds, for the same office was worth £5000 in 1696.[33] The Six Clerks of Chancery enjoyed some social prestige. They acted as attorneys for clients in the Chancery Court and their other function, carried out in practice by a host of under-clerks, was the copying and recording of the documents relating to Chancery proceedings. The revenue came from the substantial fees charged for these services.

On 23 June 1673 William Parkyns married Susanna Blackwell at St

Mildred's Church, Bread Street.[34] The Blackwells were a Hertford-shire family who had been strong supporters of parliament during the civil wars, but past political differences were not an obstacle to an alliance with a family of known royalist sympathies. The match appears to have been suitable in other respects. Although Susanna's father was a merchant tailor, several other members of the family had held legal positions, and she had besides considerable expectations as co-heiress with her sister Anne to the estate of their cousin Richard Blackwell, owner of two-thirds of the manor of Bushey in Hertfordshire.[35] The couple lived for the first few years of the marriage in the parish of St Giles-in-the-Fields.[36] A daughter Susanna (no date recorded) was born, and a son, Blackwell, in 1678.[37]

In 1677 Richard Blackwell died and William and Susanna took possession of one-third of his estate. It was a good inheritance, comprising a manor house with orchards and gardens, two subsidiary houses or cottages, about 70 acres of arable and pasture land, mostly let out in small holdings, together with the manorial rights and dues arising from the estate.[38] Early in 1678 the family moved from London to the manor house, and here Susanna spent most of her time, caring for her household and growing family. Three more children were born at Bushey between 1682 and 1692.[39] The survival rate must have been higher than the average for the time in this family, for all five children were living in 1696. William divided his time between Bushey and London; he continued to prosper and bought land in Coventry, Warwickshire and Leicestershire; and was spoken of with respect as 'a gentleman of estate'.

During the exclusion crisis of 1678–81 William Parkyns was a fervent supporter of the Duke of York's right to the succession. Burnet says that he was, 'very hot for King James at the time of the Exclusion, and had gone violently into the passions of the Court at that time'.[40] His services to the Court party were in due course rewarded by Charles II, who conferred a knighthood on him on 10 June 1681.[41] The years from 1681 to 1688 were the most prosperous and probably the happiest of Sir William's life. He was made an Alderman of St Albans and was a much respected figure in Hertfordshire. In 1684 he bought the second third of the Bushey estate from his sister-in-law Anne and her husband Rowland Pitts, thus doubling his property in Hertfordshire. By this time he was keeping a coach-and-four, a sure sign of affluence, and never, he said at his trial, kept less than eight horses in his stable. The inventory of his possessions taken after his death shows that his home was comfortably, indeed luxuriously, furnished by the standards of the day.

A quartet of conspirators

Sir William was well known about the Court as well as in legal circles, and numbered among his friends such distinguished persons as Sir John Holt (later Lord Chief Justice) and Jeremy Collier, the eminent nonconformist divine and writer who spoke of Sir William as, 'a man of sense'. Lord Powis, one of the catholic peers imprisoned at the time of the Popish Plot, also knew Sir William and introduced him to the Earl of Ailesbury. The earl evidently liked him, for he says that 'he passed always for a most honest moral man, a good gentleman of his county . . . and a man of sweet temper naturally, but too much addicted to the bottle'.[42] Sir William's reputation for honesty was not entirely deserved, for he was not above some sharp practice in property dealing. For instance, in 1679 he sold a piece of land in Northampton to Francis Arundell, without telling him that it was already mortgaged. Arundell 'enjoyed the same very quietly' until after Sir William's death, when he was shocked to find that it was not, as he had thought, freehold. He wrote plaintively to the Treasury asking that the mortgage be paid off out of the estate so that he could continue in enjoyment of the property.[43] Ailesbury thought it was wine that led Sir William into bad company and so into the rash and treasonable activities that were to cost him his life. There may have been some truth in this, for he was a convivial man and spent much time in taverns, while his inventory lists a prodigious number of 'bottels'. Another consequence of his drinking was the gout, that scourge of our ancestors. Towards the end of his life he was severely crippled by it, so much so that he could hardly walk or hold a pen. It is possible that excessive drinking and a painful infirmity had impaired Sir William's judgement and 'sweet temper' and helped to drive him into a course of action that does not seen consistent with his previous life and character.

A good many staunch Tories, among them Sir William, took the oath of allegiance to William and Mary in 1689 with the private reservation that an oath taken to sovereigns *de facto* would be nullified by the restoration of James, the sovereign *de jure*. For Sir William, as for anyone holding a public office, this was simple self-preservation. Had he refused the oath he would at once have lost his office as one of the Six Clerks, his legal practice and his aldermanship of St Albans. He had a wife and family to consider and estates to maintain, not to mention the repayments on the mortgages he was in the habit of taking out on his now numerous properties. So, taking the sensible rather than the heroic course, he signed the oath to keep his livelihood. He kept to the letter if not to the spirit of it for some time, for there is no evidence of his taking part in seditious activities before 1693. He seems, however, to have been in the habit of frequenting Jacobite taverns and other meeting-places for some while before Parker's arrival in London, for he was well known to Sir John Friend, who like Sir William was 'a great bottle man'. He was soon brought to the notice of Parker, who bestowed a Captain's commission on him, and Sir William at once set about purchasing arms and other equipment for a troop of Horse.

Why this gouty, ageing and hitherto law-abiding man undertook so hazardous and unlikely an adventure as raising a troop of Horse for a rebellion is not easy to understand. He had already played for safety by taking the oath and could have continued to live securely and even prosperously under William and Mary. Quite apart from his family responsibilities he had a great deal more to lose than most of his confederates. He was no fool, and had already seen the failure of so many conspiracies that he must have known that the risk of discovery was very high. And he knew what the consequences of failure were likely to be: a dreadful death for himself and ruin for his wife and children. Such considerations as these must have weighed with Sir William in 1689, but clearly they no longer did so in 1693. In default of any documentary evidence the reasons for this change of front can only be surmised. It is probable that Sir William had been finding that life under the new sovereigns was becoming harder and less profitable. There were considerable changes in the judiciary at this time; many persons promoted (often unfairly) by King James were ousted in favour of Whig supporters of King William. Tories, especially those who were known to have been devoted to James's interests, were not looked on with much favour by the new judges and legal officials, and thus Sir William may have found his legal practice declining. It may also have been one reason why he sold his office of one of the Six Clerks in Chancery in 1693.[44]

Certainly there are signs that Sir William's prosperity was on the decline after the Revolution. He gave up keeping a coach-and-four at about this time, and increased the mortgages on his various properties to such an extent that after his death the estate was found to be heavily encumbered. He even compelled his wife to raise money on her own jointures, with the result that the only items listed as belonging to Lady Parkyns in the inventory of the Bushey estate were two brewing coppers, worth £10.

Clearly, Sir William had been spending above his income for some years before his death, but whether the money went in equipping and maintaining a troop of Horse and in contributions to the Jacobite party funds is a matter for conjecture. Undoubtedly he must have hoped that his own fortunes would be restored along with those of his exiled king, and this must have been one of the reasons why he entered into the conspiracy. There was also the lure of legal advancement, even perhaps the Chancellorship, for who could tell what rewards a grateful monarch might bestow on a faithful supporter who had risked all for his sake? These are obvious and mundane motives, but underlying them was a sincere conviction that King James's cause was a just one. It was, finally, this belief that led Sir William Parkyns to choose the dangerous path of conspiracy rather than live safely under a monarch whom he regarded as an illegal usurper. There can be no doubt of his sincerity; he states his belief uncompromisingly in the paper written on the eve of his execution: 'I looked upon it as my duty, both as a subject and an Englishman, to assist him [King James] in the recovery of his throne, which I believe him to be deprived of contrary to all right and justice; taking the laws and constitution of my country for my guide.'[45]

These four men can be considered as a representative sample of the kinds of person who were conspiring to bring back King James in the 1690s. Among them Sir William Parkyns stands out as one of the better sort of Jacobite; he may have been 'indifferent honest', but the sincerity of his beliefs and the courage with which he stated them at the end redeem his minor faults. Although there were many more honest and less self-interested men than he in the party, there was also much too high a proportion of rogues and self-seekers for any of the conspiracies of the period to have had a chance of success. They were all fated to be betrayed from within.

4

The secret armies

THE JACOBITES' HABIT of counting their chickens before they were hatched makes any estimate of their numbers totally unreliable. Likewise the government, partly from a nervous fear of the hidden enemy in their midst, and partly for propaganda purposes, tended to exaggerate their strength. Hence it is impossible to calculate how many men would actually have taken up arms for King James had he landed in England. Some were determined enough but a great many more, although happy to indulge in seditious talk and to drink the king's health over the water, were not prepared to risk life and fortune for his sake. Nevertheless, Whig fears of a widespread fifth column were far from being unjustified, as from 1689 onwards the Jacobite party provided a rallying-point for all sorts of persons who thought they had been happier, better off or more powerful under James. There were of course plenty of grievances to be exploited, and naturally Jacobite propaganda made the most of them. In spite of the victory of La Hogue, the war throughout the summer of 1692 had gone badly for the English and their allies; the country was being drained of money and men and there were complaints that it was always the English who were in the forefront of the fighting and who consequently bore the heaviest losses. To help pay for the war, taxation had reached unprecedented levels and this, combined with a steady fall in land values and a series of bad harvests, had caused considerable hardship among the lesser gentry and the tenant farmers, and real suffering among the 'labouring poor'. Trade too was seriously affected by heavy losses in merchant shipping, which suffered severely from the depredations of French privateers, against whom the navy was unable to provide adequate protection. In addition, the debasement of the coinage was already causing considerable economic difficulty and increasing the hardships of the poor. All these ills and others besides were according to Jacobite propaganda directly attributable to King William and his foreign war; it was scarcely surprising that their party attracted a good geal of support, sometimes open but more often secret, from a wide spectrum of society that ranged from catholic peers to modest artisans.

Thus the Tories, who in the previous reign had stood firm for hereditary right, were inevitably and often unjustly thought to be inclined towards King James. Toryism and high anglicanism tended to go together, and William had done much to antagonise the High Church by his policy of preferring Low Churchmen in place of the dispossessed non-jurors. The country squires and lesser gentry also tended to be Tory and High Church; it was thus natural for them, in particular for those who had been ousted from office by Whig supporters of the government, to sympathise with and sometimes to take part in the Jacobite movement. The non-juring clergy were similarly suspect, as were laymen who had refused the oath of allegiance. Many catholics understandably favoured a monarch under whom they had at last begun to enjoy some measure of religious and political freedom. So too did some dissenters, whose hope of increased toleration under the Calvinist William had not been fulfilled.

There was plenty of opportunity for discreet seditious talk. While the non-juring clergy conducted services, often in private houses where King James could be prayed for in secret, the lay Jacobites usually met in taverns and coffee houses and sometimes formed themselves into 'clubs', that is, loose associations of like-minded people rather than established bodies with rules and subscriptions. Taverns were especially favoured, partly because they had private rooms where treason could be talked in relative safety; many a plot would be endlessly and usually fruitlessly discussed over the wine in these upper rooms, while there would be much drinking of toasts to the downfall of the 'Rotten Orange', 'Hook Nose' or 'The Little Spark' and other uncomplimentary nicknames for King William. The proceedings always ended with a round of healths to King James and his family, a favourite toast being 'To LIMP', a dispiriting combination of letters standing for Louis, James [I], Mary and the Prince of Wales. The most notorious Jacobite taverns were the 'Blue Posts' in Spring Garden, close to where the Admiralty Arch now stands, the 'Dog' in Drury Lane, the 'Fountain' in the Strand and the 'Bear' in Holborn. Soldiers were occasionally sent to raid these and other establishments and wholesale arrests would be made, but the sentences following these raids were seldom severe and more often than not the arrested persons would have to be released for want of evidence, or at worst received light sentences.

Although Jacobitism was most prevalent among the upper and middle classes, there was also a good deal of disaffection among

41

certain sections of the working class, arising from poverty and unemployment. This was by no means confined to James's ex-soldiers and sailors, many of whom would have gladly taken up arms again for their 'rightful King'. The gradual relaxation of the strict laws governing apprenticeships had led to overcrowding and consequent unemployment in the skilled trades, notably weaving and allied crafts. The weavers had been especially hard-hit, and their well-known poverty was thought to render them peculiarly open to Jacobite propaganda; thus in 1693, 'numerous copies of a ballad exhorting the weavers to rise against the government were discovered in the house of a Quaker'.[1] Unemployment had greatly increased the numbers of highwaymen and footpads who infested the roads, often operating in large gangs. The notorious highwayman James Whitney, hanged in 1692, attempted to escape punishment by offering to reveal the names of no less than forty of his gang who, he alleged, were pledged to fight for King James. In November of the same year nine butchers on their way to Thame were held up by nine highwaymen 'who, having robbed them, made them sit in a row and drink King James's health'[2] Luttrell's diary for the years 1692–4 abounds with accounts of Jacobite highwaymen, not all of them as light-hearted as the incident of the nine butchers; it would seem that King James could have recruited a small army from among the 'gentlemen of the road'. The bad harvest of 1693 caused much discontent among the landless labourers and the unskilled workers who formed the bulk of the population and the resulting hardships may well have inclined many of them to hope for a change of regime, especially as the adherents of King James were at pains to point out that the failure of the harvest was a divine visitation, a punishment for the sin of rebelling against the Lord's anointed and hereditary king. How much active Jacobitism there was among this class can only be conjectured, since the opinion of the 'labouring poor' was seldom heard or asked for; it can be assumed, however, that a good many countrymen would, had the occasion arisen, have obediently followed their landlords when they marched to join King James.

There was, then, plenty of discontent and dissatisfaction with Dutch William throughout the country, all of which was reported to Saint-Germain as general disaffection and an ardent desire for the return of James. But what the Jacobites, with their infinite capacity for wishful thinking, do not seem to have understood was that the grumbling was an expression of discontent: it was far from being desperation. And only real desperation would have led the English to rebel against a protestant king, however foreign and unpopular, in favour of one whose brief reign had plainly demonstrated that he had scant respect for their hard-won religious and civil liberties. Nor did they wish to see the country plunged again into civil war, which would inevitably have followed a serious attempt at a restoration of the catholic Stuart dynasty.

Although most Englishmen appear to have been antagonistic or indifferent to a restoration, there was still a sufficiently large minority of faithful Jacobites to give some hopes of a successful coup. Brice Blair's account of his recruiting activities, given after his arrest, shows that the Jacobite party included all sorts and conditions of men. Besides the officers who had already accepted commissions, Blair states that he had engaged 'in words' fifty or sixty men for Sir John Friend's regiment.[3] To help him he enlisted the services of Thomas Bertram, a Yorkshireman and a catholic, who had been a trooper in Parker's Irish regiment and who, like Blair, had returned penniless to London after the failure of the Irish campaign. Bertram was no doubt glad enough to share in Sir John Friend's bounty and made himself very useful to Blair. Both men had an extensive acquaintance among the indigent ex-officers in London most of whom, as Blair remarked, 'begged at that time'. In addition to these ex-officers Blair engaged a number of civilians, small tradesmen or artisans, whose occupations he obligingly gives. They include a stocking-maker, a hatter, a watch-maker, a tailor and a clerk to the stock-market. The financial status of these persons is indicated by the fact that none of them was sufficiently well-off to own a horse. 'Some had as much money as would buy a horse, some said they would borrow a horse, and some said they would go into the first stable and take a horse.'[4]

The provision of horses for such of the recruits who could not mount themselves was a pressing problem for the organisers, as horses were essential for the mobility upon which the success of the rising would depend. Shortage of money and the need for secrecy forced them to adopt haphazard methods of obtaining them and of keeping them hidden, for the authorities were constantly on the watch for large concentrations of horses and were empowered to seize them at the first sign of public disturbance: 'as to the keeping of horses, Sir John [Friend] said it was dangerous and they would certainly be seized, but the best way was to have a list of what horses were in and about London stables, and seize them upon occasion'.[5]

This does not seem a very practical suggestion for mounting a regiment at very short notice, and in fact it was never acted upon. Goodman and Porter met the difficulty by hiring a remote mansion near Barnet, called The Blue House, where there was stabling for fifty or sixty horses. Here the rebels would be able to muster their men and horses unobserved and wait for the signal to ride to the coast to meet their king.[6] The better-off rebels were to supply or hire horses according to their means. Thus Sir William Parkyns had stabling for at least a dozen at Bushey, but only five of his animals were suitable for military purposes.

Besides the fifty or sixty men that Blair recruited for Sir John Friend, he obtained promises from a number of persons in and around London who were prepared to raise and mount their own contingents. He deposed that Kelly 'at the Red Lion in Smithfield, promised me 35 Irishmen, all ready mounted'. Another man, Wrae, who kept a tobacco and brandy shop in Moorfields and who was to be Blair's Quartermaster, promised 'to bring me in a considerable number, whereof a great many could mount themselves'. Jennines, at the 'Three Crickets' in Crooked Lane, was to supply twenty men already mounted. Two more persons were each to raise a troop, but the numbers are not specified. Another, Ricsone, promised the support of 'all or most of the Jacobite bailiffs and their followers in and about Town'.[7] This last indicates that there must have been a good deal of Jacobitism among minor officials. Blair also mentions in passing that several other persons, such as Captain Fisher, another of James's ex-officers, were raising troops. It could have been that Blair was including some innocent men in his enumeration, for he was concerned to save his own neck by producing as much evidence as possible; he may, too, have been taking the opportunity to pay off some old scores by falsely accusing persons against whom he had a grudge. But even allowing for some exaggeration, there must have been several hundred men in and around London horsed and armed in readiness for King James's landing.

Blair also gives some details of the amount of support forthcoming in other parts of England. Thanks to Parker's previous activities in Lancashire and neighbouring counties, there was said to be 'a great body of horse ready in the North'. Mr Hall, a merchant of Deal, had forty men ready that would mount themselves. Throughout East Anglia there were said to be little knots of Jacobite gentry waiting for the word to rise. Norwich was 'very loyal to King James' as was Lynn and several other Norfolk towns. Drumming up support for the rising was a paying proposition for several indigent Jacobites besides Blair. Mr Pits, a non-juring parson who had lost his benefice and had moved to Long Melford in Suffolk, where he practised medicine under an assumed name, wrote to Blair offering for a suitable reward to supply a list of gentlemen in Suffolk and Norfolk who 'would prove very zealous in king James's service'. For extra pay he would do the same in Cambridgeshire and the Isle of Ely. Pits did produce a list of persons in these counties who were said to be ready to assist King James on his landing, 'either with their persons or their purses, or both', but he is vague as to their actual numbers. Most were farmers or country squires, 'not only of the meaner sort, but the better sort of gentry'.[8] The rebel army was to be further strengthened and spiritually supported by a troop of non-juring parsons, which godly lambs were to be led by a Colonel with the unfortunate name of Slaughter.

Blair has to admit that not all the persons he approached would give firm promises; for example Barnesley, an ex-Lieutenant of Horse, who kept a coffee house 'over against the turnstile in Holborn', and who was offered a Major's commission, 'sometimes refused, sometimes accepted'.[9] Blair does not mention any outright refusals, and it is quite clear that he and the other agents had many verbal promises of support both in London and the country. But events were to prove that they were, as always, over-optimistic about the determination and sincerity of those who made the undertaking. No doubt many of these promises were given in a moment of bibulous enthusiasm and repented of in the sober morning. Then again, the less honest of the Jacobite agents must have been tempted to exaggerate the number of their recruits; it put money in their pockets, and most of them were abysmally poor. For one reason and another, then, no estimate of the numbers who could be counted on to rally to King James if he landed in England can be reliable. There is a mythical quality about these secret armies and, significantly, they failed to materialise when the time for action came. The stocking-weavers, the hatters and the non-jurors stayed quietly at home and waited upon the event, and no great body of horsemen rode out of the north.

While preparations were being made for the rising in England, James was being bombarded with appeals to apply once more to Louis for the loan of ships and men to support his landing. A French force of 30,000 men, it was generally agreed, was essential if he were to keep a foothold in England long enough for the Jacobite army to muster and rally to his side. And there was need for haste as well as secrecy for with every week that passed the danger of the government's getting wind of the Jacobites' plans increased. As early as December 1693, Brigadier Sir George Barkley, one of James's most trusted officers, was urging him to be ready to invade by March next year at the latest. At the same time a Captain Williamson sent in a similar memorandum which included an urgent message from Sir John Friend: 'Sir John Friend desires, with much earnestness, that your Majesty may make a descent, at farthest, in the Spring'. He goes on to say that His Majesty's friends, and with them his cause, may all be ruined by too long a delay, for it will not be possible to keep their plans secret for much longer, and he assures the king that he will be met on landing by at least one regiment of cavalry, reinforced by Colonel Slaughter and his troop of non-juring parsons. Furthermore, Sir John says, he has 'great influence' with the two regiments of militia destined for the defence of the Tower in the event of regular troops being sent to the coast to counter the invasion. Friend's enthusiasm then outruns his discretion, for he adds as a further inducement that he 'hopes to seize the Prince and Princess of Orange and carry them to your Majesty at St. Germains'. A firm line has been drawn through this sentence, indicating that the proposal was not for His Majesty's eyes.[10]

Encouraging as Sir John's assurances were, they were insufficient to convince Louis that he would be justified in hazarding 30,000 men, together with the necessary ships and transports, in a venture that had signally failed two years earlier; he could not afford to risk another La Hogue. And possibly Louis had taken the precaution of obtaining independent reports of the state of feeling in England, which would have been considerably less optimistic in tone than those of James's partisans. Thus an anonymous agent, writing to a friend in Paris in 1694, and who may or may not have been sent over to England on a fact-finding mission by the French government, gives a much more sober estimate of the amount of support James could count on if he landed in England. This man had travelled up and down the country for several weeks, apparently in order to test the strength of the Jacobite party. His report makes it quite clear that enthusiasm for a restoration had been much over-estimated. Many of the country gentlemen interviewed had, it is true, expressed sympathy for King James and dissatisfaction with King William, but few said that they were prepared to take an active part in a rebellion. Most said it would be too dangerous and too difficult, and a number of them said that the chances of success were too remote for it to be worth while making the attempt. The local Justices of the Peace and other officials were in the main government men, were continually watchful of persons suspected of Jacobite tendencies and had extensive powers for dealing with any sign of incipient revolt. Detection, or a failure of the whole enterprise, could all too easily result in widespread arrests of suspects with the possible consequence of hanging, or at best imprisonment and confiscation of their property. Understandably most of the country squires thought it safer to stay at home and grumble, rather than risk all on a doubtful venture. The writer of this report had even taken the trouble to ascertain the feelings of the common people who, according to the Jacobites, were groaning under the yoke of the foreign tyrant and longing for the return of their true king. But the report gives a very different picture, for it seemed that the common people were in general antagonistic towards King James and had no desire for his return. For them this signified a renewed danger of 'popery and tyranny', the old, deep-rooted fear that Whig propaganda played upon so successfully. Moreover, they had little faith in James's promises of religious and civil liberty, held out to them in his latest Declaration.[11] Though they might grumble at King William and his taxes, his government was still preferable to that of a papist king.

Reports such as this may well have influenced Louis's refusal to lend James an army in the winter of 1693. In February 1694 James sent a message to his friends in London by a Mr Cross to the effect that there was no hope of French support in the immediate future. Cross was instructed to thank all the king's friends for their loyal support and to tell them that, although King Louis found it impossible to spare the required number of men at present, he still hoped to be able to assist them at some future time. His Majesty was very sorry for the delay, and added that the French king was quite as disappointed as himself that circumstances had made it necessary. He trusted, however, that his loyal friends would, 'continue to hold themselves in readiness for his return at a later and more favourable time'.[12]

Without French support even the most enthusiastic of James's supporters knew that he would have little chance of success. And they do not seem to have taken into account, when they made the request for it, that it would have been very difficult for Louis to have spared 30,000 men and adequate naval forces at this time. His armies were heavily engaged on the continent, while the main body of the French fleet was needed in the Mediterranean to supply and reinforce the army destined for the subjugation of Spain. In the spring of 1694 the French fleet had sailed from Brest, closely followed by a large contingent of English and Dutch warships, which successfully block-aded the French in Toulon harbour until well into the winter. The rest of the English fleet spent the spring and summer of that year cruising up and down the Channel coast and harassing the French ports, so that a considerable French army had to be employed in defence of this area. Thus even with the great military and naval might at his command, it would scarcely have been feasible for Louis to mount an attack upon England that year. Meanwhile, the war in Flanders went on its apparently endless way; by comparison with the lamentable succession of defeats of the previous two years, this had been a better summer's campaign for the English, and it helped to reconcile them to the expense and strain of King William's war. It also obliged the French to deploy ever larger numbers of men in the Low Countries – another factor in Louis's decision not to comply with James's request for the loan of an army. The English Jacobites seem not to have taken these difficulties into account; possibly they were under the impression that Louis's resources were inexhaustible. Only Charnock, who was both more intelligent and more realistic than the rest, repeatedly said that it would be useless to attempt a rebellion until the French fleet had broken out of the Mediterranean and returned to Brest, for only then would a French invasion become possible.

Once again the hope of immediate action had receded, but His Majesty's loyal friends in England were not unduly discouraged and went on preparing for the day when the situation would change in their favour. Recruiting continued, and arms and accoutrements were secretly bought and hidden away, while King James's agents came and went across the Channel with almost complete immunity. The most notorious of these, Colonel Parker, remained at liberty in London for some time and was in constant contact with Charnock and the other conspirators. His whereabouts must have been carefully concealed by his friends, for the King's Messengers searched diligently for him in London and in Surrey, where his wife had a house, and set up a special watch for him on the coast of Kent. But it was not until 10 May 1694 that he was finally run to earth in Bloomsbury and committed to the Tower, where he was kept at first in solitary confinement.[13] Later, however, he was given permission to see two lawyers and his wife. With the help of his friends, she took advantage of the relaxation of the strictness of her husband's imprisonment to engineer his escape. A sum of £400, to which Sir John Friend was said to have contributed £100, was collected and used to secure the connivance of Parker's keeper. His wife brought him some women's clothes and a long rope, which she concealed in the skirt of her gown. Parker escaped in a manner befitting so resourceful a character; he got out of his room by climbing up the chimney on to the roof and let himself down by means of the rope; then, wearing the clothes his wife had brought him, he walked calmly out of the Tower.[14] The keeper, who was afterwards prosecuted, no doubt earned his huge bribe by letting him out. The escape must have taken place at night so that the somewhat sooty appearance that Parker must have presented after his climb up the chimney would not have been noticed.

Parker did not, as might have been expected, make immediately for the coast, but stayed for some time safely hidden in London, where Goodman reports that he saw him soon after his escape:

and then he told me that he would be sure to correspond with me and Porter, and I should receive his letters of Mr. Charnock, or Mr. Harrison; and he accordingly did; and in his letters he still gave us hopes, and said he would certainly send us notice to be in readiness, time enough for us to be serviceable to the design of the invasion'.[15]

Even the intrepid Parker must have realised that by now it had become too dangerous for him to remain much longer in London. Shortly after this conversation with Goodman he made his way to the coast and got safely over to France. So far as is known he did not reappear in London, but his influence, through his copious correspondence, remained with the conspirators. His wife was smuggled out of the country soon afterwards, and joined her husband at Saint-Germain.

The disappearance of Parker from the scene made it necessary for the English Jacobites to choose a new leader. The choice fell upon Sir John Fenwick, a man of some social standing, and much in favour with King James. Fenwick came of an ancient Northumbrian family; his marriage to Mary, eldest daughter of the Earl of Carlisle, had further increased his social status. Like Sir William Parkyns, Fenwick had been a strong supporter of the Duke of York's right of succession to the crown at the time of the exclusion crisis and he remained a staunch supporter of James. In 1685 he had represented his native county in James's first and only parliament. Fenwick had gained some military experience fighting in the English army in Holland during King James's reign, and by 1688 had risen to the rank of Major-General. During the course of this campaign William of Orange had occasion to administer publicly a severe and humiliating rebuke to Sir John, which aroused in the latter a bitter and lasting resentment and a personal hatred for William that seems to have been one of the chief reasons for Sir John's ardent espousal of the Jacobite cause. After the Revolution he remained in England and became one of the most persistent plotters against William and Mary, but although he was an aggressive person he lacked the ability to carry out any undertaking with success and this obviously made him a much less dangerous conspirator than he might have been. Sir John Fenwick's career after the Revolution was stormy. As early as 1689 he was arrested and sent to the Tower for fomenting disturbances in the north, but was soon released for lack of evidence. Not long afterwards he was to be seen swaggering with his fellow-Jacobites in their favourite part of Hyde Park, popularly known as the Jacobite's Walk. Here, one day in 1691, Fenwick demonstrated his animosity towards the ruling house by refusing to doff his hat to Queen Mary as she passed by in her coach, and rumour had it that this piece of disrespect was accompanied by a much ruder gesture. The incident was widely publicised and caused much indignation on the queen's behalf. William, furious at the insult to his wife, ordered the gates of Hyde Park to be closed against known Jacobites from henceforth. Fenwick was in trouble with the authorities again in 1692; a warrant was out for his arrest on a charge of having taken part in the invasion plans of that year, but this time he escaped imprisonment. When the King's Messengers arrived at his house to arrest him, Sir John left by a back window – so hurriedly that he left behind his breeches and a pocketful of guineas.[16] He appears to have got out of this particular scrape without further trouble, for he was living openly in London in 1693.

The Jacobites were never very fortunate in their leaders and Sir John Fenwick was no exception. The Earl of Ailesbury knew Fenwick well and had a certain affection for him, but was not blind to his faults. 'His temper', he remarked, 'was most good, but his headpiece was not of the best'.[17] Sir John's headpiece certainly does not seem to have been adequate when it came to arithmetic. According to Goodman he had been asked by Saint-Germain to send over estimates of what forces there were in England and where, and in what strength, they were garrisoned. But says Goodman, 'he having made a mistake in his accounts' caused Parker to write to Goodman asking him to procure more accurate information, since that supplied by Sir John Fenwick was unreliable. Goodman, much more efficient, promptly suborned one of the clerks in the Secretary of State's Office who had access to the figures, which were then relayed to Saint-Germain with tolerable accuracy.[18]

Fenwick's house in London was a noted meeting-place for the more irresponsible of the Jacobite gentry; here they would foregather in the evenings to drink King James's health and discuss plans for his return. The principal topic of conversation, however, seems to have been the rich rewards they hoped to reap in return for their services. Ailesbury was sometimes present at these gatherings and describes one of them in his lively way: 'one evening I was sitting at Sir John Fenwick's house . . . and there came several of these flashy gentlemen', who proceeded to apportion the principal offices of state among themselves to the great satisfaction of all present except Ailesbury, who was grieved to see all these 'flashy gentlemen', Sir John among them, 'making court for employment for themselves as if King James had been at Whitehall'. Ailesbury was rather patronisingly offered a fairly minor post in this cloud-cuckoo-land, but he refused it politely and took his leave, remarking as he went, 'Gentlemen, there is an old proverb, "first take the bear, then divide the skin".'[19] The earl, a sensible and witty man, had a strong personal devotion to the memory of his late master, King Charles, and to his brother King James. He never took the oath to William and Mary, and had been actively involved in the plans for a restoration in 1692. But he had a poor opinion of most of the Jacobites, and after 1693 seems to have tried not to get himself involved in their wilder schemes. 'Their heads', he said, 'were ever filled with chimeras, noise and nonsense.' And he added, sadly, that although 'most had loyalty as well as zeal, ambition triumphed most'.[20]

The Jacobite activities in London during the spring and summer of 1694 seem to have attracted little attention from the government. In July public attention was focused on Lancashire, when eight local gentlemen were arrested and charged with conspiring to raise a rebellion for King James. Parker's earlier activities in Lancashire have already been referred to; he was succeeded there by another agent, James Lunt who, according to his own very unreliable account, was busy in 1693–4 distributing King James's commissions. Lunt, like Parker, did a good deal of travelling between Saint-Germain, London and Lancashire. It was at Saint-Germain that he learned, so he said, of a plot hatching in London against the life of King William. He averred that this knowledge troubled his conscience and after consulting various persons, including his friend Taffe, an Irish ex-priest, he resolved to prevent the murder if he could. For reasons that he never made clear Lunt, together with Taffe, informed the Secretary of State, not of the plot against King William, but of the revolt brewing in Lancashire. Shrewsbury acted upon the information at once. He despatched a posse of King's Messengers and a troop of dragoons commanded by a Captain Baker to Lancashire with orders to search the houses of suspects for hidden arms and other incriminating evidence. Taffe accompanied the expedition and caused the Messengers considerable embarrassment by his habit of pocketing any small article that took his fancy during the house searches.

Little of significance was found, but nevertheless eight gentlemen were arrested on the testimony of Lunt and Taffe, supported by that of two carriers, Womball and Wilson. These last deposed that they had transported large quantities of arms to the houses of the gentlemen concerned. Five of the prisoners were brought to trial at Manchester in October 1694. The trial aroused much public sympathy among the Mancunians, who were notoriously anti-government. Feeling was further aroused by the notable pamphleteer Robert Ferguson, who had recently published a paper accusing the Whig government of fabricating the evidence in order to represent themselves as the nation's bulwark against Jacobitism (and, by implication, Toryism). Ferguson's arguments could be very inflammatory. There were angry demonstrations outside the court when the trial began; stones were thrown at the crown witnesses, and there was much ado to get them into the court unharmed. In the event, the trial turned out to be something of a fiasco from the government's point of view, for the defence was able to prove that the crown witnesses were completely unreliable. The chief witness, Lunt, was unable to identify two of the accused in court although he was supposed to have had extensive dealings with them over the past two years; the rest of his evidence was so full of contradictions as to be useless. Taffe, disappointed of his expectations of a large government reward, revenged himself by destroying the crown case. He alleged that Lunt, in collusion with Captain Baker, the officer in charge of the troop of dragoons, had invented the whole plot for their own gain; he declared that he had overheard them planning to forge the commissions, drop them in the accused men's houses, and then 'discover' them in the course of their search. Had the prisoners been convicted, Lunt and Baker would have been able to claim all or part of their property.

The evidence of the other two witnesses, Womball and Wilson, was also vague and contradictory and was therefore discredited. Not surprisingly, the case for the prosecution fell apart, and the five gentlemen were acquitted amidst tumultuous rejoicing by the Mancunians. They were not, however, completely freed from suspicion, for Chief Justice Eyre dismissed them with the admonition to 'go and sin no more, lest a worse thing befall you'. There was no additional evidence upon which to try the other three Lancashire gentlemen, who had been confined to the Tower, and they too were released shortly after the Manchester trial.

A parliamentary enquiry into the Lancashire Plot followed. The Commons voted by 133 to 97 that there had been grounds for a prosecution. The Lords concluded likewise that there had been a potentially dangerous conspiracy, but that there was insufficient evidence to warrant a prosecution. This in effect was a face-saving operation on the part of the government, which had not come too well out of the affair. Emboldened by their acquittal, the Lancashire gentlemen proceeded to prosecute Lunt, Womball and Wilson for perjury and obtained a conviction. But they were not severely penalised and were shortly afterwards released, to disappear into obscurity. Thus ended the Lancashire Plot.[21] It had, to all appearances, turned out to be a mare's nest, and it had the effect of lulling public fears of a dangerous fifth column in their midst. For some time afterwards the government ceased to interpret every rustle in the undergrowth as a sign of imminent conflagration, and there was some relaxation of vigilance. Thus the Lancashire Plot was not without influence upon subsequent events, for it enabled the Jacobite conspirators to carry on their seditious activities in relative freedom from detection. Had the authorities but known it, they had covered their tracks quite effectively in Lancashire. Standish Hall in that county had been used as their headquarters by both Parker and Lunt, but no evidence was found there. Sixty years later, a workman making some alterations to the house discovered a bundle of old papers sealed into a hole in a wall. They proved to be a copious correspondence between Parker, Lord Melfort and other persons at Saint-Germain, dated between 1692 and 1693, together with lists of persons committed to taking part in the rising; there were also fifty blank commissions for officers in the rebel army.[22] It was fortunate for the Lancashire gentlemen that these documents did not come to light at the time of their trial, for if they had, they would not have got off so easily.

There were signs that a rising was being simultaneously planned in Warwickshire. At some time in 1694 Sir William Parkyns had almost certainly concealed a considerable quantity of arms at the family seat in Marston Jabbett. Although evidence for this comes in the first instance from a not very reliable source, it was amply confirmed at Sir William's trial two years later, when the cache was discovered. Sir William's nephew Matthew Smith, the son of his sister Anna, and old schoolfellow of Charnock, was a contemptible rogue who took advantage of his relationship with his uncle to hang on the fringes of the Jacobite coterie, gathering scraps of information in order to sell them to the Secretary of State, Lord Shrewsbury; most of this was gossip picked up in taverns or from news sheets, as Shrewsbury quickly realised. He soon tired of Smith and his exhorbitant demands in reward for worthless information and after paying him a few small sums he discarded him. Smith, in revenge for this rejection, published in 1697 a book purporting to contain copies of his correspondence with Shrewsbury, in which he alleged that the latter had wilfully suppressed the information contained in the letters, because he was a crypto-Jacobite. The accusation was not generally believed, and certainly not by King William, who regarded Shrewsbury as one of his most trusted servants. Nevertheless, Shrewsbury was so distressed by the suspicion that his health, never of the best, was seriously affected; he resigned from his office on grounds of illness shortly afterwards.

Smith certainly had some knowledge of his uncle's affairs, and he used it to prove that the rest of his information was genuine. He claimed that in December 1694 he had written to Shrewsbury to tell him that there was a quantity of arms hidden at Sir William Parkyns's house in Marston Jabbett, and urging that a search be made at once. Smith must have known the house well. He tells Shrewsbury that the searchers would find it empty except for one servant (this would have been Richard Evans, Sir William's ex-coachman, who acted as caretaker). Every room in the house should be searched, 'but particularly the two garrets over the two rooms, where you are to go up by a staircase in the hall, and look for the arms in the space between the two chimneys . . . they are very fine arms, enough for a troop'.[23]

Shrewsbury never ordered the search; it is possible that he never received the information, for Smith was thought to have forged most of the letters that he published in 1697. Or it may have been that Shrewsbury, after so many abortive house searches in Lancashire, was sceptical of the truth of Smith's message. But on this occasion Smith was telling the truth. At the time of the trials in 1696 just such a quantity of arms was found at Marston Jabbett and in circumstances fatally compromising for Sir William. Now, it was known that Sir William had bought arms for the troop he had been raising in London, but the weapons found in Warwickshire cannot have been intended for the use of these men. They would have been needed at very short notice, and it would have taken at least a week to convey them from Marston Jabbett to Hertfordshire or London. The arms spoken of by Smith must therefore have been intended for persons in or near Warwickshire, and it seems likely, as Smith said, that they had been bought and stored at the time of the Lancashire Plot, or even earlier. From this it can be inferred that the ramifications of that conspiracy were wider than had been supposed. Clearly too Sir William Parkyns, as well as being heavily involved in the plans to remove King William, was assisting in plans for a rising in the Midlands and the north. In this connection, it may be significant that he sold his office as one of the Six Clerks in 1693 for a considerable sum. He probably devoted most of it to the Jacobite party funds and to the purchase of arms.

5
'If it be not now, yet it will come'

IN EARLY DECEMBER 1694 Queen Mary was suffering from what appeared to be a minor indisposition. Little anxiety was felt at first by her physicians, but on 21 December smallpox was diagnosed and she became seriously ill. On 28 December she died. Her untimely death – she was only thirty-two years old – plunged the whole nation into mourning, and no one lamented her more profoundly than her widower. Mary's devotion to William had not, to outside observers, seemed to have been fully appreciated or reciprocated by him; he had not always been the kindest of husbands: 'she was generally thought to submit to the King's humours and temper more than she had reason to do, considering the insolent treatment she frequently received from him, which she was never known to complain of herself, but I have often heard her servants speak of it with great indignation'.[1]

William was a very private person; his lifelong habit of reserve and his occasional outbursts of irritation with her led people to suppose that he did not truly love his wife. To the astonishment of all, even his closest friends, his sorrow was as passionate as it was sincere; no one had thought the little man had so much grief in him: 'The King's affliction for her death was as great as it was just; it was greater than those who knew him best thought him capable of; he went beyond all bounds in it: during her sickness, he was in an agony that amazed us all, fainting often and breaking out in the most violent lamentations: when she died, his spirits sunk so low, that there was great reason to suppose he was following her: for some weeks afterwards, he was so little master of himself, that he was not capable of minding business or seeing company'.[2] To the end of his life William mourned Mary's loss. He kept the anniversary of her death as a day of mourning, shutting himself away and spending the day in prayer and meditation. When he died, the attendants who prepared his body for burial found that he was wearing under his shirt Mary's little gold ring around which was entwined a lock of her brown hair.[3]

As well as being a profound emotional shock, the queen's death seriously affected William's political position. While she lived there was still a Stuart in the direct line of succession on the throne of England, even though William was the executive partner in their joint rule. Thus she provided a focus for the loyalty of many who found it difficult to accept his more remote claim. Without Mary, his position was much less assured. Moreover, as well as being the hereditary heir, Mary had other attributes that were of inestimable value to William. She had the Stuart charm and good looks, but none of their less endearing characteristics; her modesty, piety, kind-heartedness and open friendly manner did much to mitigate the unpopularity accorded to her morose and withdrawn husband. Although not unintelligent, she was a woman whose interests were homely, and she had little liking for statecraft; but she brought to the partnership a warmth and humanity that were lacking or seldom apparent in King William. Burnet, who knew them both well, put this succinctly when he said, 'he was to conquer enemies, and she was to gain friends'.[4].

Thus Mary's death could have been a political as well as a personal catastrophe for both king and nation: 'What this unexpected Accident may produce as to the present Government, many are the discourses, and a little time may shew', wrote John Evelyn, expressing the general anxiety.[5] It was largely due to William himself that this anxiety was soon resolved. For once, and briefly, the barriers between him and his English subjects were down, and king and people were united by their grief for the dead queen. It had been generally supposed that William had only cared for her because she had helped him to the throne, and his often brusque manner to her in public had not done much to correct this impression. His violent grief at her death undeceived everybody and evoked real sympathy from the whole nation. Mingled with this sympathy there was considerable anxiety over William's own health; for several weeks he was so ill that it was feared he would soon follow Mary to the grave. This was an alarming prospect, not only for the English but for the Dutch and their allies as well, for William was the linch-pin upon which the conduct of the war depended; if he died there was every likelihood that the Allied campaign against Louis would collapse, and that both England and Holland would lose their bulwark against the French. The parliamentary delegation that came a few days after the death of the queen to offer William an address of condolence, after expressing with tears the grief and sympathy of both Houses, begged him, 'most humbly . . . that you would not indulge your Grief, upon this sad occasion, to the Prejudice of Your Royal Person; in whose Preservation, not only the Welfare of your own subjects, but of All Christendom, is so nearly concerned'.[6]

William broke down as he thanked the delegation for their sympathy and their concern for his own and the public good. He would try, he assured them, not to be found wanting in his public duty, but added pathetically that just now he could 'think of nothing else apart from the great loss we have just suffered'. The sympathy and concern for himself of both parliament and people were some comfort to the stricken king. They must too have given him some reassurance that he was not in any danger of losing his crown as well as his wife. 'I hope that Your Majesty will draw some consolation from the resolute declaration of the Parliament for Your Majesty', wrote the Dutch Pensionary Hensius, clearly expressing the relief of the Allies that they were not going to lose their leader. Although William's health never completely recovered from the shock of Mary's death, he began albeit slowly to pick up the threads again. Within a month he was able to attend to affairs of state, and even to go hunting at Richmond on Saturdays. It became apparent that he would live to rule alone; 'a little time' had shown that his reign was not dependent upon Mary's life.

After Mary's death there was a marked cooling of enthusiasm for King James on the part of several highly placed persons who had hitherto been suspected of Jacobite leanings. Marlborough in particular ceased to correspond with Saint-Germain at this time. Princess Anne was now the heir to the throne and it seemed likely that she would succeed to it before many years had passed, for William, although only forty-four, was not expected to live to a great age; there was besides always the possibility that he might die by violence or in battle. Marlborough, who with his wife Sarah had gained complete ascendency over the mind of Anne, had thus only a few more years to wait to become the most powerful man in the kingdom. It cannot therefore have seemed to him worthwhile to jeopardise such a future by continuing to give clandestine support to Anne's unlucky father. He was not alone in this, for other persons of high rank such as Shrewsbury, Godolphin and Russell, all of whom had been corresponding with Saint-Germain in 1692, were by now firmly attached to William's interest.

Political considerations apart, there were economic factors contributing to the stability of William's rule. By contrast with the more unsettled conditions of 1692, and in spite of high taxation and a mounting currency crisis, the national finances were in a healthier state. The Bank of England, founded in 1694, had for the first time put the government's finances on a secure footing; it also offered security of investment and a guaranteed rate of interest to those who subscribed to it. Predictably the Bank, after some initial difficulties, was a complete success and was supported by Whig merchants and Tory landowners alike. It was in fact to prove 'as important in attaching men of property to the new regime as the dissolution of the monasteries had been one hundred and fifty years earlier'.[7] The Bank was also to prove important in detaching many men of property from their allegiance to King James, for it had by now become clear on which side the bread was buttered. Thus even many die-hard Tories who would have fought for James in 1692 were, by 1695, more concerned for the security of their investments than for the sanctity of divine right.

The cooling in the upper levels of the Jacobite party was not reflected in the lower strata: the dispossessed had nothing to lose and the truly zealous never gave up hope; and the Jacobites' claim that there was still widespread disaffection and discontent was not without some justification. The *rapprochement* between William and his people had already begun to fade by the spring of 1695, and there was as always discontent with the progress of the war and the high taxation that it caused. Matters were made worse by the continuing depreciation in the value of the silver coinage, a problem that by 1695 had reached crisis proportions. For some years the price of silver had been higher on the Continent than in England. The export of silver derived from clipping and melting silver coins had thus become very profitable, and in spite of the fact that it was accounted treason and punishable by hanging, it had become almost a minor industry in the back streets of London. Since a clipped or defaced coin was not worth its face value and had to be assessed by weight rather than by denomination, the resulting depreciation affected all sections of the populace, and particularly the poor. Because obstruction of the government in any form was considered by the Jacobites to be helpful to their cause they were much given to coin-clipping.

This activity was often combined with the printing of Jacobite propaganda, and since it was a home industry it was usually carried out by women. Some idea of its extent and persistence can be gained from Luttrell; as early as September 1692 no less than three hundred clippers and coiners were reported by him to be operating in London.[8] In November of the same year copies of King James's Declaration, together with a quantity of coin clippings, were discovered in a house in Covent Garden. Two women were arrested and sent to Newgate.[9] Hanging usually followed conviction for this offence; clippers and coiners almost invariably figured among the lists of persons executed at Tyburn throughout the years 1690–6, but this severity had little or no deterrent effect. Naturally, the pamphlets emerging from the secret presses did not neglect to lay the blame for the currency crisis and its attendant evils at the door of King William's government; but as usual the Jacobites greatly exaggerated the general discontent and disaffection.

The Jacobite conspirators took no action for about a month after Mary's death; probably they were hoping that nature would spare them the trouble of eliminating him, but as soon as it became apparent that William was not going to die, fresh schemes were hatched for his removal by force. Early in February 1695, Charnock visited Goodman and told him that 'he had something to propose to him'. Goodman must have shown interest, for Charnock then took him to see a Mr Waugh (or Waw), who assured them that he was in daily expectation of a commission from King James authorising the capture of William. There followed a number of meetings to discuss ways and means, sometimes at Goodman's house, but more often at taverns or coffee houses. Sir William Parkyns, Porter and on one occasion Brice Blair were present at these later gatherings. The final plan, arrived at after several alternatives had been considered and rejected, was to attack the king when he was hunting at Richmond and take him prisoner. The conspirators do not seem to have given any thought as to how they were to dispose of their captive, and it was Goodman who asked, 'What then? For we ought to have regard to some end or other in such an undertaking, for I was not willing to offer anything to his person.'[10] Although nothing as yet had been said about killing the king, Goodman clearly realised that this way of solving the problem of his disposal must have been in the minds of the confederates. Waugh then suggested that they have a coach in readiness to carry the king to Deal, where there was a fort manned by Jacobite sympathisers who he knew would hold the prisoner safely until such time as a boat could be found to carry him to France. Once in France, there would be no difficulty in conveying him to Saint-Germain where, presumably, he was to be laid like a trophy of the chase at the feet of James. The entire operation, Waugh estimated, would require no more than twelve men and would cost £2000 to carry out. Not surprisingly, Goodman thought the whole scheme quite impractical, and moreover did not believe that King James would ever send the required authorisation for it.[11]

Goodman's account is confirmed by Francis De La Rue, who was present at some of the meetings. De La Rue was the son of a French soldier who had lived forty years in England and had successively married two Englishwomen, so that Francis was half English. After the Revolution the elder De La Rue had returned to France and had entered the service of King James, where he was a Major in his regiment of Guards. Francis remained in London where he became acquainted with most of the Jacobite fraternity. He seems to have been tolerated but never fully trusted by them; he did, however, manage to gain the confidence of Porter, who told him of the plan to capture William and later took him to several of the meetings where this was discussed. The rest of the company were evidently wary of De La Rue, for he complained that 'there was much whispering in corners' when he was present. Much of his evidence, therefore, is hearsay and not altogether reliable, but his habit of adorning his lengthy testimonies with colourful detail makes him an interesting witness. The conspirators at this stage seem to have shrunk from using the ugly word 'murder' and to have gone no further than discussing the kidnapping of the king. It is De La Rue who first reports the more sinister development. According to him, William would never have reached France alive, for it had been decided that should the guard put up any effective resistance, his assailants would put a bullet through his head and say afterwards that he had been killed by a random shot. Typically, it was Porter who advocated this course, pointing out that it would solve the problem of getting the victim transported to France. De La Rue, although he later expressed pious horror of the whole plan, was certainly involved, for Goodman at one point suggested sending him and Charnock to Deal to arrange for the hire of a boat to carry William to France.[12]

By mid-March the expected Commission had not arrived and the conspirators began to grow impatient, as it was known that William would shortly be leaving for Flanders where he would remain for the rest of the campaigning season. Porter and Sir William Parkyns were for proceeding without the royal sanction, but Charnock and the rest said they must wait for it. According to Goodman they were still planning to abduct and not to kill the king, but were having difficulty in finding a captain who would hire his boat for so dangerous an enterprise. One man did agree, but he asked so exhorbitant a price that 'it was not in possibility to comply withal'. Then almost on the eve of William's departure a meeting was held at the Fountain Tavern by Temple Gate. During it Sir William was called out to speak to a boatman who after a whispered consultation with Sir William and Porter agreed to hire his boat for a more reasonable sum. The bargain was struck and all was put in readiness, but to the disappointment of the conspirators their quarry departed for Flanders the very next day and so the whole plan had to be abandoned. Shortly afterwards Goodman heard that King James, when he heard what had been intended, was exceedingly angry that they 'had used his name to what he had not promised'. Goodman and Porter, at his command, sent a full report of the affair to Saint-Germain.[13]

At his trial in 1697 Sir John Fenwick attempted to prove his innocence by claiming that he had been instrumental in foiling this particular scheme. He told a not very credible story of how one day in late April 1695, when he was walking in the Court of Requests, he was accosted by Sir William Parkyns, Charnock and Porter. They asked him if he had heard anything about a Commission from King James authorising the capture of King William. A Mr Crosby, they assured him, had just returned from France; Crosby had actually seen the Commission signed, and was surprised that it had not yet arrived in London. Fenwick professed to be much shocked by this report. Crosby, he declared, must be lying, and 'it was a scandal upon King James', who he was quite sure would never give an order for so base an action. Furthermore, said Fenwick, 'they could intend nothing less by seizing the King than to murther him', and he held forth at some length on the iniquity of such a scheme. Sir William, unmoved by Fenwick's expostulations, then announced that an attack on the king was planned for that very Saturday; it would be at Richmond as he returned from hunting there. It would be their last opportunity for some time, as it was known that William would shortly be departing for Flanders. Sir William, backed by Porter and Charnock, then declared that they were determined that the king 'would never go out of England alive'. Fenwick, according to his own account, persuaded the conspirators to do nothing further in the matter until the next Saturday, and even got them to agree to dine with him at the Fountain Tavern on that day. They kept the appointment, rather surprisingly, and Fenwick, even more surprisingly, detained them there, 'discoursing upon the business and shewing them the baseness of their action and the impossibility of their succeeding', until it was too late to set out for Richmond. Early next morning, to the great relief of Fenwick, King William left for Flanders.[14]

Sir John Fenwick was fighting for his life, and told this story to prove that he had never been involved in any plot to kill the king which, to do him justice, he was never seriously accused of. It is probable, however, that he knew something of what was going on in April 1695, and may have heard rumours of the meeting at the Fountain Tavern described by Goodman and had decided to make use of this information for his own purposes. But the tale is much too thin to be anything but the product of a limited imagination, for who could possibly believe that three determined assassins would allow themselves to be detained by Fenwick's dinner and 'discourse' until it was too late to set out on their momentous enterprise? In fact the story did nothing to help Fenwick's case for, as the prosecution pointed out, it could not be substantiated. By that time both Sir William and Charnock were dead, and Porter, as the principal witness for the crown, would have had no motive for confirming it. But Fenwick was right in one particular, when he said that Crosby must have been lying about having seen a Commission for the capture of William signed at Saint-Germain. It seems certain that no such order was ever signed by King James. Crosby's part in this affair is somewhat mysterious; he may have been sent by one or other of the conspirators to get James's authorisation to proceed with their plans, and it is also possible that he was a government spy or *agent provocateur*. Crosby had recently been arrested for high treason but, rather suspiciously in view of the serious nature of the charge, had been released on bail. He then made straight for Saint-Germain and had an interview with James, in the course of which he apparently propounded a scheme for the murder or capture of William.

James has often been accused of being privy to, even if he did not instigate, the various plans to kidnap or kill his usurper. His partisans, especially those who knew him personally, always emphatically denied that he would ever have entertained such an idea; indeed, they all report that his invariable response to any such suggestion was an indignant veto. William was James's supplanter and arch-enemy, therefore to defeat him in battle was justifiable; but William was also his nephew and son-in-law, and James, whatever his faults, was not the man to connive at a cold-blooded murder, least of all of a member of his own family. Brice Blair's comment that 'he did not think it was in his nature' was echoed by most of the soldiers later sent from Saint-Germain to help organise a rebellion, and by many persons in England, such as Ailesbury, who knew James well. Moreover, quite apart from considerations of honour, even James, whose intelligence was not of the brightest, had sense enough to realise that the mere suspicion that he had commanded the murder of his rival would do great harm to his cause. For these reasons, then, any plans of this kind were carefully kept from him. When he did hear of them, as for instance from the dubious Crosby, his reaction was unequivocal: he was furious, and immediately dismissed Crosby from his presence with the command never to appear before him again. Afterwards he said the man must have been mad to come to him with such a suggestion, or else he was a spy sent by the Prince of Orange.[15]

Crosby returned to London in mid-April and stood his trial, but was acquitted for want of evidence against him.[16] There is no proof that he had been suborned and used as an *agent provocateur*, but James's guess was a shrewd one if Fenwick's statement about Crosby's assertion that a Commission existed was correct. Certainly James's very different account, which has a ring of truth, makes Crosby's assertion look distinctly suspicious. It is significant too that his name is not mentioned in connection with the later and more important conspiracy. If he had even been suspected of being a spy the conspirators would have avoided him and kept him out of their conclaves. And as far as the government was concerned, he had served his turn and was of no further use.

King William's departure for Flanders and James's firm refusal to sanction a personal attack on him had effectually discouraged the conspirators for the time being. But there was still the hope that Louis might be persuaded to provide James with an army large enough to ensure a restoration. The conspirators calculated that a force of about 10,000 men would be sufficient to enable James to secure a foothold in England. Once this was achieved, supporters from all over the country would rally to his side, and he would be swept back to his throne almost before the usurper, fighting in Flanders, was aware of what was happening. Speed and secrecy, therefore, were essential to the success of the operation. But first an emissary had to be sent to France to give both Louis and James a first-hand report on the current state of feeling in England and of the amount of support that could be counted on once James had landed. Charnock was selected as the person best qualified to undertake this mission, probably because he had a reputation for being a persuasive and eloquent speaker. But because he was a relatively obscure person Charnock would need to have his credentials vouched for by someone of standing at Saint-Germain; without a proper introduction, there was every likelihood that he would be taken for yet another of William's spies. James's Chamberlain at Saint-Germain was Lord Powis, and his son, Lord Montgomery, lived in London and was a frequenter of the little coterie of Jacobites that gathered round Sir John Fenwick; he was also a close friend of the Earl of Ailesbury. Montgomery, then, was the obvious person to provide Charnock with an introduction to Lord Powis and through him to James; but he was not, it would seem, personally acquainted with Charnock or any others among the conspirators and so it was necessary to approach him with this request through Ailesbury. Charnock had been too often rebuffed by the noble earl to make the approach himself, so Sir William Parkyns undertook to arrange matters for him. Although Ailesbury had a low opinion of

Charnock's social pretensions he thought well, even affectionately, of Sir William. He therefore agreed, albeit somewhat reluctantly, to act as intermediary between Montgomery and Charnock.

In his memoirs, written twenty years after these events, Ailesbury is very careful to say that he knew nothing of the real reason for Charnock's journey to France; so far as he knew, Charnock needed the introduction because he intended to go to Saint-Germain 'to seek his fortune'. Ailesbury was writing from a safe exile in Brussels, but even after the lapse of twenty years it would have been highly impolitic for him to admit any knowledge of Charnock's real reason for seeking the introduction from Lord Montgomery. Jacobitism was still a live issue, and the earl had a son and property in England. Both the son and the rest of his family could have found themselves in serious trouble if Ailesbury had been truthful about his own participation in the two meetings that followed Sir William's request. These meetings were treated as events of crucial importance by the prosecution at the trials of the participants, for they provided evidence that the rebellion was already being planned in the early summer of 1695, and they mark the beginning of the plot that was to come to a head in the following February. There seems little reason to doubt the testimonies of the crown witnesses, and they are substantiated by supporting evidence from several minor witnesses. Although Ailesbury's account of the proceedings is almost certainly inaccurate as regards his own part in them, it is by far the most detailed and entertaining, for he gives a characteristically lively account of a Jacobite dinner party. Ailesbury states in his memoirs that he consented, at Sir William Parkyns's request, to act as intermediary between Montgomery and Charnock. He goes on: 'I desired Sir William to bring him (Charnock) to dinner next day, and I would engage my Lord Montgomery to meet him at my house. But Sir William, who loved the bottle, desired we might meet at a public house, and I was so foolishly complying as to consent.'[17]

Sir William's reason for refusing the earl's invitation to dine at his house may partly have been because he feared he might be insufficiently free with the bottle, but there were additional reasons for the meeting to take place elsewhere. He had a private intention of making it a larger party and could not of course bring uninvited guests to the earl's dinner-table. Accordingly, he persuaded Ailesbury to bring Montgomery to dine with him and Charnock at the King's Head Tavern in Leadenhall Street. As 'dinner' in those days was a midday meal, the appointment was for two o'clock. The entertainment at the 'King's Head' was not, in the opinion of the two principal guests, either enjoyable or rewarding, and is is evident from Ailesbury's account that they thought they had been slumming, both socially and politically. In the first place, they had been given to understand that Sir John Fenwick, whom they both knew well, was to be the only other guest. But Fenwick brought with him a notoriously silly youth, Peter Cook, son of Sir Miles Cook, a Master in Chancery. 'This Mr. Peter Cook had a zeal beyond knowledge, and I never could be quiet for him thrusting himself upon me', was Ailesbury's irritable comment on this addition to the party. Next, he was disconcerted to find that Sir John Friend was also included, for he knew that, like Sir William, he was 'a great bottle man' and he did not trust his discretion. All this was tiresome enough, but worse was to come, for 'Sir William Parkyns brought thither, unknown to me, that monster of a man, George Porter . . . and I was enraged to the last degree, and at table, with a miserable dinner, I scarce opened my lips.'[18]

According to Ailesbury, nothing of importance was talked about during the meal, and he says that he and Montgomery left as soon as it was over. As they went out, they met Goodman on the stairs, coming to join the party. He had been invited, but had not been able to come until after dinner, at about half past three in the afternoon. As to what took place later, all Ailesbury says is that 'I heard that some of the company staid till four in the morning. What they did I do not know, but no doubt the bottle went round.'[19] He met Montgomery a few days later, who complained that 'he had been with ill company and had had a very bad dinner'. And Montgomery, it seemed, had been much too irritated by the whole proceeding to oblige Charnock with an introduction to his father at Saint-Germain.

Notwithstanding Ailesbury's insistence on his own innocence, it is clear from the testimonies of several others who were present that there had been a good deal of seditious talk both before and after the dinner at the 'King's Head' and that he must have taken part in at least some of it. Porter, for instance, deposed that: 'Several things were talked of before dinner, concerning the best ways of bringing back King James; and after several proposals having been made, it was agreed on by the whole company to send Captain Charnock to King James, which he accepted of.'[20]

Peter Cook deposed that: 'When Lord Ailesbury and Lord Montgomery were going away from the meeting in Leadenhall Street, Charnock followed them to the coach side and said to them, "Well, my lords, it is your intention that I should go over?" and they answered, "yes, sure, if you think fit".'

Although this statement of Cook's need not necessarily be taken as evidence that the two lords had known of the purpose of Charnock's journey to France, it is most unlikely that they could have been ignorant of it; Goodman as well as Porter swore that they had both taken part in the decision made after dinner. Moreover, they both consented to attend a further meeting and must have had some ulterior motive for doing so, for plainly they would not have been willing to meet this company again just for the pleasure of it. And there could be no doubt about the traitorous nature of the decisions arrived at after dinner. Charnock, in the name of all present, was to ask King James to 'borrow 10,000 men of the king of France, viz. 8,000 foot, 1,000 horse and 1,000 dragoons'. He was also instructed to tell James that there were very few forces left in England and that there were 'a great many people dissatisfied, and that therefore they could not choose a fitter time'. The demands of the conspirators, it may be noted, were now considerably reduced. In 1692 a force of 30,000 men had been asked for, but now they evidently realised that it would be unrealistic to ask for so great a number; a request for the loan of only 10,000 men would, they thought, stand a much better chance of acceptance by Louis. As Porter said, the company agreed that 'if the king of France meant well to King James, he could not refuse him so small a number of men'.[22] Charnock then pointed out that it would be useless to ask for a French army unless both James and the French could be assured that there would be adequate support for it in England once a landing had been effected. After some further discussion he was instructed to tell James that he would be met on landing in England with a body of at least 2000 Horse, and that these would be augmented by still larger contingents once the news of his arrival became known. To ratify and confirm this promise the whole company then rose to their feet and drank a solemn pledge to the success of the undertaking – with the exception of Peter Cook, whose legs by this time were so unreliable that he had to drink his pledge kneeling on his chair with his elbows on the table.

The promises of support and the terms of the message to King James were agreed upon solemnly enough but Charnock, who had a cooler head than most of his associates, knew that the bottle had gone round too often for these decisions to have been made in complete sobriety; he refused to set out on his errand until there had been an interval for calmer reflection. And, as he rightly remarked, he would be going on a fool's errand if he could not give King James absolute assurance that he would be met on landing by at least 2000 mounted men. The company were still sober enough to see the sense of this, and arranged to hold a confirmatory meeting in a week's time. A change of venue was considered advisable and so the second meeting took place at a tavern kept by a Mrs Mountjoy. Ailesbury had thought poorly of the entertainment at the 'King's Head'; he was even more affronted at finding himself in this dubious establishment.

'It was', he reports', 'a tavern, but a poor one, and kept by one Mrs. Mountjoy, a woman who I found to be of moderate reputation, and the few who served her were of her sex . . . Bad wine, I suppose, there was sufficient, and for eating she sent out for provisions after we arrived.' The place, as Ailesbury indicates in his prim way, was no better than a cheap brothel. Lord Montgomery arrived, but at once pleaded urgent business elsewhere and excused himself from the meeting. The earl, in spite of his patrician distaste for the place and the company, did manage to derive some amusement from the situation. 'The mistress of the house passing for what I have hinted at', he says, 'and Mr. Peter Cook for a devotee, we placed that mixture at the upper end of the table, and that made me laugh. The woman and her maids were in the room as long as I stayed, and that was all our discourse . . . I went away very soon.'23

Once again his lordship had conveniently forgotten that there had been any more serious discourse, and that he did not in fact leave the tavern until the purpose of the meeting had been achieved. According to Porter and several other witnesses, 'Mr Chernock [sic] had desired the meeting to be satisfied before he went whether they kept to their former resolution of meeting king James with 2000 horse, and they all agreed to it, and desired to beg of king James to make what haste he could.'

As Ailesbury was leaving, Charnock followed him to his coach and begged him 'for the love of God' to persuade Montgomery to give him the introduction to his father. The earl returned a noncommittal answer, and drove off. Soon afterwards he went to Tunbridge Wells where he stayed for three months mainly, he said, to avoid the solicitations of the Jacobites. In spite of Ailesbury's repeated assurances of his own innocence, it is impossible to believe that he had attended these meetings without knowing anything whatever of their true purpose. Moreover, the fact that Charnock, on his return from France, brought letters to Ailesbury from King James indicates that he was expected to come back with messages. Had Charnock really gone to Saint-Germain to seek his fortune he would hardly have returned so soon. According to Peter Cook, admittedly not a very reliable witness, Charnock had sought out Ailesbury immediately after his return from his mission, in order to report results.24

Charnock went to France in late May, taking with him a long and detailed memorandum for King James setting out the conspirators' view of the current feeling in England, and stressing the need for prompt action by James and the French government: 'The persons from who I am sent to you (viz. the Earl of Ailesbury, Lord Montgomery, Sir John Fenwick, Sir William Parkyns, etc.) say that the inclination of the people to the present government is changed into an universal defection.'[25] It is significant that the names of Ailesbury and Montgomery head this list, but whether both or either of them had consented to it is a matter of conjecture. Certainly they both denied having done so, but this was only to be expected.

The memorandum enumerates the various groups that the signatories confidently expected would join King James as soon as he landed in England. The list of those supposed to be disaffected to King William is substantially the same as that sent to James in 1693 (see chapter 2). The bulk of the English army, the writers say, is engaged in Flanders; very few contingents, and those scattered about the country, are left for the defence of England. For this reason 10,000 men would be quite sufficient to support a landing; the French king, it was thought, could quite easily spare that number of men. Finally, James was given full assurance that he would be met in England by at least 2000 horse, and that they would be augmented by contingents from all over the country as soon as his presence there became known. All was in readiness, and all that the king's friends needed to know was the time and place of his landing. Then they would flock to his side, and the rest would follow.[26]

This document demonstrates once again the Jacobites' ignorance of the true state of feeling in England, for it claims that almost all sections of the population were ready to rise against the foreign tyrant William, a statement for which there is no real evidence. That James's advisers at Saint-Germain were even more ignorant is less surprising, for they were dependent for information upon Jacobite sources; and the death of Queen Mary had given them fresh hopes. As early as January 1695, Secretary Carryl, Melfort's successor at Saint-Germain, sent a long memorial to James and Louis, setting out the reasons why a restoration would stand a better chance now than ever before. William's right to the throne, Carryl says, was universally held to be invalidated by Mary's death, since now King James, the Prince of Wales and Princess Anne all had a prior claim. William's only hope of keeping the crown was to import a large foreign force to cow the English into accepting him as sole ruler; he was alleged to be making preparations for this already. The English would never submit to having a ruler imposed upon them by force, much less by a foreign force, and so they would immediately rise in rebellion against William and would be ready to welcome James and a French army as deliverers from foreign tyranny. The time, Carryl declared, had never been more propitious, for the whole country was on the verge of revolt. The High Church party in particular was said to be ready to declare for King James, for they feared that William was planning to dis-establish the Church of England, as he had the Episcopal Church in Scotland in 1691. Even the dissenters would rebel in defence of their country and their liberties.[27] The document is a typical example of the blinkered outlook of James's advisers, for Secretary Carryl seems quite unaware that parliament had already and without demur ratified William's right to rule alone. Nor is there any evidence that William had ever thought it necessary to import an army to defend his claim. And he was far too astute a politician to antagonise the majority of his English subjects by dis-establishing their national Church. As to the assertion that the English would be bound to rise and defend their country against a foreign army, no one at Saint-Germain appears to have considered that this would apply with much greater force to an invasion by the army of a country with which England was already at war. There must, however, have been some more sober counsellors at Saint-Germain, for no action was taken in response to Carryl's memorandum.

But His Majesty's loyal friends, both in England and in France, were never inactive for long. On the heels of Charnock's message came another memorandum, dated 28 June 1695 but unsigned. It requests that 'some directions be given to such as Your Majesty does most particularly confide in, what your friends in general must do, supposing the Prince of Orange to be killed in France, or that he should die before Your Majesty can be able to make a descent; it being natural to believe that either the Princess Anne or a commonwealth would be advanced, unless obstructed by Your Majesty just at this juncture'.[28]

This has been interpreted by James's enemies as a veiled allusion to an intended assassination of William, the inference being that James was fully aware that it was being planned. But this is putting a malicious construction on what was a perfectly sensible request. William was fighting a war, and in time of battle was ever careless of his own safety; he had been wounded once at the Boyne, and might at any time be killed by a chance bullet. Although there had been some improvement, his general health had never been good since an attack of smallpox in early life had left him with chronic asthma. Clearly then the possibility that he might die at any time was one that had to be considered by his enemies as well as by his friends, and it was quite reasonable for the Jacobites to take steps to deal with this contingency. There is in fact no record of James having taken any action in response to this memorandum, but doubtless he and Louis had given the matter some consideration.

Unhappily for the Jacobites, their reviving hopes were fated once again to be disappointed. Charnock returned from a three weeks' journey to Saint-Germain bearing a dispiriting message from James: 'His Majesty took it very kindly, but could not do anything that year.'[29] The main reason for James's inability to take action at that time was much as it had been the previous year and, from a tactical point of view, the time for asking for the loan of even a small French army was even less propitious than it had been then. The bulk of that army was heavily engaged in Flanders, and by now even the mighty French nation was beginning to suffer from the strain on its manpower and resources that the long war had imposed. Moreover, the best part of the French fleet was still bottled up in the Mediterranean by the English, so that it would not have been possible to provide adequate transports and naval cover for a descent upon England. And William was then making tentative peace overtures, which were being given careful consideration by Louis and his ministers. Although these came to nothing, and the War of the League of Augsberg was to continue for another two years, there was still in the summer of 1695 some possibility of a Peace Treaty between England and France. It was thus hardly the moment to jeopardise the success of the negotiations by making an unprovoked attack upon England. James's more realistic advisers at Saint-Germain, such as Middleton, were doubtless well aware that the time for requesting French aid was more than usually unpropitious, and that they must bide their time until the situation changed; the hot-heads in England, on the other hand, seem not to have taken these factors into consideration.

Strategic and political considerations were in themselves quite sufficient to warrant Louis's refusal to help James at this time. But there was another and almost equally important factor, and that was James himself. The James of 1695 was very different from the man he had been even in 1688. There are strong indications that the crisis of the Revolution had brought on some kind of seizure from which he never fully recovered, and a number of physical symptoms point to this. The attacks of severe nose-bleeding from which he suffered during his abortive attempt to defend his crown in 1688 might well have been the outward sign of a cerebral disturbance or a mild stroke. It is significant too that on his arrival in France he was reported to speak with a pronounced stammer, which had never been remarked on before; this also is a common reaction to severe stress. James's physical health had always been good; he was noted for his energy and industry, and at the age of sixty-six was reportedly hunting with the vigour of a man of twenty. But from his early youth he had been subjected to a series of stressful and often traumatic experiences well beyond the common lot and his intelligence was not of the best. Moreover, the mild obsessionalism that in earlier life had made him a good and hard-working administrator became as he grew older his dominant and most unfortunate characteristic: it drove him into a situation with which he was no longer fit to cope.

All accounts of James's behaviour during the weeks immediately preceding his flight to France indicate that he was then behaving in an uncharacteristic way. From a decisive and determined man, convinced of the rightness of his policies and prepared to carry them out in the face of opposition, he seems to have become almost overnight a confused, frightened and rather pathetic old person, who had lost the power of making any decision not directly related to his personal security. The nose-bleeding cleared up and the stammering disappeared soon after his arrival in France, but the change in personality remained. It was not the gross deterioration of extreme senility, but all the subsequent accounts of James at Saint-Germain depict a priest-ridden, garrulous and rather simple old gentleman, with little or no sign of the drive and determination that had been so evident before his downfall. These accounts vary from the malicious to the affectionately indulgent, but all convey the impression of a person who is no longer taken quite seriously. All the writers too remark on his apparent indifference to his misfortunes and, after the failure of the Irish campaign, his lack of interest in a restoration. To his detractors this was a sign of senility; to his friends, Christian resignation. The truth may well have been that it was an unconscious refusal to face a situation with which he was no longer equipped to deal.

One of the most illuminating descriptions of James at Saint-Germain is given by Rizzini, who had been Modenese Envoy at the Court of St James, and who had known James in his heyday:

He lives always surrounded by friars and talks of his misfortunes with indifference, as if he did not feel them or had never been a king; in this way he has entirely lost the respect of the French and those who knew him in Flanders (forty years previously) say that he was quite another man then, so great is the change they find in his Majesty, who, however, is as affable and courteous to everyone as could be desired.[30]

Time and adversity had worked sad changes in the Golden Boy who had charmed the ladies of the French Court forty years before. James, it was said, had exchanged three kingdoms for a Mass; perhaps it was by a merciful dispensation that he appeared content with the bargain. His biographer James Clarke, speaking of the effect upon him of his failures and misfortunes, says: 'These constant ill successes of all the King's endeavours, had long convinced him, that Providence had marked out no other way for his sanctification than that of suffring [sic] for which reason those attempts that he had made of late were rather at the Sollicitation of his subjects, or that he might not be defective in his duty to the Prince his son, than out of any earnest desire to make the same figure in the world as he had formerly done.'[31]

More concerned with repentance for his sins than with restoring his fallen fortunes, James became increasingly pre-occupied with his religious exercises. From 1692 onwards he paid regular and prolonged visits to the monastery of La Trappe, where he took full part in the monastic life and spared himself none of the hardships, except that on medical advice he allowed himself to supplement the spartan diet with an occasional egg. His queen was similarly devout, and their religious interests formed another bond in a marriage that against all probability turned out to be a very happy one. But in James, for all his shortcomings, there was a certain sweetness of nature that became more evident in adversity; it won him the lasting affection not only of his young and beautiful wife, but also of Louis XIV. However, the Court at Saint-Germain can never have been a cheerful place, for James filled it with monks and friars, to the discomfort of the secular members, who found themselves crowded out by clerics. The Trappist atmosphere that James succeeded in imposing on it, the quarrelling factions and the pervasive air of hope deferred, not to mention a chronic shortage of money, must have made it gloomy indeed.

The unfailing affection and consideration that Louis accorded to his unfortunate protégé was one of his more endearing traits. But he cannot have failed to notice the apathy into which James had fallen, for the two kings met frequently. It must have occurred to Louis that James was now hardly the man to a lead a hazardous expedition with the energy and *élan* necessary to carry it to a successful conclusion. Neither would he have presented a figure with much appeal for the protestant English. This consideration, quite as much as the current difficulty of providing adequate support for a landing, may have influenced Louis's decision not to provide help at this juncture. However, James was able to assure his friends in England that this refusal was not absolute; the attempt was only put off 'till a fitter time'. Deteriorated though he might be, James was still a valuable pawn in Louis's hands, and he never let his personal affection for him blind him to political reality. He would keep him in reserve until the 'fitter time' came for a move against his opponent William.

Charnock, returning from his unsuccessful mission to France on 15 June, found several of his confederates in Newgate, where they had been confined as disturbers of the peace. The more irresponsible of the Jacobites were wont to celebrate the birthdays of the exiled royal family with copious potations, which often ended with a public display of loyalty. The birthday of the young Prince of Wales was 10 June, clearly an occasion for celebration. Fenwick, Goodman, Porter and his servant Thomas Keyes, together with a number of kindred spirits, foregathered at the Dog Tavern in Drury Lane. Many Jacobite songs were sung and many healths drunk to the prince and his parents until the revellers, flown with wine and loyal enthusiasm, unwisely attempted a more public demonstration. Luttrell reports that: 'With kettle drums, trumpets, etc., they caroused, and having a bonfire near the place, would have forced the bystanders to have drunk the said prince's health, which they refusing, occasioned a tumult.'[32]

Keyes's trumpet must have contributed to the uproar, for he had been a trumpeter before entering Porter's service, and when the conspirators' business was over would often entertain them with a tune. The crowd that collected to watch the proceedings was certainly not going to be enticed into drinking Jacobite toasts. They chased the demonstrators back into the tavern, where a fight took place which nearly wrecked the place before the Jacobites were driven out into the arms of the hastily summoned Watch. Porter, Goodman, Keyes and several others were arrested and committed to Newgate, but were released about a month later on payment of a fine. Fenwick too was arrested but was let out on bail, mainly because he had been too drunk to emerge from the tavern and contribute to the uproar in the street.

If the Jacobites had hoped to gain more adherents by this exhibition they must have been sorely disappointed. The London crowd left them in no doubt as to where their loyalties lay – they were solidly for King William; there was, certainly on this occasion, no sign of the 'almost universal defection' so confidently reported to Saint-Germain. Indeed the 'Jacks', as they were contemptuously called, seem not to have been taken very seriously and were regarded as noisy nuisances rather than a danger to the peace of the realm. The law took a similar attitude; although the revellers had been arrested on a charge of treason they were punished as disturbers of the peace rather than as political offenders. The populace accorded a similar reception to several other Jacobite demonstrators. For example, on 12 August Trooper Bishop, of the Earl of Oxford's regiment, staged a one-man rebellion when he 'rode through the City with sword and pistol in hand saying King William was dead, and he would kill any that should deny it; but the mob soon brought him down, and being carried before the Lord Mayor, he was committed to Newgate'.[33] The Earl of Oxford's regiment was rumoured to be riddled with disaffection, but Trooper Bishop's exploit was extravagant even for a Jacobite; he was fined 100 marks and ordered to stand three times in the pillory.

In order to let Porter know of the discouraging result of his mission Charnock had to seek him out in Newgate. According to Porter, Charnock also brought back letters from King James to Ailesbury, Fenwick, Sir William Parkyns and 'several other persons of quality whom he did not name'. As usual these persons of quality remain discreetly anonymous. Throughout this affair there are dark hints and rumours of treachery on the part of various highly placed persons in King William's government; it is significant that when the plot was discovered not one of these persons was called to account for having taken part in it. Whether the conspirators were using their names to get backing from Louis, or whether the grandees were using the lesser men as catspaws will probably never be known; certainly, if Marlborough, Shrewsbury, Godolphin or any of those whose names were whispered had had anything to do with the plot they covered their tracks very efficiently; none of the rumours of their disaffection was substantiated and William himself always refused to listen to such slanders.

During the summer and autumn of 1695 the conspirators made no definite plans; they were waiting for the 'fitter time'. In August came the news of the Allied victory at Namur, the only resounding success of the whole long war. Although fighting was to continue for another two years, after Namur the tide turned in the Allies' favour, and this went some way towards reconciling the English to the hardships that the war imposed. The bells were rung for William on his return to England in November; once again he was temporarily a popular hero, and in return for his subjects' enthusiasm he seems to have made more effort to behave graciously towards them. He went on a progress shortly after his return, and was received everywhere with acclamation. If there were Jacobites among the crowds that gathered to see him pass, they were careful not to advertise themselves.

Although the Jacobites had had to put off taking immediate action, they were not inactive. Sir William Parkyns's house in Bushey was conveniently situated for conspiracy, being at the London end of the straggling village street and well screened by orchards and gardens.

There was a good deal of coming and going here during the late summer and autumn. One of the more notable visitors was the veteran conspirator Robert Ferguson, who stayed there at least once, and used Sir William's house as a distribution centre for the stream of subversive pamphlets that flowed from his pen. Of all the odd characters thrown up by the numerous conspiracies of the seventeenth century, Robert Ferguson was the strangest. He was consistent in one thing only: he devoted a long busy life to conspiring against the reigning king. Born in Scotland, the son of a cavalier, he took holy orders early in life and became successively a presbyterian, an independent and finally an episcopalian. He was a prolific writer, and in earlier days had written many of the pamphlets issued by Shaftesbury (Dryden's 'false Achitophel') in furtherance of his scheme to inflame popular opinion against King Charles. He had also written a number of perfectly orthodox religious treatises. He was heavily involved in (if he did not instigate) the Rye House Plot of 1683. In 1685 he fought against King James in the Monmouth rebellion. In 1688 Ferguson was one of the most ardent supporters of the Revolution, but no sooner were William and Mary established on the throne than he changed sides and became a Jacobite. Although much of Ferguson's life abroad was spent as an impoverished fugitive, and in England he was hunted by the authorities and frequently imprisoned, he lived to a ripe old age and died in his bed, to the last industriously plotting against Queen Anne. His appearance was as strange as his life. A vivid thumbnail portrait is given in one of the proclamations offering a reward for his capture: 'A tall, lean man, dark brown hair, a great roman nose, thin-jawed, heat in his face, speaks in a Scotch tone, a sharp piercing eye, stoops a little in his shoulders; he hath a shuffling gait that differs him from all men, wears his periwig down almost over his eyes.'[34]

Ferguson's sincerity and devotion to whatever cause he espoused is unquestionable. Unlike so many of the persons with whom his subversive activities obliged him to consort, he was never known to betray an associate and for this reason was implicitly trusted by them. In the summer of 1695 he was living precariously in London, flitting from one lodging to another and on several occasions narrowly escaping arrest; he wrote several inflammatory pamphlets at this time proving, with much scriptural justification, that William's usurpation of the throne was contrary to the laws of God and man. It was therefore the Christian as well as the moral duty of every Englishman to depose him at once and restore the rightful king. Although Ferguson was active in promoting rebellion and attended a number of meetings where this was discussed, he was never involved in the plot against the king's life. Indeed, this was carefully concealed from him, for it was known that he would have set his face against a deed that he considered underhand. When, much later, he did get wind of it he is reported to have informed Saint-Germain with a view to getting it prohibited; but by then it was too late to stop the attempt being made.

Among the visitors to Bushey Manor was Job Hewett, who arrived there about the end of September, bringing with him a bundle of Ferguson's pamphlets for distribution about the country. Hewett seems on several occasions to have acted as a messenger between London and Saint-Germain, where his uncle, Captain Holmes, later to take an important part in the Assassination Plot, was an officer in King James's bodyguard. Another uncle, who rejoiced in the soubriquet 'Old England' Holmes, and who was described by Matthew Smith as 'an old, fat, lethargy man', was some kind of factotum or hanger-on of Sir William's. 'Old England', from his nickname, must have been a traditionalist and probably a Jacobite, but he does not appear to have taken an active part in the conspiracy. He was useful however, and according to Smith spent most of that summer at Bushey, his chief function being to bring Sir William's spare horses up and down from London. Matthew Smith was also at Bushey intermittently during the summer. He was there when Hewett arrived with the pamphlets and as the house was already full, they had to share a bed. Smith, running true to form, attempted to make use of this opportunity to pump Hewett for information about various matters, and particularly the whereabouts of Ferguson, as he knew that a substantial reward had been offered for the latter's arrest. But Hewett refused to be drawn, knowing that Smith would carry any information straight to Shrews-bury. After the discovery of the conspiracy, Smith alleged that on this occasion Hewett had told him that he was to be a cornet in Sir William's troop of Horse, and had divulged some interesting details about the plot to kill the king. Hewett stoutly denied that he had ever told Smith anything of the sort. Smith, he said, was in the habit of hanging about the Jacobites' favourite taverns in the hope of gleaning scraps of saleable information. Hewett had encountered him several times, and always answered any leading questions by putting him off with tales from the news-sheets, or even inventing some himself. Clearly, Smith was gullible as well as inefficient, for when these two were confronted at the trial of Sir John Fenwick Hewett, 'so exposed Smith that he had nothing to say for himself'.[35]

As the year advanced, Sir William and his confederates began to hope that the 'fitter time' for King James's return was approaching, and they intensified their preparations for it. Abraham Sweet, an Excise Officer who had been for some three years on friendly terms with Sir William, spent a good deal of his time at Bushey. Walking in the orchard and garden, he and Sir William had many conversations about King James's return but never, Sweet deposed, had Sir William been so positive about its imminence as he was shortly before Christmas 1695. 'Great things were expected of him by King James', Sir William told Sweet, and he had made full preparations to meet him when he landed, which would be very soon; the troop of Horse that Sir William had been raising was now complete; it consisted 'all of old soldiers', as well as several gentlemen volunteers who were to ride with him. In addition, he had spent much money on the purchase of thirty saddles and other gear for his men.[36]

The saddles and arms that Sir William, according to Sweet's evidence, bought for his troop must have been safely concealed somewhere in or about Bushey or London, for they never came to light. They could not have been the arms that he had bought and concealed at his house in Marston Jabbett at the time of the Lancashire Plot in the spring of 1694, for these would not have been immediately available for a troop in London or Hertfordshire. Towards the end of September Sir William was clearly becoming worried lest the weapons hidden in Warwickshire should be discovered, for the government, perhaps through Matthew Smith, might at any moment get wind of them and the conspirators were never safe from spies and *agents provocateurs*. If Sir William came under suspicion of traitorous activity, both the Bushey and Marston Jabbett houses would be searched and the hidden arms discovered; it was therefore necessary to find a safer place of concealment for them.

To this end, Sir William made use of Charnock and his Warwick-shire connections. A sister of Charnock's had married a farmer called Heywood, who was one of the tenants on the Warwickshire estate and lived at Callidown House, three miles from Marston Jabbett. Char-nock, who must have known all about the cache of arms, wrote at Sir William's request to his brother-in-law, explaining that Sir William was shutting up the manor house and needed somewhere to store a few items of furniture. Most of it had already been removed, but there remained a few things for which Sir William had no space; as he did not want to risk leaving goods in an empty house, he would be much obliged if Heywood could store these things until they could be disposed of. Heywood agreed to this seemingly innocent request and shortly afterwards the 'goods' arrived and were stored in an empy attic. They comprised three large wooden boxes, very heavy and carefully nailed up, a bed, some pieces of tapestry and a few other odds and ends – miscellaneous objects doubtless included to lend colour to Sir William's story.[37] Heywood does not seem to have been sufficiently inquisitive to tamper with the nailed-up boxes, for he swore to complete ignorance of their contents. When they were opened some months later, they were found to contain three dozen cavalry swords, thirty-two carbines and twenty-five brace of pistols. There can be little doubt that these were the arms reported by Matthew Smith to have been hidden by his uncle at Marston Jabbett in 1694 and, as he said, there were enough weapons to equip a troop of Horse. But who was to use them and for what purpose was never discovered. They were certainly hidden at too great a distance to be recovered at short notice by Sir William's troop of old soldiers.

Throughout that summer and autumn Sir William was commuting regularly between Bushey and London. At first he used the George Inn, a large new establishment in Holborn, as his London base; there was ample stable-room at the 'George' for the five or six horses that Sir William was in the habit of bringing up to town, usually with the assistance of 'Old England' Holmes. After he left the 'George' he continued to keep his horses there, and the frequent comings and goings of these animals was later to be regarded with justifiable suspicion, for it was thought, rightly, that they were not for their owner's sole use. Later in the year, perhaps for reasons of economy, but more probably for the greater convenience of conspiring, Sir William joined Charnock at his lodgings in Norfolk Street in a house kept by a Mrs Conant. Norfolk Street has only recently disappeared under a new 'development'. Built in 1684, it was one of a series of little streets of flat-fronted red-brick houses running down from the Strand to the riverside. It was conveniently close to the Temple and to most of the Jacobites' favourite taverns. Porter joined Sir William and Charnock there soon afterwards, and the three men lived together on close and convivial terms. 'We used', said Porter in his evidence, 'frequently to visit a tavern in the evenings, or drink a bottle of wine in our chambers.' Mrs Conant must have been a Jacobite sympathiser, for she can hardly have been unaware that her house had become a meeting-place for the conspirators; her lodgers kept open house for the other members of their gang, and there was much coming and going in Norfolk Street at this time. It was a safer place in which to talk treason than a tavern, and there was a good deal of discussion over the wine as to the best way to bring back King James. For the inner ring of the conspiracy this inevitably involved the removal of King William and, according to Porter, who took a prominent part in the deliberations, murder and not kidnapping was their avowed object, 'and we thought the quickest way to bring in the king, and restore him to his crown, was by knocking king William on the head; and there were several meetings about the best way of doing it'.[38]

Several plans were considered, all of them impractical, and all requiring a considerable number of men to carry out. Characteristically, it was Porter who proposed the wildest of them: a troop of heavily armed men, equipped with long ladders, was to attack Kensington Palace one dark night. First killing the guard, they were to use the ladders to climb into the king's bedchamber, kill him as he slept and then set fire to the palace to cover their crime. But this project was thought by the rest to be too difficult and dangerous to be given serious consideration. Another plan was to attack King William as he was returning from chapel through Hyde Park. His coach was to be set upon as it passed through the gates; it was calculated that thirty or forty men could easily overcome the guards, kill the king and make their escape before the alarm could be raised. But the most favoured place for the murder was Richmond Park. Here, the conspirators thought, it would be easy to attack the king when he was hunting, for he would be unlikely to have the guard with him then and any companions he might have would be few and lightly armed. Thus the conspirators talked and planned over their wine, but even the hot-head Porter realised that the time for action had not yet come, for there would be little point in killing King William before King James could be at hand to take his place. They must wait, as Charnock repeatedly told them, until the French fleet could leave the Mediterranean and join the rest of the French ships at Brest. Not until then could the Jacobites hope for French support for James's landing. In the meantime, all they could do was wait, talk and plan, and watch the comings and goings of their prospective victim.

PART II

The plot

6
'King James is a'coming'

TOWARDS THE BEGINNING OF DECEMBER, reports began to come in that the French fleet at Toulon was at last fitting out preparatory to evading the English blockade and sailing to Brest, then as now one of the chief French naval bases. This move was possible because Admiral Russell and a large part of the Mediterranean fleet had been recalled in late autumn to defend the Channel coast. Admiral Rooke was left in command in the Mediterranean, but had too few ships for the double task of assisting the Allied forces in Spain and maintaining the blockade at Toulon; he was also handicapped by a serious shortage of supplies. The concentration of the French navy at Brest was regarded by the English and their allies as a serious threat to their sea-power, communications and trade; the Jacobites viewed it rather in the light of Birnam Wood coming to Dunsinane, for to them it presaged the downfall of the usurper William. Louis would now have plenty of ships at hand for the projected advance upon England.

Admiral Russell was ordered out to intercept the French fleet, but adverse winds kept his ships in port from mid-December until the beginning of February, thus enabling the French to slip through the straits of Gibraltar and reach Brest unmolested. This manoeuvre caused some alarm to the English, for the enemy fleet was now in full strength almost on their doorstep. In the event, however, it was a protestant wind that kept Russell's ships in port. Burnet says that: 'This was then thought a great unhappiness, but we found afterwards, that our preservation was chiefly owing to it; and it was so extraordinary a thing, to see the wind fixed at the south-west during the whole winter, that few could resist the observing a signal providence of God in it.'[1] The wind was indeed providential, for had Russell's ships been able to sail for the Mediterranean, the coasts of England would have been very inadequately defended against invasion from across the Channel.

To the Jacobites the arrival of the French fleet at Brest was a sure sign that their hopes of enlisting French help would soon be realised;

as confident as ever they took no trouble to conceal their jubilation and boasted openly that their king would soon be enjoying his own again, thereby causing considerable public disquiet, as Burnet reports: 'We were all this winter alarmed from many different quarters, with the insolent discourses of the jacobites, who seemed so well assured of a sudden revolution, which was to be both quick and entire, that at Christmas, they said, it would be brought about within six weeks.'[2] This was why Abraham Sweet the Excise Officer said that he had never had so much assurance from Sir William Parkyns of King James's coming as he had that Christmas: 'for at, or since that time, he told me that he had it from the king's own hand, that he would come'. Goodman too believed the invasion to be imminent. He was in regular correspondence with Parker at Saint-Germain, and 'always or most commonly in his letters he told me for a sign, when the Toulon fleet should join the Brest fleet, I might certainly depend that we should be invaded here'.[3]

Almost the only person in England to remain unperturbed by the boastings of the Jacobites was William himself. Absorbed in his preparations for the forthcoming campaign in Flanders, he paid little attention to them; besides, he was not a man to worry about things that did not interest him, or which came between him and his over-riding passion in life, fighting the French. For this reason perhaps, the government took no steps to investigate the alarms and rumours of invasion that by Christmas were common talk in the taverns and coffee houses of London.

William's preoccupation with the war probably led him to under-estimate both the danger from France and his own growing unpopu-larity with his politicians. The elections of 1695 had returned a predominantly Whig Parliament. William had never fully trusted the Whigs, suspecting them, not without justification, of trying to set further limits to the powers of the crown; many of them, he thought, were republicans at heart. He therefore tended to favour the Tories, who at least could be trusted to uphold the institution of monarchy; moreover, his policy had always been to attempt to maintain some balance of power between the two parties. William was thus not altogether pleased with the results of the election and, not surprisingly, by the autumn of 1695 he was at loggerheads with the Commons on several issues. His proposal to grant huge tracts of royal lands in Wales to the Duke of Portland was refused by the Commons. The Bill for the Regulating of Trials for Treason was at last passed by both Houses, although William and the Court party had never been in favour of it; it was thought to endanger the personal safety of the

JAMES the second by the grace of God King of England Scotland France and Ireland defender of the Faith &c. To Our Trusty and well beloved Greeting. This is to autorize you to raise and command a Troop of Horse as Captaine in the Regiment Commanded by Our Trusty & wellbeloved   and to obey the orders from time to time according to the Disciplin of war. Given at Our Court at St. Germains the *twentieth* day of *June 1692* And in the *eight* — year of Our Reigne.

By his Majestys Comand.

1. Officer's commission of 1692, signed by James and counter-signed by Melfort, with a blank space for the officer's name. One of fifty commissions and other documents found concealed in a hole in a wall at Standish Hall, Lancashire, in 1752. The commissions distributed in 1693–4 would have been similar to this.

2. The royal exiles at Saint-Germain, by Pierre Mignard. The painting was commissioned by Louis XIV. It shows the young Prince of Wales James Edward (the Old Pretender), Queen Mary Beatrice, the baby Princess Louise Marie ('la Consolatrice') and a much aged James. The family went to Versailles for sittings because the 83-year-old artist was unable to make the journey to Saint-Germain.

3. William III. Copy of a portrait attributed to W. Wissing. It shows William in middle age.

4. Nine Jacobite plotters, from a German engraving in the Sutherland Collection. These are the conspirators who did not escape punishment. The dates of their executions are given in the new style, that is ten days later than the seventeenth-century dating.

5. Part of a view of London from the river, from an engraving by S. and N. Buck, 1749, showing Norfolk Street on the north bank with a glimpse of the Strand at the top of the street. Much of this area was built in the 1680s, hence the uniform appearance of the houses.

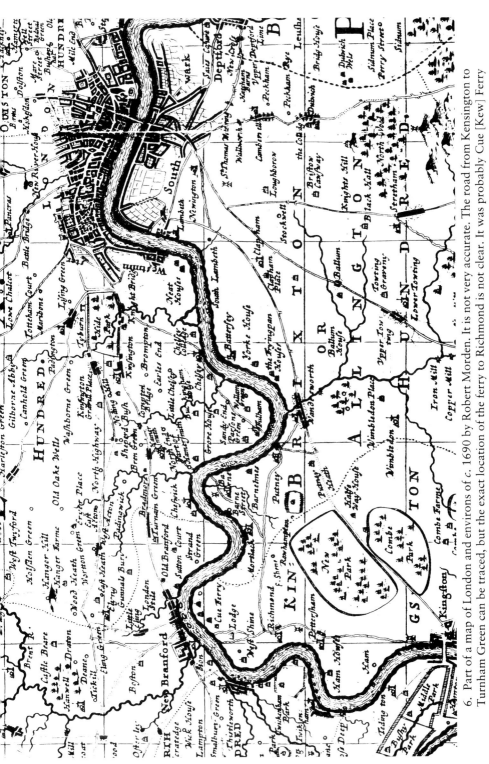

6. Part of a map of London and environs of c. 1690 by Robert Morden. It is not very accurate. The road from Kensington to Turnham Green can be traced, but the exact location of the ferry to Richmond is not clear. It was probably Cue [Kew] Ferry and was close to where Kew Bridge is now.

7. The conspirators in conference, with the musketoon on the table. An identical weapon, said to be the one associated with the Assassination Plot, can be seen in the Armoury of the Tower of London. It was an early form of revolver and could fire six or eight shots without re-loading.

8. Lord Chief Justice Sir John Holt, by R. van Bleeck *c.* 1700.

9. Ink and wash drawing of a public execution. No date or title is given, but from internal evidence it is roughly contemporary with the Assassination Plot, and must have been of Tyburn where the 'triple tree' or triangular gallows was situated. Note the priest and the shorthand writer in the cart with the condemned men.

monarch. In December the Commission appointed to enquire into the Massacre of Glencoe at last reported its findings, laying the blame for the massacre fairly and squarely on the Scottish politicians who had ordered it. But although it was widely held that death should have been the penalty for so terrible an atrocity, William contented himself with removing the chief offenders from office. It is possible that he did so because he was not entirely free from responsibility in the matter, having signed the original orders (without realising their full implications) for the proceedings against Glencoe. Of course this leniency did nothing to enhance his popularity, particularly in the Highlands. William's proposal to remedy the devaluation of the coinage by royal proclamation without reference to parliament also caused much offence, and was defeated. These and other minor defeats justified Clarke's statement that 'The Prince of Orange's affairs began not to have so favourable an aspect as formerly; that the new-called parliament were reasty and refractory on several points.'[4]

There were other causes for dissatisfaction, notably the heavy losses of merchant shipping due to the activities of French privateers. There was much parliamentary criticism of the inadequate convoy system, which left the merchant ships almost unprotected. English commerce too was suffering from unfavourable exchange rates caused by the depreciation of the coinage. Price rises and inflation, the inevitable concomitants of war, were also causing much hardship, particularly among the poor. In addition, there was widespread complaint against the Dutch merchants, who were thought to enjoy trading advantages over their English counterparts. But over and above these causes for discontent there loomed the coinage crisis, which had reached almost catastrophic proportions. By early 1696 silver coinage had depreciated in value by almost 40 per cent. Although the reform of the currency was endlessly debated in parliament throughout 1695, it was not until January 1696 that a Bill for a recall of the clipped coins and a re-issue of milled money was finally passed; even so, it was 1699 before the coinage could be described as stable. The resulting hardships and difficulties were inevitably blamed on King William and his government while the Jacobites, as was only to be expected, took full advantage of the general discontent to 'blow the coles as much as in them lay'.[5]

Reports of widespread disaffection in England poured into Saint-Germain and were duly relayed to the French Court, where they were listened to with increasing interest. James was persuaded to rouse himself from the apathy into which he had fallen and to exert himself to make one more bid to regain his crown. At the earnest request of his friends and advisers he applied once again to Louis for the loan of men and ships, and this time he was not refused. James's request had come at a timely moment. The peace negotiations had broken down some time ago, and the war in Flanders was not going well for the French. The strain on their finances and man-power was beginning to tell and they, like their opponents, were weary of the long war. A descent upon England, if successful, could be the master-stroke that would end it almost within weeks. If James were to be re-established on his throne, Louis would have a dependent and friendly ruler in England in place of his arch-enemy William. The defeat of William would mean that England would be neutralised and that, without English support, the Allies would no longer be able to hold out against the French. Even if this latest attempt, like its predecessors, did not succeed, little or nothing would be lost and something would be gained; for the mere threat of an invasion from France would be sufficient to cause William to recall a large part of his army from Flanders and thus enable Louis to regain the initiative. Win or lose, from the French point of view the game was well worth the candle. So Louis readily agreed to lend James the 10,000 men and sufficient transports and naval cover, but with one all-important proviso: not one French soldier was to embark for England until there was definite assurance that the rebellion in England was already under way. He promised, however, that his army would set sail the moment they heard that the rising had begun. In view of the failure of the Irish campaign and the abortive attempt of 1692 this was not unreasonable. Louis had burned his fingers twice and was not prepared to risk a third failure. Unless and until he heard that the English had taken the initiative he would make no move to help them.

Shortly after Christmas another emissary arrived at Saint-Germain with more messages urging James to act without delay. This man, called Noseworthy, alias Powell, was a well-known and well-connected Jacobite who needed no introduction to James's court. Immediately after his arrival Noseworthy had a brief private interview with James and Queen Mary, at which he gave a verbal and rather hurried account of the state of affairs in England. Noseworthy expatiated volubly on the general discontent prevailing in all parts of the country and on the almost universal support that James could count upon; he added that there were not more than 14,000 regular soldiers left in England and they were scattered up and down the country. In short, the time had never before been so propitious, and the king was urged by all his friends to take advantage of it before it was too late. Noseworthy was so earnest and persuasive on the subject of his friends' readiness to take up arms for him that James, according to Clarke, got the impression that they were only waiting for his command to start the rising and would not wait for the landing of the French troops: 'The King', says Clarke, 'not having leasure [*sic*] to stay with him at that time, so as to come to a fuller understanding', hurried away to his prayers, telling Noseworthy to put his report in writing so that it could be shown to the French king. It so happened that the two kings met on an informal occasion before Noseworthy had had time to send in his report. James took this opportunity to tell Louis of the interview with Noseworthy, from which he had been given to understand that the English would rise without waiting for the landing of the French. On hearing this Louis immediately put in hand the arrangements for assembling the men and ships in readiness for the invasion.

Two or three days later James received Noseworthy's report. To his dismay, it stated categorically that the English had no intention of taking up arms until he and the French army had landed. They pointed out that to do so would seriously endanger the success of the whole enterprise. The Jacobite troops were scattered and mostly untrained, and it would take time to assemble them in sufficient numbers to be effective. If for any reason, such as contrary winds, the French landing were to be held up even for a few days the rebels could easily be cut to pieces by the regular troops before help could arrive. And if that happened James would be unable to conquer England with 10,000 foreign soldiers. James was now in an embarrassing position, for he knew that if Louis saw Noseworthy's report he would probably countermand the orders for the invasion. So he said nothing of it to Louis and the preparations went ahead. Clarke's account of what he somewhat euphemistically calls the 'misunderstanding' between the two kings is derived from James's own memoirs.[6] It is not altogether convincing but there could have been some truth in it, insofar as haste and wishful thinking might have led James to misinterpret Noseworthy's verbal message; clear thinking had never been James's forte, but he was in general a truthful man. Nevertheless, he does seem on this occasion deliberately to have misled Louis in the matter of Noseworthy's written report. This was certainly dishonest but it was understandable, since James's future and that of his dynasty was at stake, and he knew that without French help he would have no chance of a restoration. The more surprising thing about this curious incident is Louis's prompt acceptance of James's assurance that the English would rise before he landed. It seems most unlikely that Louis would have mobilised a whole army without some further and more reliable confirmation of the Jacobites' intentions. He may in fact have known that James, whether deliberately or not, had misled him, but decided to go ahead with his plans not because he had any real hope of effecting the restoration, but simply for the strategic advantage the diversion of English troops would give to the French. Be this as it may, men and ships soon began to converge on the Channel coast; by mid-January 12,000 men with their transports were assembled at the ports of Calais and Boulogne. The secret of their destination was well kept. The troops' movements were reported on in England but little attention was paid to them, for it was assumed that the men were sent there to await embarkation for Flanders.

Meanwhile James and his advisers, full of confidence in the imminence of his restoration, were taking steps to coordinate the Jacobite forces in England. The secret army was scattered throughout the country and consisted mostly of small contingents officered by amateur soldiers such as Sir John Friend and Sir William Parkyns. The nominal commander was Sir John Fenwick, but he had neither the ability nor the experience for so vital a position. It was therefore deemed advisable to send over some person of proven military skill and experience to direct and control this motley army. The choice fell upon Sir George Barkley, one of James's most trusted commanders and military advisers. Barkley was of Scottish descent, and had been a professional soldier all his life. A proclamation for his arrest of 1696 describes him as: 'a tall thin man, about sixty years of age, of a ruddy complexion, lame of his right hand'.[7] Barkley had fought well in the Irish compaign, during which he rose to the rank of Brigadier. In 1691 he had been sent by James to Scotland to assist in fomenting a rebellion there, an assignment well suited to him for he had a talent for intrigue; Burnet says he was 'engaged in many ill things' at that time. After the French defeat at La Hogue, Barkley returned to Saint-Germain and served as Lieutenant in the small Jacobite army paid with French money; since this army (or rather royal bodyguard) consisted mostly of officers many of them, including Barkley, had to accept some reduction in rank. Barkley was well fitted for his difficult and dangerous assignment, for he had the reputation of being bold, ruthless and a skilful tactician. To assist him in his task and to stiffen the Jacobite army, about eighteen picked men were to follow him secretly to England.

According to Barkley's own account of his part in the plot, James had decided to appoint him to go to England as early as November 1695.

He says that, one day during that month:

'King James is a 'coming'

The King haveing call'd me into his closet, was pleased to tell me he was resolved to make an attempt for recovering his kingdoms next winter, that his friends in England had satisfied him that the dispositions ther were great and the time seasonable. But the forces the King of France could spare would not be sufficient without the help of his own subjects . . . Many English would rise, but they would want officers who had some experience in the war; that he intended to send me to London some time before, to discours with his friends, and to take measures conjunctly with them, to have all in readiness . . . and that for heading those raw and inexperienced men, he intended to send over a number of Officers, who should be engaged to follow such orders as I should give them.[8]

It was not until 27 December that Barkley had a final interview with the king, at which his appointment was confirmed and he was invested with a Royal Commission authorising the raising of the rebellion. He left for England that same night taking with him only Major Holmes, who was to be his adjutant and inseparable companion. Holmes had useful connections in London as he was brother to 'Old England' Holmes, hanger-on and errand-man to Sir William Parkyns. Barkley was also provided with £800 with which to pay his men and buy such equipment and horses as might be required; he complained later that this sum was quite inadequate. To cover the reason for his sudden departure from Court it was given out that he had gone to Paris to be cured of the clap. The two men arrived safely in London ten days later. Here they established themselves in lodgings over a confectioner's shop close by Kensington Palace and awaited the arrival of their followers.

During the next two weeks about eighteen officers and men were infiltrated into London. Most of them were from James's personal guard, seasoned soldiers who had fought in the Irish campaign and later for the French in Flanders; there was a preponderance of catholics among them; also a sprinkling of men who had drifted over to Saint-Germain and who had no particular employment but some experience of soldiering. Before leaving, each man had a short personal interview with King James and was told that he was being sent to England to assist and reinforce the rebels there. It is quite clear from what these men said later that there was never any mention of any plot against the life of King William, much less that they would be required to participate in it. The necessity of keeping secret the reason for their departure was impressed upon them and so the men, as they left Saint-Germain in ones and twos, put it about that they were weary of King James's service and were going to seek their fortunes elsewhere. But inevitably the sudden disappearance of so many

89

persons from the little Court aroused a good deal of speculation and gossip. When this reached James's ears he was extremely angry, and gave out at his levee that 'whoever should be found to make mention of any of those gentlemen, that were gone for England, or be inquisitive about them, that he should be severely punished, and never received into favour again'.[9] This seems effectively to have silenced the gossips, for the rumours did not reach any of William's spies and the presence of James's soldiers in London went unremarked by the authorities.

Although there were well-organised arrangements for conveying illicit travellers between Saint-Germain and London, the journey was not without some risk and discomfort. No one was allowed in or out of England without an official pass, and strict watch was kept at the ports for proscribed persons. But in spite of these precautions the Jacobites were able to come and go with comparative ease and safety because their conveyance had become a profitable trade for the many smugglers who operated from the remoter parts of the coast, especially in Kent and Sussex. Considerable anxiety was expressed by the authorities about the ease with which this trade was carried on, for it was well known that shallops and other small craft crossed the Channel almost daily with illegal cargo of all sorts. The Customs officers were neither able nor willing to do much to stop it. They were, according to a report by the second Secretary of State, Sir William Trumbull, 'neither diligent nor honest' and were very inadequately supervised,[10] although not in his opinion underpaid. Thus the inefficiency of the Customs service enabled the Jacobites to establish a number of well-known routes for safe and easy travel in and out of England. The best of these was set up some time in 1693 by William Berkenhead, the most reliable of their travel agents. Since almost all the persons with whom this history is concerned travelled to and from France under his auspices, it seems justifiable here to describe in detail how this very efficient service was operated.

Berkenhead worked in conjunction with a farmer called James Hunt, who lived about half a mile from the shore in one of the remoter parts of Romney Marsh. Hunt was already running a profitable side-line in smuggled French goods, mainly silks and laces and other luxury articles; the return cargo was usually wool. Berkenhead first approached him with the suggestion that for a suitable reward he should convey letters to and from Saint-Germain concealed in the parcels of smuggled merchandise; there would also be occasional passengers who would pay well for the service. Hunt found the smuggling of human contraband even more profitable than silks and laces and he and Berkenhead soon established a regular passenger service between Romney and London. Berkenhead or one of his assistants usually accompanied the travellers to and from London, and arranged an efficient system of post-horses. There were also several safe houses along the road where rest and refreshment could be had. The third partner in this enterprise was Captain Gill, owner of a shallop (or 'owler' as the smugglers' boats were called)[11] which plied regularly between Romney Marsh and Calais. Gill was a 'fat, greasy fellow' who took good care of his own preservation, declaring that 'he would not be hanged for any B—— in Christendom'.[12] His crew of twenty were heavily armed and could beat off any attack by the excisemen; the boat besides was equipped with ten oars a side, which enabled it to out-distance pursuers with ease. Gill would certainly have been hanged if he had been caught, but he seems to have operated with impunity for many years until he vanished into obscurity. The service was certainly profitable, for Ailesbury says that Hunt was reputed to have made £3000 within a few years, 'what with guests at so dear a price and starving them, as also by running of goods'.[13] Ailesbury paid a surreptitious visit to Saint-Germain in 1693, and was obliged to wait at Hunt's house for ten days before Gill's boat arrived to carry him to France. He commented most unfavourably on the hospitality provided there and complained bitterly of being half starved by Hunt and his 'scraping wife', as well as being grossly over-charged: 'I was forced to do what God knows poor people practice but too often, to sleep much not to think of an empty belly. I lay there ten nights and had not a meal of meat, bad butter, cheese worse . . . once a fisherman brought some small flounders dressed with base butter; once he gave me a cat instead of a rabbit.'[14] The earl paid ten guineas for his ten days' stay, an exorbitant charge in those days.

Barkley and Holmes, as well as all their followers, travelled to England by way of Gill's boat and were escorted to London from Romney Marsh by Berkenhead. One of these followers, George Harris, who later turned King's evidence, gives in his deposition a detailed account of his commissioning by King James and of how he and his companion travelled to London.[15] Harris had been an Ensign of Foot in James's Irish army and since 1691 had served in the king's guard. On 14 January 1696, Harris and his comrade Hare were summoned to a private interview with the king which took place, perhaps for reasons of secrecy, in the queen's bedchamber. The only other person present was Parker, who was now at Saint-Germain and was taking an active part in the preparations for the rebellion. Both James and his advisers knew the value of the personal touch and

James, who had always taken a great interest in administrative detail, had evidently taken upon himself the task of briefing the men who were being sent to England. The king began by telling Harris and Hare that he knew that they had served him faithfully and well for a long time, and that they now had an opportunity of doing him some further service. They were going to be sent to England to assist Sir George Barkley, under whose orders they would be. Sir George, the king went on, would 'take care of them' in London and would see that they got their pay. His Majesty then told them that he had ordered money to be given them for the journey, ten *louis d'or* apiece, which should be sufficient to get them to London. He warned them to say nothing of the reason for their departure, and advised them to tell their friends that they were leaving because they were tired of the king's service and were going to seek their fortunes elsewhere. Also, they must travel under assumed names. James, after consulting a list which he pulled out of his pocket, told Harris that he would be known as Jenkins, while Hare's alias was Guinney. As soon as they arrived in London they must seek out Barkley, who would give them their orders. They would find their commander, the king told them, in Covent Garden Square between the hours of six and seven o'clock at night; he would be waiting for them under the Piazza; they would easily identify him in the dark by the white handkerchief hanging out of his pocket. On this conspiratorial note the interview ended and Harris and Hare were led off by Parker to collect their journey money. Parker told them that they should set out at once for Calais, and wait there for Captain Gill's boat. Lodgings had been arranged for them, and should their crossing chance to be delayed an agent in Calais had been instructed to pay for their lodgings for as long as might be necessary.

Harris and Hare were held up for some days in Calais but eventually, 'the wind coming fair', they were able to embark and landed at one o'clock in the morning. Captain Gill took care to see that his passengers were not intercepted by Customs officers; the two men were escorted on the half-mile walk to Hunt's house by Gill himself and fifteen of his crew, 'armed like soldiers, each having his firelock and collar of bandileers'. Because strangers riding across the Marsh in daylight would arouse suspicion the travellers, after waiting for two hours for their horses to arrive, set off in darkness for the next stage of the journey to London. The regular stopping-place was at the house of a man called Tucker, or Teuker, at Sandways Lane. This must have been some distance along the road to Rochester, the next stage, for the ride took them five hours. At Tucker's house Harris and Hare were able to rest during the daylight hours. Late in the evening they were joined by Berkenhead who was to escort them to London. Riding through the night, the three men arrived at Rochester at seven o'clock the next morning. Rochester was a busy town where travellers attracted no notice, so they were able to go on in relative comfort by the public coach as far as Gravesend; from there they took a boat to London. Here Berkenhead established his charges in lodgings at the 'Sign of the Unicorn' in Brownlow Street and departed to attend to the next contingent. Unfortunately the landlady of the 'Unicorn' immediately recognised Hare, with whom she had been acquainted some years ago, so he had to drop his alias of 'Guinney' and go under his own name. But although she may have suspected that he and Harris were proscribed persons she did not inform upon them. Possibly Berkenhead, with his usual efficiency, had taken care to select lodgings kept by persons who, if not active Jacobites, were at least sympathetic to the cause and so would be unlikely to betray their lodgers. Certainly the presence of so many of King James's soldiers in London went unnoticed by the authorities.

On Mondays and Thursdays between the hours of six and seven o'clock in the evenings, Sir George Barkley took up his station in Covent Garden, lurking in the shadows of the Piazza with the white handkerchief dangling conspicuously from his pocket. Covent Garden at that time was still an open space, with the Piazza running round two sides and a clock tower or 'dial' in the centre. Here Barkley waited for his men to come and find him; it must have been a chilly vigil for an ageing man, for the weather was unusually wet and cold even for February. Harris relates that he and Hare went to look for their commander on the first evening after their arrival and were dismayed to see no sign of him. Next morning Berkenhead, who seemed to manage to be everywhere at once, met them by chance in the street and told them that Sir George would be at his station that evening and would be expecting to see them. That night 'it rained very hard', but the two men made their way through the downpour to Covent Garden where they found their leader sheltering under the Piazza with Holmes and Berkenhead. Barkley, first making solicitous enquiries about the well-being of the royal family at Saint-Germain, gave Harris and Hare their instructions. First of all they must be careful to stay in their lodgings during the day and not advertise their presence in any way. And they must not come any more to Covent Garden for fear of arousing suspicion; Major Holmes would bring them their further orders when the time came. As to their pay, Barkley had to tell them that he had no money for them at present but Major Holmes would shortly be bringing them some.

Holmes duly appeared at their lodgings several days later and paid each man a guinea, and a few days afterwards gave them each four guineas. This, Harris explains, amounted to a month's pay at five shillings a day, the current value of the guinea being thirty shillings. Harris and Hare seem to have obeyed Barkley's injunction not to stir out in the daytime, but not the order to stay away from Covent Garden. Loneliness and boredom drew them there at nights in the hope of meeting some of their comrades. Loitering near the dial in Covent Garden one evening, they were delighted to encounter four of their fellow-soldiers from Saint-Germain. 'The discourse', says Harris, 'was of keeping themselves in their lodging and not stir out in the daytime.' The 'discourse' was probably a good grumble, for all these men had been cooped up in their lodgings for some days with nothing to do but wait for orders and watch the bustle of the city from their windows. The days must have seemed long and tedious for men accustomed to an active life and a crowded Court.

Four of the officers from Saint-Germain were not under the command of Barkley. After a brief stop in London to report their safe arrival they made their way northwards to join the Jacobite army in that area. The Jacobites in Lancashire and Yorkshire had gone to ground after the discovery of the Lancashire Plot, but the contingents organised by Parker in 1691–2 were apparently still in being and were awaiting the summons to assemble. King James, according to Harris, 'had given a regiment of twelve troops to Mr. Curwin' in the north.[16] The four who went north were to be officers in this regiment and to 'put it on a good footing'. It was confidently expected that the rebellion would receive wide support in the northern counties, where it was believed that 'the greatest part of the inhabitants of these districts are well affected towards His Majesty and may join him without any hindrance'.[17] Plans were made for the capture of Newcastle, which it was thought would not be difficult, for the defences were ruinous and the inhabitants said to be disaffected. This, besides providing the rebels with a strategic port, would have effectually paralysed the coal trade with London and other major cities.

Barkley had not been many days in London before he met Charnock and learned of the conspiracy against the life of King William. The meeting was probably engineered by Major Holmes and his brother 'Old England'. One evening Charnock excused himself from going to the tavern with Porter and Sir William, saying that he was engaged to meet some gentlemen that had newly come over from France. He was going to meet Barkley and Holmes. Barkley, in his account of the conspiracy, tells how he met Charnock and became involved in it.

Barkley's report was written eighteen months after these events took place, and is very condensed; probably for this reason it does not always correspond exactly with the other evidence, but such parts of it as can be confirmed appear to be accurate and bear out the testimony of other witnesses. Describing this first meeting he says: 'Soon after my arrivall . . . I came aquainted with Mr. Charnock, who at our first meeting complained to me, that he and some others had a design on foot, which would have undoubtedly have facilitated the King's return, but that His Majesty would never permit them to put it into execution.'[18]

Charnock was too discreet to reveal any details at this stage, but Barkley must have expressed a desire to know more, for a few days later Charnock introduced him to Sir William and they both outlined the plan to him, assuring him that they 'wanted nothing for perfecting it but His Majesty's leave'. The scheme appealed greatly to Barkley, for he saw in it the only way in which the present stalemate between the English rebels and King Louis could be resolved: the sudden disappearance of William would set things in motion on both sides of the Channel. But Barkley was too wary and too experienced not to realise that it would be a difficult and dangerous operation to carry out successfully. He says of it that

it was to form a partie to fall upon the Prince of Orange, which I did much approve of, if it could be carried on with that secresie and conduct as a thing of that consequence ought to be; upon which I immediately asked them, if it was possible to find so many good men as would be requisite, and would undertake a brave action without asking of questions, and urged several other difficulties which then occurred.[19]

Barkley's report was written with the object of exonerating James from any knowledge of, much less participation in, the conspiracy. He makes it quite plain that he, and he alone, was responsible for putting the scheme into operation; and he knew very well that James would have vetoed it had he known what was afoot. Indeed, at that very time James had ordered the arrest of a mysterious Mr Vane who appeared at Saint-Germain out of the blue and without credentials with yet another proposal for the murder of William. There was nothing new in this, for a number of such plans had been mooted over the past few years and Barkley cannot have been ignorant of them, or of James's invariable response to such suggestions. He must have had a shrewd idea that he would find at least one conspiracy brewing against the life of King William in England, but it is quite certain that nothing of this was put in his orders, and that he had no definite knowledge of it until he met Charnock. Confirmation of this comes from another quarter. Knightley, one of his officers arrested after the discovery, says in his deposition that shortly after arriving in London he met Barkley in Covent Garden, and that Barkley said that 'he had done the business his master sent him about, but that he had something put into his head, by which he could do the king further service, and asked him if he could get him half a dozen of honest fellows, and explained himself that he meant gentlemen'.[20]

Barkley was already recruiting men for the enterprise, but it is significant that he did not tell Knightley what he needed them for at this stage. He was well aware that even the most devoted of James's adherents, although they would gladly lay down their lives for him in battle, would have qualms about taking part in a murder, a deed contrary to the soldier's code of honour. Barkley, who was both ruthless and unscrupulous, knew that his men might refuse to obey him unless they could be convinced that both he and they were acting under royal orders as set out in the Commission. It would therefore be necessary to interpret the Commission in such a way as to imply that it authorised a personal attack on King William. Barkley evidently felt that legal advice was necessary on this point and, having a lawyer to hand in the person of Sir William Parkyns, he showed him the Commission. It was short and was couched in such general terms as to leave a certain latitude in its interpretation:

James R.
Our Will and Pleasure is and we do hereby fully autherise, strictly require, and expressly command our loveing subjects to rise in arms and make war upon the Prince of Orange, the Usurper of our throne, and all his adherents, and to seize for our use all such fortes, Towns, Strongholds within our dominion of England, as may serve to further our interest, and to do from time to time such other acts of hostilitie against the Prince of Orange and his adherents most to our service, we judgeing this the properest, justest and most effective meanes of procureing our restoration and their deliverance; and we do hereby indempnify them for what they shall act in pursuance of this our Royal Command. Given at our Court of St. Germains en Laye. 27 December 1695.[21]

For Barkley and Sir William the all-important clause in this document was 'to do from time to time such *other acts of hostilitie* against the Prince of Orange'. Between them, they very soon decided that they would be justified in 'stretching the sense' of it to include an attack on King William; the indemnifying clause at the end could also be made to apply to a murder as well as to acts of war. Even Barkley, however, realised that the deed should be given some semblance of fair fight and that William should not be attacked when he was entirely defenceless, for he says, 'Presuming therefore upon the Commission I had from His Majesty, to make war upon the Prince of Orange . . . I thought myself sufficiently authorized . . . to attack that Prince when his guards were about him.'[22]

Although he states that he showed the Commission to both Sir William and Charnock, Barkley's memory was at fault here. Porter asked Charnock one day if he had read it and was told that he had not, but that Sir William had. Porter, choosing his moment, applied to Sir William: 'I asked Sir William Parkyns one evening as we were smoking our pipes by the fireside, whether he had seen the Commission? He said, he had, and . . . it was for raising and levying war on the person of the king.'[23] This, according to Porter, was the interpretation put on the Commission by Barkley and Sir William. But Charnock, knowing how damaging this would be to King James, strenuously denied that the Commission could have contained any such phrase as 'to levy war on the *person* of the Prince of Orange'. It was, he said, 'an expression of which the impropriety shews the falsity; it could never have come out of the mouth of a soldier, nor enter into any commission, but smells of the gown and the green bag, and of hints given to mend an evidence, and to bring it to what they would be at'.[24]

The reference to Sir William could hardly have been clearer, and indicates that Charnock knew that he and Barkley had 'stretched the sense' of the Commission for their own purposes. The fact that Barkley from then on kept the document carefully in his own pocket and allowed no one else to see it is significant. If his officers had been allowed to read it they might well have disagreed with the version given out by Barkley and would probably have refused to take part in an enterprise which was both against their principles and without James's sanction.

It happened that Porter had been confined to bed with an attack of gout and so had not been present at the first meetings with Barkley. The latter had heard something of Porter's unsavoury reputation, and at first was unwilling to have anything to do with him. Not that he doubted his loyalty, but he had been told that he was 'much given to drink, and open minded, and therefore not fit to be trusted with a thing of that great consequence'. But Sir William and Charnock insisted that Porter could not be excluded; he had been involved from the first, and knew all their secrets. As to his trustworthiness, they both assured Barkley that 'their lives were as dear to them as I could esteem my own', and that they would never have involved Porter in the conspiracy if they had not felt sure of his reliability. As things turned out, Barkley's distrust of Porter was amply justified, but he

97

allowed himself to be persuaded and was taken by Charnock to meet him at Mrs Conant's, where he was still in bed with the gout. Barkley had evidently decided to inspect Porter before including him in any further discussions, for he says that 'we did not talk of anything of consequence at that time'.[25] Porter seems to have made a better impression than might have been expected as Barkley made no further objection to him, and from then on he participated fully in the conspiracy, indeed was often supposed to be the ringleader.

By early February the French preparations for the invasion were well under way. Transports and warships were converging on Calais harbour, and a force of 12,000 men under General Boufflers was almost ready to embark. Rumours of these movements soon filtered through to England, but the government at first paid little attention to them, mainly because care had been taken to give the impression that the troops were going to Flanders as reinforcements for the hard-pressed French army. James was to proceed to Calais and place himself at the head of the army on 28 February, by which time all would have been in readiness for his embarkation for England. According to a report in the *Postman* he had pawned his jewels to help pay for the expedition, and had been supplied with 140,000 *livres* by King Louis, with a promise of more in case of need.[26] No date had been set for the embarkation as Louis was still adamant that the English rebels must rise before his army set sail. Since the English were equally firm in their determination not to make the first move, the resulting stalemate seemed likely to doom the expedition to failure before it had ever begun. The situation was becoming desperate; Louis was already thinking of calling the whole thing off. It was therefore imperative that someone of suitable importance be despatched at once to England to persuade the rebels that success depended on their rising first.

The Duke of Berwick was chosen to undertake this difficult and dangerous mission. James FitzJames, Duke of Berwick, was the illegitimate son of King James and Marlborough's sister, Arabella Churchill. Military genius ran in the Churchill family; Berwick was one of the most brilliant commanders of his age, and in later life rose to be a Marshal of France. He was a man of courage and integrity and a devout catholic. His loyalty to the cause of his exiled father was unswerving, and the trust and affection with which James rewarded that loyalty was one of his more pleasing traits. Although only twenty-one years old at the time, Berwick had distinguished himself in the Irish campaign and subsequently had made a name for himself as a talented commander fighting for the French in Flanders. He was well

98

known and respected in Jacobite circles for his courage, loyalty and acumen, and was thus more likely to be listened to than some of James's more controversial advisers. His mission was a dangerous one as he had been a familiar figure about the Court not many years before and might be recognised and arrested. Besides he was not an easy person to disguise, being good-looking and phenomenally tall and thin. Travelling alone under an assumed name, Berwick crossed the Channel in Gill's boat early in February. His identity was successfully concealed from Hunt, who did not know the name of the 'tall young gentleman' – of whom he had been told to take especial care – until sometime afterwards. Escorted by Berkenhead, Berwick arrived safely in London where his presence was successfully concealed from all but a few trusted friends. He lost no time in making contact with the 'principal noblemen' known or suspected to be disaffected. Rumour had it that he met them at a masked ball where, between dances, he pleaded his father's cause in whispers; luckily he escaped detection, but his carelessness of his own safety gave considerable anxiety to his friends including Ailesbury, who pleaded with him several times to return to France while he still could.

Berwick was disappointed to find that support for the rebellion was neither so general nor so enthusiastic as he had hoped. He found that while many of the English would like to see King James restored to his throne, they would not welcome him back if he came supported by a large French army. They argued that an enemy force once established in England would not be easily got rid of, and they had little faith in Louis's promise that it would be withdrawn as soon as the restoration had been effected. In consequence, the French landing was likely to provoke a prolonged and bloody war, a prospect dreaded by English-men of all parties. In this atmosphere of distrust and hesitation it is not surprising that Berwick's efforts to persuade the English Jacobites to make the first move met with no success. His argument that they were losing precious time and endangering the whole enterprise by their refusal, and his assurance that James would embark with the army the moment he heard that the rising had begun, fell on deaf ears. The Jacobites were not going to take so grave a risk and stood firmly to their decision to wait for the French landing. Berwick was too intelligent and too experienced a soldier not to admit that he thought they were in the right. He says:

To say truth, their reasons were good; for it is certain that as soon as the Prince of Orange had discovered their plot, or had good information of the design, which could not long remain concealed, considering the perparations that would be necessary for transporting the troops, he would have immediately ordered out a fleet and blocked up the sea ports of France.[27]

And both Berwick and the Jacobites knew that, thanks to the protestant wind that had kept it so long in port, there was a powerful fleet available for this purpose.

Berwick's mission had failed, and it began to look as if King James would never embark for England. Only one tenuous hope remained of breaking the present deadlock. Three days after his arrival in London Berwick met Barkley and learned of the plot brewing against King William. Barkley, knowing that Berwick would never agree to a murder, was careful· to explain that the plan was to take the king prisoner: 'he said that with fifty men he would undertake to beat off the guards and seize upon his person'.[28] He was full of enthusiasm for the scheme, which in his opinion was the surest way of ensuring King James's return. Berwick was less enthusiastic, thinking it too difficult and dangerous to have much chance of success. Nevertheless, he could not but agree with Barkley that the capture of William might be the precipitating factor that would set everything in motion without further loss of precious time. For neither Louis nor the Jacobites would hesitate to take advantage of the resulting confusion to sweep James back to the throne left vacant by the sudden disappearance of the usurper. It was a desperate measure, but with the whole scheme hanging so precariously in the balance Berwick did not feel justified in doing anything to prevent Barkley and his confederates from making the attempt, as he records in his memoirs: 'though I did not look upon the affair to be as certain as they concluded it was, I thought myself in honour bound not to dissuade him from it'.[29]

Berwick has been much censured by Whig historians for apparently condoning the Assassination Plot – it was considered to be a serious blot on an otherwise blameless reputation. But in fact he never knew that the plan was to kill and not to capture William. He would certainly have done his utmost to prevent Barkley from going ahead if he had. Honour bound him first and foremost to the cause of his father, and in the circumstances he no doubt felt justified in not vetoeing the plot. All the same he seems to have viewed it with some distaste, and to have had no wish to be associated with the conspirators. This consideration, and the increasing risk that his presence in London might be betrayed, determined his immediate return to France. A week after his arrival he set out under the escort of Berkenhead for Romney Marsh. They stopped to rest at Teuker's house in Sandway Lane where they were joined by Parker who was on his way to London, whence he was clearly expecting to accompany Berwick to the north. According to a deposition by Porter, Berwick had been appointed to command the rising in the north[30] and Parker, with his previous experience in those regions, would have been an invaluable aid to him. As things had turned out, however, the rising would have to be delayed, and it was essential for Berwick to return to France and report on his mission. He did not think fit to send Parker alone to the north and so the latter had a wasted journey, returning straightaway to France with Berwick.[31] It was, incidentally, the last time that either of them set foot in England. The return journey was uneventful except for one brief alarm. Berwick, who had fallen asleep on a bench in Hunt's house while awaiting the arrival of Gill's boat, was awakened by a posse of armed men. At first he took them for soldiers come to arrest him, but to his great relief he saw Gill among them and realised that they were the boat's crew come to escort him to the shore. Landing safely at Calais, Berwick proceeded to Paris to report the result of his journey to King James. Unfortunately, an accident to his carriage delayed him until after James had set out for Calais, and they met on the road. Having heard what Berwick had to say about the state of affairs in England, James ordered him to proceed at once to Paris and report to the French King. What, if anything, Berwick told his father of Barkley's plot is not known, but even had James wished to countermand it, by then it was too late to do so. Berwick arrived none too soon at the French Court, for Louis was on the point of ordering the dispersal of the forces assembled at Calais. But on hearing of the the plot to take William prisoner he changed his mind and directed that the ships and men should remain there for the time being. If the plot succeeded they were to sail at once for England; if it failed they would be diverted to strengthen the forces fighting in Flanders.

According to a much later report in an English newspaper, Berwick was so confident that James would soon be restored to his throne that he told Louis, before leaving Paris to join James at Calais, that he had every hope of returning in three months' time as Ambassador Extraordinary. It would then give him great pleasure to thank Louis in person for his help in bringing about his father's restoration.[32] Whether or not Louis shared this confidence, he was at least prepared to wait upon events in England. James meanwhile went on his way to join the army at Calais. From there, on such days as that wet and stormy February allowed, he could see the cliffs of Dover and watch for the signal fires, the pre-arranged sign that the moment had come to embark on what was to be his last venture.

7
'A hunting we will go'

BARKLEY'S PREOCCUPATION with the most secret 'plot within a plot' did not cause him to forget that he had been sent to England to coordinate a general rising. Within a week of his arrival in London, envoys were being despatched to make contact with the little groups of Jacobites waiting for news and instructions in various parts of the country; it was now urgently necessary to ascertain that their loyalty had not wavered and that they would be ready and equipped to rise at a moment's notice. Matthew Smith was, unusually for him, correct in saying that 'all methods are concerted', for in spite of the difficulties imposed by the need for secrecy, bad roads and slow transport, the Jacobite system of communications worked remarkably well. During the first two weeks of January a good many men were riding up and down England carrying secret messages and instructions; so discreet were these envoys, indeed, that there is definite evidence for the activities of only two of them, Sir William Parkyns and his companion, Captain Scudamore.

It was important that the persons sent on these missions should be of some standing within the Jacobite party, and that they should be known to the local leaders. Sir William's standing among the London Jacobites was unquestionable; Matthew Smith's assertion that 'no man was in greater favour with King James, or more likely to be great should there be a change'[1] was perhaps exaggerated, but nevertheless his uncle William was by this time a person of some importance in the party and had immediately won the confidence of Barkley. He was thus a most suitable person to be entrusted with messages to the Jacobites in the Midlands. And Sir William, besides being the son of a Warwickshire J.P., had inherited the family estate at Marston Jabbett and owned property in Coventry and Leicestershire, so that he was well known in both counties and could give as the official reason for his journey the need to attend to his various properties. His travelling-companion, Captain Scudamore, was the son of a Yorkshire squire and had fought for King James in Ireland. He was well known for his devotion to the Stuart cause, and had been arrested in 1690 on suspicion of being connected with the Ashton Plot, but had later been released for lack of evidence.[2] Scudamore was said to have been active among the Yorkshire and Lancashire gentry in 1692 when Colonel Parker was recruiting in those counties, and would thus have had many useful contacts in the north.

James Eubanks, Sir William's groom, giving evidence at his master's trial, gives an interesting account of how he accompanied him and Scudamore on their mission, of the purpose of which he was clearly ignorant. He told the court that one evening early in January, Sir William and Scudamore had ridden down to Bushey and that Sir William, as soon as he arrived, had sent for the groom and ordered him to get horses ready for a long journey early next morning, a Thursday. Sir William and Captain Scudamore would be travelling northwards, and Eubanks was to accompany them. Abraham Sweet was at Bushey that evening; he appears to have spent a good deal of his time there, apparently combining his duties as Excise Officer with some sort of employment by Sir William. Sweet deposed that Sir William had confided to him that he was setting off for Leicester in the morning to meet 'some of the king's friends, some of them were to ride almost as many miles as he did';[3] a statement that shows that the conference must have been arranged beforehand. The little party set off early on Thursday morning and by nightfall had reached Stony Stratford, where they put up at an inn. Riding all through the next day, they arrived at Leicester before dark and put up at the 'Angel', the principal inn in the market-place.

Throughout the next day, Saturday, a number of persons came to visit Sir William and Scudamore in their private apartments at the 'Angel'. Eubanks was closely questioned about the identity of these visitors but could name only one of them; significantly, this was Captain Yarborough, a Yorkshire gentleman and a well known Jacobite. The only other person mentioned by Eubanks was a 'gentleman dressed in black' who told him he was a minister, but did not give his name. This gentleman must almost certainly have been a non-juror, and was probably one of the non-juring parsons who were to form the troop led by Colonel Slaughter. Yarborough's boy, gossiping with Eubanks, told him that both these gentlemen had ridden all the way from York to attend the meeting. This was all that could be got from Eubanks. When pressed for further information, he said rather huffily that he had been much too busy to notice his master's visitors. 'I had my horses to see to, and besides, it was market day, and there were a great many people went up and down stairs.'[4]

Eubanks must have known what kind of company his master kept but like a discreet man and a good servant he turned his back and attended to his work.

Whatever discussions may have taken place upstairs at the Angel Inn can safely be assumed to have been quite unconnected with Leicester market, or with Sir William's properties. Market day, incidentally, was a good choice for a clandestine meeting as the comings and goings of strangers would be much less noticeable than on an ordinary day. The conference must have been satisfactorily concluded by Saturday night, for early on Sunday morning Sir William, Scudamore and Eubanks set out on their long ride home. They covered their tracks discreetly by taking a different route, going by way of Bedfordshire and stopping for the night at the small village of Brickhill. They were back in Bushey by eight o'clock on Monday evening.[5] The distance covered in this four days' journey was about 200 miles, a long ride in wintry weather for an ageing man who suffered severely from gout. At his trial, Sir William claimed that it was impossible he could have even thought of leading a troop of soldiers, for his gout was so disabling that he 'could scarce go upon my feet or hold a pen'; but if he was capable of undertaking the arduous ride to Leicester and back and be none the worse for it, he can hardly have been as much of a cripple as he would have liked the court to believe.

Sweet was at Bushey Manor when the travellers returned and was obviously eager to hear the result of the meeting. Sir William told him with satisfaction that 'he had met the gentlemen, and all things went well, and that the West was as well inclined to King James's interest as the North'. Clearly the meeting had been a momentous one, and the Jacobite communications network must have covered a wide area. Sweet had worked at one time in the West Country, and told Sir William that he knew many of the gentry there; he asked with slightly suspicious interest when the next meeting in that region would be and offered to carry messages to the persons concerned; there would be no difficulty about this, he added, for he could easily get leave from his employers, the Commissioners of Excise, to go and visit some friends in the west. Sir William at this point may have begun to have doubts of Sweet's loyalty or else he did not think it wise to entrust him with so important and dangerous an errand. He put him off, saying that there was no need to trouble himself in the matter, for the correspondence was all settled and the meeting-places appointed. Neither did he name any of the persons summoned to the meetings, merely telling Sweet that 'they were all gentlemen of estate, and one of them a lord's brother'.[6]

Who these 'gentlemen of the West' were is one of the many enigmas that surround the Assassination Plot. By comparison with the well-documented Jacobite activities in the northern counties, there is little evidence of serious disaffection in the west. Certain Jacobites in Shropshire, it is true, were reported at the time to be courting popular favour by accepting clipped money, elsewhere unacceptable, in payment of rents; the Tory squirearchy tended to be sympathetic to King James, but there is little to show that they went much further than drinking his health in private. King William's proposal, defeated by parliament, to bestow huge tracts of land in Wales upon his friend the Earl of Portland had certainly aroused considerable hostility among the Welsh gentry, but there too, there is little evidence of active Jacobitism. Possibly the gentlemen of the west were more discreet than their northern counterparts, in which case Sir William's statement that they were 'as well inclined to King James's interest as the North' was justified. On the other hand, this may have been yet another example of Jacobite wishful thinking.

Sir William, his mission satisfactorily accomplished, returned to his lodgings in Norfolk Street which by now had become the scene of considerable activity. Among those who came and went at Mrs Conant's house were several troopers of the Earl of Oxford's regiment, which at that time was on guard duty at Kensington Palace. Disaffection in this regiment had been rumoured in the past, and was said to be rife among the older men who had served under King James. Two of its troopers had been arrested in 1693 for publicly drinking confusion to King William and Queen Mary;[7] Trooper Bishop, arrested in the following year for riding through the City proclaiming the death of King William, also belonged to this regiment. Brice Blair reports in one of his statements that early in January 1696 he 'chanced' to get into conversation with another of the Earl of Oxford's troopers, an Irishman called Bale, to whom he remarked 'by way of jest' that he had heard there were a great many Jacobites in his regiment. Bale answered that 'he believed a great many of the older men were Jacobites in their hearts', but he gave Blair clearly to understand that he was not one of them.[8] The encounter with Bale cannot have been as fortuitous as Blair claimed, for he was evidently looking for likely men in this regiment.

That the Earl of Oxford's regiment was on duty at Kensington Palace at this particular time was seen by the conspirators as a most fortunate circumstance, and they lost no time in taking advantage of it by attempting to suborn several of the older men who had served under King James. Charnock and De La Rue, and occasionally Porter, took to inviting these older soldiers into Mrs Conant's house, ostensibly for a friendly drink. Mrs Conant herself had some acquaintances among the men. One of them, who was later arrested, declared under oath that he knew her and that one day when he was passing her door she called him into the house. He found several of his comrades there, sitting about and drinking, but he virtuously denied that any traitorous healths had been drunk.[9] Another of the arrested soldiers even stated, most improbably, that the only healths drunk at this gathering had been to King William. There were several such small meetings at Mrs Conant's house at which De La Rue, Charnock and one or two more of the inner ring were present, including Sir William, who seemed to be enjoying himself in the company of the military. He asked Knightley, who was there on one occasion, 'whether he did not wonder to see him among so many soldierlike men?'[10] How far the conspirators were successful in their attempts to corrupt the men of the guard is uncertain; it is most unlikely that they would have been told in detail about the plan to murder William as this was far too dangerous a secret to be entrusted to any but those who would take an active part in it. Brice Blair said that he had heard through his friend Bertram that Charnock and Porter 'had made themselves sure of a number of the Earl of Oxford's regiment',[11] but this probably meant that it was hoped the men would come over to King James when he landed, rather than that they had undertaken to cooperate with the assassins. There were, however, rumours that some of the royal guard had secretly agreed to go out with their guns unloaded on the day appointed for the murder. These rumours were never confirmed although four troopers were later arrested on suspicion of being concerned in the plot; they were dismissed from the regiment, but there was insufficient evidence to warrant a prosecution.

The amateurs, Sir William, Porter and Charnock, had for several years been endlessly discussing ways and means of removing King William, but as none of their plans were really practical they came nowhere near being put into operation. However, Sir George Barkley, besides being a determined and skilful commander, was a professional intriguer. Once having made up his mind that the success of James's restoration was contingent upon the removal of William, he set about organising the operation with a speed and thoroughness that cannot but compel admiration. His first step was to find out what other individuals or groups were hatching similar plots, and if they were, whether they were trustworthy enough to be made use of. Father Johnson, a Benedictine monk and one of the most active of the agents from Saint-Germain, introduced him to Captain Fisher, a close

106

associate of Blair's, who had been given one of King James's commissions to raise a troop of Horse. Fisher was reputed to be concocting yet another plan to murder William, and this seems to have been an independent enterprise unknown to Sir William, Porter and Charnock. Barkley had an interview with Fisher shortly after his first meeting with Charnock, taking the precaution of doing so under his alias 'Bartlet'[12] and being careful to say nothing of his association with the other conspirators.

Fisher readily told Barkley of his own plan: to raise a body of men to attack the king in his coach as he passed through the gates of Hyde Park on his way to church on a Sunday morning. The plan would be easy to execute, he assured Barkley. There was a little house by the park gates where a small body of men could lie in wait for the coach to pass through. As soon as it was through the gates they would rush out and close them, thus cutting off the following guards. Meantime, another party would make a frontal attack on the coach and the small advance guard, despatch the king and any other occupants of the coach, and make their escape with all speed. Fisher was full of enthusiasm for this scheme and declared that he would personally guarantee to immobilise the coach by shooting the leading horses, 'though he should fall down dead in the doing of it'. Barkley did not think much of this plan, which in fact had already been discussed and dismissed as impracticable by the other conspirators. He saw at once that it would be almost impossible to carry out in daylight, when Hyde Park and its environs would be full of people, although he admitted that it might be done at night; but this again would not be easy, since the king seldom or never left the palace at night. Undeterred by Barkley's cool reception of his plan, Fisher went on to outline several alternative proposals, including one already brought forward by Porter. This was to attack Kensington Palace very late at night, overcome the guard, place long ladders against the king's window and send up a few men to murder him as he slept. After this the attackers were to fire the palace to cover their crime. Barkley, not unnaturally, thought this idea so fantastic as not to be worth a moment's serious consideration, and indeed the impracticability of Fisher's schemes roused his immediate distrust; he determined then and there to keep him at arm's length and to exclude him from any future plans. He did, however, make discreet use of Fisher as a source of information about the king's movements and asked him particularly to let him know when the king went hunting, 'pretending that I had a mind to see him hunt'.[13] This mistrust was well-founded as Fisher was the first to betray the Assassination Plot but thanks to Barkley's caution, he could give so little definite information that no attention was paid to him at the time.

Various other plans to hamper the government forces and facilitate a take-over were given careful consideration by Barkley. He had been in contact with Sir John Friend, and on his advice sent Fisher to see whether it would be possible to capture the Tower. This was one of Sir John's favourite projects; he was convinced that the regiment guarding the Tower was disaffected and would come over to King James as soon as he landed in England. But Fisher found the Tower to be strongly guarded and the troops there, contrary to report, very loyal to King William. So, as he euphemistically put it, 'it was thought convenient to desist from that enterprise'.[14] Another of Sir John Friend's suggestions was to burn down the Victualling Office, which supplied the navy. If·the Victualling Office were to be put out of action, the fleet would be unable to put to sea to intercept an invasion. But, like the Tower, it proved to be too securely guarded to be attacked without a much greater force than Barkley had at his disposal, and he therefore abandoned both projects and concentrated instead on the more feasible one, the removal of King William. To that end, as he says in his own account of the affair, 'I made it my business to know that Prince's days of council and recreation, and how many guards he had about him when he went abroad . . . I haveing once engaged in this affair I was resolved to try every way to bring it about.'[15]

The first week of February saw the emergence of what could be described as the Executive Committee for the planning of the Assassination Plot, under the chairmanship of Sir George Barkley. In addition to his henchman Major Holmes and the original conspirators, Sir William Parkyns, Charnock and Porter, several more men were now drawn in. One of these was Ambrose Rookwood, sometime Brigadier in King James's little army, and one of the officers sent over from Saint-Germain. Rookwood came of an ancient family, well known and respected for its loyalty and devotion to the Catholic Church. His grandfather, another Ambrose Rookwood, had been closely associated with Guy Fawkes and was executed in 1605 for his part in the Gunpowder Plot; it was a strange twist of fate that brought the grandson to the gallows for a very similar offence. The younger Rookwood was a loyal and disciplined soldier of King James, a devout catholic and a man of honour. He was drawn into the plot, in spite of his abhorrence of what he considered to be a cowardly and unsoldierlike deed, because he felt that he had no choice but to obey the orders of his superior officer, Barkley: 'his soldier I was, and as such I was to obey and act according to command', he said in his last statement.[16] But if he had known beforehand what he was to be involved in in England, Rookwood said, he would 'have begged his majesty's pardon for not coming'.

Another member of the inner conclave was Alexander Knightley, already mentioned as having been approached by Barkley and asked to find six reliable gentlemen willing to do some service for King James. Like Rookwood Knightley disliked the plot, the full details of which he only learnt on the eve of the attempt; but having already committed himself to Barkley's service without knowing what was afoot, he thought himself obliged to go through with it, 'on a punctilio of honour'. Knightley brought in Captain Edward King, another catholic ex-officer living penuriously in London. King does not seem to have had any moral scruples about taking part in an assassination. He was present at most of the subsequent meetings and was to make himself very useful when it came to planning the final details. It had earlier been proposed that Goodman, since he had been much involved in the earlier deliberations and conspiracies, should be included; but according to the evidence of De La Rue, Goodman was not approached, 'because he would not be contented without being made acquainted with the whole scheme and design thereof, therefore they did not communicate it to him, not thinking him easy to comply with their method, but would be troublesome in opposing their project, to make them comply with his manner'.[17] So nothing was said to Goodman of the plot; probably because, in addition to thinking him too opinionated to fall in with their plan, Barkley and the rest thought that since he was likely to oppose it, he might even betray them.

There was much meeting and consultation during the next few days. For reasons of security the venue was often changed; sometimes it was Mrs Conant's house, but more often different taverns, such as the 'Globe' in Hatton Garden, the 'Sun' in the Strand or the 'Nag's Head' in Covent Garden. These gatherings were occasionally augmented by other persons, notably Sir John Friend, Robert Ferguson and De La Rue, but the plot was never discussed in their hearing. De La Rue was not fully trusted, and it was known that Ferguson, although violently opposed to William and his regime, would never have consented to his murder. Indeed, he was said to have got wind of it sometime later and to have written to Saint-Germain to get it vetoed, but by that time it was too late. As for Sir John Friend, he too had heard rumours of the plot, and with more sense than he is usually given credit for had declared that 'he was sorry for it, for he was afraid that it would ruin

109

King James's affairs, and all his friends'. Sir John suspected that he was being excluded from a secret and expressed his annoyance at this in no uncertain terms. He was present one day at a dinner at the 'Nag's Head' when Father Johnson came in and drew Barkley and Porter into a corner of the room, where they held a long whispered conversation. Sir John was incensed by this secrecy, and protested that 'he desired to be fairly dealt with, that he was as ready to serve the king as any man, and that he fancied there was something behind the curtain that was being concealed from him'.[18] The indignant Sir John was no doubt placated with some excuse, but he was never told what was 'behind the curtain' for the good reason that apart from his well known disapproval of the plot he was also known to be indiscreet when in his cups, a not infrequent occurrence.

Time pressed for the conspirators, for at any moment the government might get wind of the projected invasion, or Louis, discouraged by the inactivity of the English Jacobites, might give the order to dismantle the expedition and recall James to Saint-Germain; there was also the ever-present risk of the plot being betrayed by an informer. Barkley therefore set to work at once to organise the attack on King William. The first thing to be decided upon must be the time and place of the assassination. Throughout their previous discussions the conspirators had always come back to Richmond as the most favourable place for it, knowing that while he was hunting the king would have few guards with him and so would be at his most vulnerable. Barkley too had already been considering this possibility when he asked Fisher to let him know when the king went hunting. He soon concluded that Richmond, or somewhere along the route between there and Kensington, would be the best place to mount the ambush and that it must be on William's hunting day, Saturday. The final decision was taken on or about 11 February, and Barkley determined that by the following Saturday, 15 February, he would have everything in readiness. If it should happen that the king did not go out that day, the attempt must be postponed for a week until 22 February.

The next step was to make a careful survey of the route and to ascertain the procedure followed by the royal hunt. Fighting the French was William's main purpose in life and most of his energy was devoted to it. Hunting was almost his only form of relaxation and in spite of his physical frailty he had been from his early youth an enthusiastic and indefatigable huntsman. Richmond, easily accessible from Kensington and with its great park well stocked with deer, was his favourite hunting-ground; only illness or pressure of work kept him from enjoying an afternoon's sport there when he was in London.

'A hunting we will go'

The royal hunting-parties were a regular feature of Court life and always took place on a Saturday, a day of relaxation then as now for kings and courtiers. Although William's health had deteriorated since Mary's death, he was still fit enough to ride and shoot for a short winter afternoon. The hunts were comfortable and leisurely affairs, carefully organised so as not to overtax the King's failing strength, and the route and timing were well known and seldom varied.

Punctually at ten o'clock William's field kitchen, with its attendant cooks and serving-men and a small advance guard, would start out from Kensington for Richmond. Between half past ten and eleven o'clock the king would enter his coach and trundle out of the palace yard, attended by a guard of twenty-five men. Following the coach there would be a large party of courtiers on horseback who were to take part in the hunt. The road to Richmond went by way of Hammersmith and Turnham Green. Since there was at that time no bridge across the Thames at Richmond, the entire cortège had to cross the river by a ferry near Brentford. This took some time, as the ferry could not accommodate the whole party and would have to make several crossings before king, guards and courtiers had all reached the Surrey side. Hereabouts, presumably, the royal kitchen would be set up to provide some refreshment for the hunters before the afternoon's sport began. Hunting would thus be unlikely to start before mid-day and would have to cease when the short February afternoon began to close in. After the hunt the courtiers would scatter and make their own way back to London. William was in the habit of repairing to a hunting-lodge not far from the ferry, kept by a Mr Lattin. Here he would rest and eat a light meal before setting out in his coach for home. Dusk would be well advanced before he reached the ferry and it would be quite dark long before he reached Kensington. Since much of the road, at any rate as far as Hammersmith, ran through open country it would not be difficult to find a suitable place for an ambush somewhere along the route.

The whispered conversation at the 'Nag's Head' which had so annoyed Sir John Friend was no doubt concerned with this question, for immediately after it Barkley instructed Porter to take King and Knightley with him and make a careful survey of the route taken by the royal coach on its return from Richmond to Kensington, with a view to finding the best place for a surprise attack. There could be, of course, no question of making the attempt on the outward journey, first because the king would be accompanied by a large party, and secondly because it would be broad daylight. Porter, King and Knightley set out on their expedition that same evening but went no farther than the Rose Tavern in Hammersmith, at that time a small village on the outskirts of London. Here they spent the night, setting out early next morning to reconnoitre the ground. King, who was evidently chosen for his knowledge of the locality, led his two companions first to Turnham Green, then a large open space crossed by the road to Brentford. Around the perimeter of the Green the country was sparsely inhabited but as the road approached Brentford there was a scatter of cottages and taverns. The three men rode slowly across the Green, taking careful note of the terrain as they went. As they approached Brentford they came to a little lane leading from the main road to the Richmond ferry. Jacques Abbadie, in his *History of the Late Conspiracy*, gives an exact description of this place:

In a Bottom, where the ground is moorish and uneven, there is a Bridge where divers roads meet and cross one another; on the North side there is a road that goes round Brentford, and on the South side a lane that leads to the river; so that one may come thither from four several places. After you cross the bridge the Road grows narrow, having on one side a footpath, and on the other side a tall and thick hedge.[19]

In addition to the thick hedge there were shrubs and bushes at that end of the Green, sufficient to provide additional cover for a party of horsemen. Furthermore the lane was narrow, so that a heavy coach and six horses could not turn in it, and thus would be easily immobilised once the leading horses had been shot.

Porter and his companions were favourably impressed with the possibilities of this place for an ambush, but they did not neglect to investigate any other sites that the area might offer. Crossing the river by the ferry, they went on to explore the territory on the Surrey side. Led by King, they rode slowly along the lane that ran from the ferry to Mr Lattin's hunting-lodge. As they approached the house, King showed the other two a little wood or copse, abutting on the lane and enclosed by high and close-set palings. This seemed to them a very promising place, as a party of men on foot could easily be concealed in the wood, from which they could emerge and make a surprise attack on the coach as it passed by on its way to the ferry. At the same time, a frontal attack could be made by a party of horsemen hidden farther down the lane. Knightley was very pleased with this spot, declaring that 'it was the fittest place he ever saw'. It would be even better, he went on to suggest, if someone could be sent the night before the attack to saw half-way through the palings so that they would fall at a touch;[20] a practical idea, for the element of surprise would be lost if the men had to scramble over the high fence.

It was now past mid-day and the three scouts decided that there was no need to look further. They rode on to Mortlake, where they had a leisurely dinner at an inn before returning to London. In the evening they went to the Nag's Head Tavern, where Barkley, Sir William, Holmes and Charnock were awaiting their report. The respective advantages of Turnham Green and the little wood near Mr Lattin's house were described in detail and discussed at some length by the whole party. King and Knightley were much in favour of an attack from the wood and Barkley was at first inclined to agree with them. However, both he and Porter soon saw that it had several serious drawbacks. In the first place, horses would be useless in the wood and so the attackers would have to be on foot, which would put them at a disadvantage against the mounted guard and would also make a quick getaway impossible, because their horses would have to be hidden some distance away. There was also a real risk of the men being discovered by the rangers before they could make the attack, as they would have to remain concealed in the wood for many hours; even a casual passer-by might inadvertently detect the presence of a sizeable party of men. Another and even more important consideration was that they would be on the wrong side of the river for a quick return to London after the deed was done; the ferry crossing would take time, and the delay would much increase the risk of capture.

On the other hand, Turnham Green had several points in its favour. It was on the right side of the river for a quick retreat to London. It was also a place where it would be possible, indeed necessary, for the whole party to be mounted, and the thick hedge and bushes would provide plenty of cover for them. But the chief attraction of Turnham Green was that when the king's coach entered the lane there would be very few of the guard with it. There was not room on the ferry for more than about half-a-dozen of them in addition to the great coach and its six horses. The king usually crossed first without alighting from the coach, which would then proceed along the lane without waiting for the rest of the guard to catch up with it; and since the river was wide and the ferry slow, this would take some time. This was the deciding factor and Barkley, with the concurrence of the others, fixed upon the lane at Turnham Green as the place for the ambush.[21] With his customary thoroughness, Barkley went in person the next day to inspect the place and to familiarise himself with the ground. He also sent another of his men, Durant (or Durance), to take note of what inns and stables there were in the immediate vicinity where the men could put up their horses while they waited for the signal to assemble for the kill. It was essential not to have a large concentration of men until the last moment as this would inevitably attract attention, so they were to be scattered about the various hostelries in groups of not more than three or four and would, it was hoped, be taken for ordinary travellers; they would in any case not have to wait for more than a few hours.

Barkley estimated that between thirty and forty men, armed with pistols and 'strong cutting swords', would be quite sufficient to do the business. The contingent from Saint-Germain, including himself and Holmes, amounted to eighteen. He knew that his own soldiers would obey orders even if some of them had little relish for their task; but they had come to England, as they thought, to fight for King James in open warfare and might need some persuasion to take part in such a dishonourable deed. Thus Barkley was careful to put it about that the attack on King William had been authorised by King James; and as to the ethics of it, he assured them that 'assaulting the king in this manner was no more than attacking him in his winter quarters, or than killing him as he was passing from one town to another in Flanders'.[22] It was for this reason too that Barkley did not tell many of his men until the last moment that the object of the expedition was to kill and not to capture the king. The news shocked a good many of them, including Rookwood and Knightley. Harris too much disliked the idea. Meeting Rookwood early on the morning of 15 February, he asked him whether it was true they were to be the murderers of the Prince of Orange, and added bitterly that 'they had served a fine purpose, to be sent over on such an account'. Rookwood answered ruefully that 'he was afraid they were engaged in it, but if he had known he had been sent over for that purpose, he would have excused himself from coming to England'. Both agreed that it was a 'barbarous thing' but they had no choice but to obey orders.[23] Similar sentiments were expressed by some of the others, but the rougher element among them had no such gentlemanly scruples. One man, Cassells, looked forward with relish to avenging himself on King William, holding him personally responsible for the wounds he had got at the Battle of the Boyne.

About twenty more men would be needed to make up the number thought necessary by Barkley. These would have to be recruited from among James's partisans in London, and must be approached with discretion, for their loyalty could not be so certainly counted upon as in the case of Barkley's own men. This was a difficulty that had occurred to Barkley at the outset; he asked Sir William and Charnock at their second meeting 'if it was possible to find so many good men as would be requisite, and would undertake a brave action without asking of questions?' He was assured that they knew a number of persons who would be willing to join him, 'even at peril of their lives'.[24] Barkley therefore had to rely heavily on Sir William, Charnock and Porter to find the additional recruits he needed.

Sir William may have recommended some other persons, but was only alleged to have involved two. One, according to his own account, was his nephew Matthew Smith, but since Smith was never trusted by the conspirators his claim that he was to be included is doubtful to say the least. The other was almost certainly Abraham Sweet, who was seriously considered as a recruit by Sir William at one time but was finally rejected. Sir William Parkyns, whatever his faults, was considerate where his dependants were concerned, and because Sweet was a poor man with a large family he hesitated to involve him in an adventure that might end in injury, capture or even death by hanging. That Sir William did consider recruiting him is attested by Sweet himself, who in his deposition tells how he was summoned by his master to Norfolk Street on or about 11 February. Sir William told him when he arrived that 'there was something he designed I should have done, but on second thoughts, I was not a fit person, by reason of my family'. Sweet was not told what that 'something' was, but it can have been nothing else but to ride out to Turnham Green with the rest on the following Saturday. However, although he did not ask him to join the expedition, Sir William still found Sweet useful. He sent him back to Bushey with a message to Lady Parkyns, asking her to send up three of the strongest horses with James Eubanks on Friday 14 February. Sweet must have expressed some eagerness to be included in the conspiracy, for Sir William changed his mind and agreed to his going out on Saturday on condition that he first made some provision for his family so that they should not be left destitute if Sweet should come to harm. So he told his henchman to come up again on Friday, when Eubanks would be bringing the horses. Sweet duly returned and after he had helped the groom to stable the horses at the 'George' in Holborn he went round to Norfolk Street. Sir William took him into his chamber and asked him first whether he had left his family 'in a good condition'. Sweet had to admit that 'he had not been able to get his money in, and they had but little'. Whereupon Sir William, whose normally sweet temper seems to have been somewhat eroded by the stresses of conspiracy, was incensed and told him 'in passion' that he might as well have stayed at home. Clearly he was not prepared, on top of all his other worries, to be responsible for the ruin of the Sweet family. So Sweet was sent back to Bushey the next morning and, fortunately for himself and his wife and children, took no further part in the conspiracy.[25]

115

Sir William himself was not to ride to Turnham Green. He may have been a little chagrined at being left out after playing so prominent a part in the planning of the plot, but Barkley must have decided that gout and inexperience would have made him rather a liability in a fight and so he had been excluded. Nevertheless, there is a note of offended dignity in his reply to Porter, who asked why he was not going to Turnham Green on Saturday. He was much too busy to go out, Sir William said. He had to get his troop of horse ready to join King James who, as Porter knew, would be landing any day now. The troop of old soldiers and gentlemen volunteers was already in being and equipped; Sir William had bought thirty saddles and other necessary gear, and was said by Porter to have recently acquired thirty horses, but there was still a good deal of last-minute organisation needed before it was ready for action and Sir William was evidently determined that no piece of equipment should be lacking. Francis De La Rue provides evidence of this care. He was given to hanging about Norfolk Street in the hope of picking up information and, being a loquacious man, adorned his testimonies with much useful detail. He tells how on the morning of 11 February he 'happened' to be going down Norfolk Street when he met Keyes, the ex-trumpeter and Porter's servant. The ever-inquisitive De La Rue asked him what he was doing. 'Says he, "I am going to Sir William Perkins with a lerrying trumpet,[26] for it seems he is raising a troop of horse".'[27] Apart from the testimony of Sweet, this little anecdote is one of the few pieces of evidence for the existence of Sir William's troop as it was never discovered who was to comprise it. There can however be little doubt that it existed, and Sir William was certainly convinced that the 'lerrying trumpet' would soon sound for battle.

It was not easy to find enough ruthless and reliable men for so dangerous a mission as the murder of a king. Charnock first approached two brothers, Thomas and Bevill Higgins, who were actively involved in raising troops for the rising. But when they learned that they were being asked to take part in an assassination, both brothers refused to have anything to do with it; they did not, however, betray the secret and were even rumoured to have offered to lend some horses. Charnock next tried to enlist Bertram, Blair's lieutenant, but he would give no definite promise. Blair himself had already heard some rumours of the plot from Father Johnson and had expressed such pious horror at the idea that he was not asked to join.

Porter had more success than his two confederates. His servant Keyes had been involved from the first and would therefore be included without question. Another factotum of Porter's was Charles

Cranburne who since 1692 had been acting as his armourer, secretly buying swords and pistols on Porter's behalf; this man could be safely counted upon. Francis De La Rue, although never fully in the confidence of the conspirators, was also involved by Porter at the last moment. Another of Porter's recruits was Plowden, who was summoned from his home in Hampshire by letter, arriving in London on Thursday 13 February; Plowden had been active in the Jacobite cause, and was one of the persons to whom Parker had given a commission to command a troop of horse. Meeting Porter and some others of the band on the evening of his arrival, Plowden was let into the secret and immediately agreed to join with them. Porter also wrote to another Hampshire friend of his, Captain Prendergrass, like Plowden an active Jacobite and a catholic. Prendergrass came to London at Porter's request because, as he said in his deposition, he was an old friend, and he was under an obligation to him for some unspecified act of kindness in the past – the only recorded instance, incidentally, of anything good being said of Porter. Prendergrass was a man of integrity and honour, a fact which does not seem to have been taken into account by Porter when he asked him to join the conspiracy to murder the king. When the full secret was revealed to him on Thursday evening, Prendergrass was 'exceedingly startled at such a horrid proposal' and privately resolved to prevent it if he possibly could, but without betraying his friend. Realising that he might be suspected of treachery if he made any objection to the plan at this first meeting, however, he said nothing, and agreed to meet King and Knightley at the Rose Tavern for a final briefing on the following evening, Friday 14 February.[28]

When Alexander Knightley had first been approached by Barkley to find him 'half-a-dozen of honest fellows', he had not been told how they would be needed, except in a general way for King James's service. The two men met several times during the next week or so, and Barkley must have decided that he could trust Knightley, who deposed that 'by degrees sir George told what it was; the first was a general proposal, after that he said, that to facilitate the king's landing, it was to attack the prince of Orange at the head of his guards'.[29] It was Knightley who brought in King, whose local knowledge had proved so useful on the reconnaisance to Turnham Green and Richmond. Durant, a Flemish soldier, was another of Knightley's recruits and was immediately put to use as a spy at Kensington Palace. Barkley's confidence in Knightley was such that he took on another man, Boyce, on his recommendation, without seeing him first. According to Knightley, 'Sir George liked him very well, and desired me to engage him, and present his services to him.' Apart from these three, King, Durant and Boyce, Knightley does not seem to have introduced anyone else, so it is likely that he never succeeded in making up the half-dozen honest fellows for whom Barkley has asked.

Major Robert Lowick was another catholic ex-officer who like Rookwood became involved much against his better judgement. Indeed, it is probable that Lowick was told only that the plan was to capture King William, for to the very end he strongly repudiated the allegation that he would ever have taken part in a murder: 'if the killing of the most miserable creature in the world, or the greatest enemy, would now save my life, restore the king, and make me one of the greatest men in England, I would first choose to die, because against the law of God'.[30] This was written by Lowick on the eve of his execution and must be given some credence, for men do not usually lie when they are at the point of death especially if they believe that they would imperil their souls by so doing. Nevertheless, there can be no doubt that Lowick was deeply involved in the conspiracy even if he was never aware of its real purpose. This was testified to by all the witnesses at his trial, one of whom, Thomas Bertram, was patently reluctant to compromise him.

Thomas Bertram, when approached by Charnock, had been evasive, but he was less willing to refuse Lowick. Bertram and Lowick were both Yorkshiremen, had grown up in the same town and were distantly related. Like most of King James's ex-soldiers, Bertram was unemployed and very poor, and had besides a wife to keep. Lowick was unmarried and although far from well-off himself, did what he could to help his kinsman and his wife; he would often relieve their poverty with small gifts of money or clothing. It was no doubt his sense of obligation for these kindnesses that made Bertram agree to Lowick's proposal that he should ride with the band to Turnham Green. They arranged to discuss the matter further at a coffee house on the evening of Thursday 13 February, but Bertram failed to keep the appointment. Later, he rather sheepishly explained to an irate Lowick that his wife had prevented him from coming. Mrs Bertram was a determined woman, and she had no intention of letting her husband involve himself in a dangerous conspiracy merely to oblige their benefactor. When she learned the purpose of his meeting with Lowick she followed him all the way to the coffee house, 'crying and roaring' so loudly as to attract the attention of the Watch. As a result Bertram, who must have added his own voice to the uproar, was threatened with arrest as a disturber of the peace. He escaped the Watch, but not his vigilant wife. He must have intended to elude her and to join the band on Saturday 15 February, but she effectually prevented him by locking him in the house and tearing the shirt off his back every time he attempted to go out, and by standing guard over the door for the whole day. Thus the determination of Mrs Bertram to keep her husband out of trouble probably saved him from the gallows, but the conspirators were another man short.

A certain Henry Crymes had scraped acquaintance with Bertram; he managed to give the impression that he was a keen Jacobite, so much so that Bertram thought he would be a useful recruit. He therefore asked Crymes 'Whether he had a mind to a country journey, in company with 30 or 40 more.'[31] Crymes's reply to this cryptic invitation was that he would go as far as Bertram; but he then became so inquisitive about the object of the journey that Bertram's suspicions were aroused and he became evasive. Crymes in fact was a government agent who had somehow got wind of the conspiracy, probably through Bertram. By dint of clever questioning he had already extracted a good deal of information from him, but none of it specific enough to be reported to his employers at once. In a letter to Sir William Trumbull, the Second Secretary of State, dated 17 February 1696, he reports a conversation with Bertram:

I then pressed him to tell me the matter, which he refused. I asked him whether it was the West or North (for he had ordered me to buy a pair of boots and get ready). He still refused, bidding me guess. I then asked what number, and I might guess, who answered me, "30, not exceeding 40". I then said "Why, then the little spark must be cut off". He took me by the hand and squeezed it, and drank to me, by which I concluded it to be a dangerous attempt, for Bartrom [sic] has engaged for me and sayd they are all gentlemen that are to mount.[32]

Bertram must have realised that he had given away far too much and that it might be dangerous to let Crymes any further into the secret, so he was put off with an excuse at the last moment. This was wise, for Crymes was determined at whatever risk to himself to find out all he could. His letter continues:

I assure you the moment I know anything you shall be master of it, and let the fate of it be never so unfortunate to me, the time we mount. I shall know the man who is to do the business, who shall certainly be shot through the head by me if powder and ball will do it, and if I sink, as I can expect nothing less, I hope the Government will take care of my wife and children.[33]

Thanks to Bertram's discretion however, Crymes seems to have been unable to elicit much more information, nor was he given the opportunity of endangering his life in King William's service.

In spite of the loss of Bertram and one or two other disappointments, Barkley was able to muster about thirty-two men by the evening of 14 February, which he calculated would be more than sufficient to overcome the royal guards. The provision of suitable mounts and equipment for his men took a good deal of organising. It was essential that their horses should be strong and well-trained, that they should have curb bridles for better control in an affray and saddles equipped with holsters for their pistols. Riding-boots for those who did not possess them had also to be procured. Some of those who were better-off, like Plowden and Prendergrass, could mount themselves. With the money supplied from Saint-Germain, Barkley commissioned Holmes and Charnock to hire twenty more horses from various livery stables and instructed them to make sure that suitable saddles and bridles were provided with them. The horses were to be hired in groups of not more than three from stables well scattered about the City. The prospective riders were not to be told where to collect their mounts until the morning of the attack.

To make up the required number, Porter undertook to hire seven horses and Lowick another three. Sir William Parkyns contributed three from his own stables, which were brought up from Bushey by Sweet and the groom, Eubanks, on the eve of the attack. According to Eubanks a case of pistols and at least one pair of riding-boots came up with each horse. When he had stabled the horses at the 'George' in Holborn, Eubanks reported their arrival to his master at Mrs Conant's, and was instructed to get them saddled and ready first thing next morning, because some gentlemen, friends of Sir William, were going to ride out. Evidently Sir William thought it wise to have Eubanks out of the way for the rest of that Saturday and he gave him the day off to visit some friends, telling him that he need not return until four o'clock in the afternoon. Sir William had promised five horses, but seems not to have had enough suitable ones in his own stable as he hired two more through the agency of Mr Lewis, Gentleman of Horse to Lord Feversham, and had them stabled alongside his own three at the 'George'.[34] Needless to say, he did not tell Mr Lewis why they were wanted. Thus in one way and another, every man of the attacking party was supplied with a suitable mount by the evening of Friday 14 February.

In Barkley's opinion, the most suitable weapons for a surprise attack were pistols and heavy cavalry swords. Pistols had the advantage of being easily concealed and were less cumbersome and easier to manage than the heavy guns of the day. Swords too would not attract undue attention, since it was usual for gentlemen to wear one, especially when travelling. Few of the soldiers from Saint-Germain appear to have brought their own arms with them and so these too had to be supplied, mainly by Porter. Since 1692, when Colonel Parker was in London fomenting rebellion among the Jacobites, Porter had been surreptitiously buying second-hand arms, chiefly swords and pistols. Charles Cranburne, described by Porter as his quarter-master, bought the weapons on his behalf and had them stored at a sword-cutler's. Twenty swords and ten pairs of pistols had been acquired in this way by Porter, an invaluable addition to the scanty armament of the conspirators. On or about 11 February Cranburne was ordered by his master to collect the weapons from the sword-cutler and to clean and prepare them for use. Porter also produced a musketoon, an early form of revolver capable of firing six shots without reloading: as a mark of special favour he entrusted this to his friend Prendergrass, telling him it was to be used to fire through the windows of King William's coach. King, who was standing by at the time, said merrily that he hoped Prendergrass would not be afraid of breaking the glass.[35]

To get the actual operation under way at such short notice and in complete secrecy was a complex task, and Barkley planned it with considerable skill and cunning. On Friday evening the arms were to be distributed to the men, and they were ordered to wait in their lodgings next morning for final instructions; not until then would they be told the exact route and where to collect their horses. Some, but not all, would not even be told until the last moment what the object of the expedition was. The two spies, Chambers and Durant, would be sent early to Kensington Palace to watch for the setting out of the hunting-party. Barkley himself would be waiting for news of this in his lodgings over a confectioner's shop close by the palace gates. When it came he would proceed at once to the 'Blue Posts' in Spring Garden, the nerve centre of the operation. Here, Porter, Charnock and the other ringleaders would be waiting for him and for the signal to set out for Turnham Green, while runners would be sent to the rest of the band to do likewise. The departure of the royal kitchen with the advance guard would be the early-warning signal. Chambers was to report this, first to Barkley in his lodgings, and then at the 'Blue Posts'. The time for action would come when Durant, the second spy, arrived with news that the king had entered his coach and had set out for Richmond.

Not until then would the whole party be set in motion; they had plenty of time and so were told to ride at a leisurely pace to Turnham Green. To avoid attracting attention, they were to wear countrymen's clothes and to go in small groups of not more than three. On arrival at Turnham Green they were to go to the various taverns and stables designated by Durant, put up their horses and await the signal to mount and converge as inconspicuously as possible on the lane leading to the ferry. Barkley's station was the Queen of Bohemia Tavern, conveniently close to the river. Here he would wait until a spy posted on the Surrey side signalled that the king's coach and the guard were approaching the ferry. This message would be relayed to the waiting men, who would then approach quietly in the gathering dusk and conceal themselves behind the thick hedge bordering the lane and such other cover as the place afforded.

For the assault, Barkley divided his men into three parties of eight. Two parties, one under the joint command of Porter and Charnock, and the other led by Rookwood, were to attack the guards from either side of the lane, taking care first to immobilise the coach by shooting the leading horses. The third party, under the command of Barkley, would make a frontal attack on the coach, first using their pistols to shoot through the windows, and then their swords to despatch the king and any other occupants there might be; it was at this point that Prendergrass and the musketoon were to play a prominent part. Barkley calculated that the fight would be over in a matter of minutes as the guards would be few and soon overcome by superior numbers, while the king, even if he were armed, would have no chance against eight men. When the deed was done the murderers were to ride together at the gallop as far as Hammersmith. Here they must separate and make their way back to London as unobtrusively as possible. The horses must then be returned to their stables, and the assassins must conceal themselves as best they could until news came that King James had landed in England, when those who had a horse could emerge from hiding and ride with all speed to join him. The rest must shift for themselves until the opportunity came to fight for their 'rightful King'; and that opportunity, Barkley assured them, would not be long in coming.

Barkley very sensibly had made arrangements for his own preservation. The murder was to be the signal for James and his French army to embark and thus it was essential that the news of its successful operation be conveyed to France with all speed. The smuggler Hunt had orders to keep a boat standing by for Barkley who, taking Holmes with him, was to ride straight from Turnham Green to Romney Marsh and embark immediately for Calais. Some resentment was expressed by his confederates at being thus abandoned and exposed to the risk of capture while their leader fled safely away, but these objections were briskly dealt with by Barkley. 'You need fear nothing', he assured Porter, 'I will go away that night; I have a ship ready, and the King will be landed five or six days afterwards; if you will but keep yourselves close for so many days, all will do well.'[36] And even if by some mischance the conspirators should be caught their lives would not be at risk for, they were assured, King James would be at hand to secure their release long before King William's judges would have time to hang them. With this reassurance the conspirators had to be content, having in any case no alternative but to hide and wait upon events.

By Friday the arrangements were almost complete. George Harris's account of how he received his last orders is no doubt typical of the general procedure. On that evening he and his comrade Hare, together with five other men, assembled at an ale house in Covent Garden. Counter, another of the officers from Saint-Germain, came to them and gave each man a pair of pistols and strict orders to wait in their lodgings next morning for their final instructions. Harris must either have disregarded the order to stay in, or else was exempted from it, for he says that early on Saturday morning he went to Rookwood's lodgings to find out what was happening. Rookwood, who appeared to be in a hurry, told him to go and see Counter who would tell him what to do:

whereupon this informant [Harris] went to Mr Counter's lodgings, at a confectioner's over-against the Three Tuns Tavern in Holborn, where he lay by the name of Rumsey: he found him at home, and he told him he had orders for him from Sir George Barkley; and that he and Mr. Hare must be ready instantly, and go to Turnham Green at the sign of the Woolpack . . . There were then present major Holms, Mr. Knightly and Mr. King. Major Holms told this informant, that his horse and Mr. Hare's stood at Somerset House, and he told Knightly that Mr. Hungate's horse stood there likewise; and Mr. Knightly spoke to this informant, to take care of Mr. Hungate's horse, since they all stood together, which he promised to do.[37]

Sir George Barkley then made a brief appearance at Counter's lodgings to check that all was going according to plan. Like all good commanders on the eve of battle, he took the opportunity to make an encouraging speech to his men in the course of which he told them that they were his janisseries and that for himself, 'he hoped they would bring him the Garter'. These were not, it may be thought, remarks calculated to inspire men to a deed of courage in the face of danger, whose consequences were more likely to be fatal to themselves than to their leader. But Ailesbury's comment that with many of the Jacobites 'ambition triumphed most' seems justified in view of Barkley's hopes for his own advancement.

Porter too spent a busy Friday evening. He dined at the 'Blue Posts' with Charnock, Sir William and several others, where no doubt many toasts were drunk to the success of the morning's venture. After dinner he sent for Kendrick, one of the men from Saint-Germain who was to be in his party, ordered him to be in readiness early next morning and to bring one of his comrades, Sherborne, with him when he came to report at the 'Blue Posts' on Saturday. Porter would then tell them both where to find their horses and how to proceed. Both men duly reported and on being told (apparently for the first time) exactly what the object of the expedition to Turnham Green was, they agreed to go.[38] Thus by Friday evening, or early Saturday morning, all the men were briefed and ready for the adventure. One order, however, seems to have been disobeyed: most of them spent Friday evening in one or another of their favourite taverns.

On Saturday morning the two spies, Chambers and Durant, were at their posts at Kensington Palace, watching the preparations for the royal hunt. Barkley waited nearby in his lodgings over the confectioner's shop. The ringleaders were assembled at the 'Blue Posts', while the rest of the men stayed close in their lodgings, waiting for the order to set out. The king's kitchen was expected to start out for Richmond at about ten o'clock, but the hour went by with no word from the palace. It was eleven before Chambers arrived at the 'Blue Posts' with the welcome news that the advance party was on its way.[39] Barkley came in shortly afterwards to wait with the others for Durant's report that the king's coach, with the guard and attendant courtiers, had left the palace yard. In mounting tension they waited for the final signal, but another hour went by before Durant came running to the tavern. He brought unwelcome and disturbing news: the royal coach had been sent back to the stables, the courtiers had dispersed and the advance guard had just returned to the palace at the gallop. Neither King William nor anyone else would be going hunting that Saturday afternoon.

8

The betrayal

CHAMBERS'S OMINOUS NEWS threw the conspirators into a considerable state of consternation. Most of them feared betrayal. Charnock said that he had heard rumours of warrants for the arrest of several unnamed persons, who he thought were connected with the conspiracy. But as these rumours were so vague they were soon dismissed. Confidence was to some extent restored by Chambers's and Durant's report that apart from the cancellation of the hunt, everything at Kensington Palace seemed normal and quiet, and no alarms disturbed its normal routine. It had been given out that the king was not able to hunt because he had taken physic.[1] This reassuringly mundane reason for the king's staying indoors was quite sufficient to allay the conspirators' alarm, and they began to take heart and to consider how best to arrange for their plan to be carried out on the next Saturday, 22 February. Confidence was further restored by Porter, who persuaded them that it was very unlikely they would all be sitting peaceably in the 'Blue Posts' if they had been informed upon; more likely they would by now all have been in Newgate. On this more optimistic note the party at the 'Blue Posts' dispersed, now apparently undismayed by the morning's disappointment.

The rest of the band had meanwhile been waiting at their several stations for orders to ride out to Turnham Green. As soon as possible, Barkley sent his adjutant Holmes to inform them that the expedition must be postponed for that day. They were told to continue to hold themselves in readiness for the next Saturday; during the intervening days, orders were to keep as close as possible within their lodgings and not to be seen on the streets unless absolutely necessary. The cancellation of that day's arrangements at least gave Barkley an opportunity to test out the elaborate plans for mounting his band, and to let the men and horses get some much-needed exercise. Each man was told where his horse was stabled and commanded to take it out and ride up and down London for an hour or two and then return it to · the stable. Not more than two men were to ride together; should they happen to encounter any of their fellows, they must make no sign of recognition. There would be little risk in letting the men ride about London, for while in open country the presence of a number of strange horsemen might excite remark, they would not be noticed as they threaded their way through the crowded streets of the City. Barkley's orders were obeyed, no doubt with alacrity as far as exercising the horses was concerned, but not so strictly when it came to keeping within doors. Harris and several of the rest said that after returning the horses to their stables they spent a convivial evening in various taverns. Their officers did likewise. Having delivered Barkley's orders, Holmes went off with him and Rookwood to dine at the 'Black Lion' in Holborn. Porter, with Keyes in attendance as usual, Prendergrass and Cranburne, lingered at the 'Blue Posts', dining and drinking until six o'clock. Evidently there was no question of the superior officers keeping close in their lodgings, which indicates that they were not apprehensive of discovery and arrest.

Abraham Sweet had been instructed by Sir William to report for further orders at Mrs Conant's house on the morning of 15 February. But when he arrived Sir William had already gone out to join the party waiting at the 'Blue Posts'. He had left orders for Sweet to wait for him until eleven o'clock, but although Sweet obediently waited until then Sir William still had not returned. Instead Chambers appeared at the house and, as it was now well past eleven o'clock, the two repaired together to a tavern in nearby Covent Garden where they sat for some time over a pint of sack. Either Chambers's tongue was loosened by the sack, or else Sweet knew much more about the conspiracy than he would later admit, for Chambers made no secret of where he had been that morning or of his own watching and waiting for the king's departure. But the king, he said regretfully, had 'kept as close as a fox in his hole'. Chambers was a grim old ruffian who had served many years under King James and who had been wounded several times at the Battle of the Boyne. He held King William personally responsible for his wounds, and hated him accordingly. Sweet was favoured with an exhibition of these old injuries, together with a detailed description of how they had been come by, at the end of which Chambers declared, 'I want to revenge these on the person who was the cause of giving them to me.'

Having finished their sack, Sweet and Chambers went back to Norfolk Street, where they found Sir William and Charnock returned from the 'Blue Posts'. The four men dined together, but Sweet gives no report of the conversation on that occasion. However, it seems clear that Sir William had no intention of involving Sweet in active participation in the plot unless absolutely necessary: he sent him back to Bushey the next day and gave him no further orders for the following week. Sweet deposed that he did not see Sir William again until 20 February when he met him by chance at Watford going about his usual business. He did not see Sir William after that until they met at the Old Bailey.[2]

Sir William's groom Eubanks had been told to report to his master at four o'clock on Saturday afternoon, as he had intended to go home to Bushey that evening. But Sir William did not go home until Monday when he, Eubanks and 'Old England' Holmes took the three horses back to Bushey. Evidently Sir William, like most of the other conspirators, felt confident that the plot had not been betrayed and that he was in no danger of arrest by staying in London. This is surprising as there were several persons who knew of the plot and whose loyalty was already open to suspicion, notably Crymes and Francis De La Rue, whom Charnock for one certainly did not trust. Besides De La Rue, there were several persons such as Prendergrass who had been called in at the last moment and who, while they were loyal Jacobites and willing to take up arms in King James's cause, might not care to take part in an assassination; no one concerned in the plot to murder the king seems to have considered that these late recruits might now feel it their duty to give the authorities some warning of what was being planned, a possibility that does not seem to have occurred to any of the major conspirators. As time went on they felt so secure that little trouble was taken to conceal their meetings. 'Towards the end', Porter remarks in one of his statements, 'there was very little secrecy, and at one time there were seven assembled in Sir George Barkley's lodgings.' This confidence that they were still undetected was, as it turned out, very much misplaced.

Francis De La Rue, according to his own depositions, was actively seeking further information about the conspirators' next move during the week following 15 February. He hung about Norfolk Street, where he knew that sooner or later he would encounter one of the principal conspirators, with the object of finding out what they planned to do next. On the morning of Tuesday 18 February, he successfully buttonholed Charnock as he emerged from his lodgings at Mrs Conant's. The little street was not a good place for secret conversation, so De La Rue drew Charnock down to the nearby embankment, saying that he 'desired to have a word with him by the waterside'. Having got Charnock to the comparative privacy of the riverside, De La Rue then asked how the plot progressed and whether it was true that another attempt on the king was planned for next Saturday.

Charnock had for some time had doubts as to De La Rue's trustworthiness and he was not to be drawn by such obvious fishing for information. He attempted to put De La Rue off the scent, saying that he thought it most unlikely that there would be another attempt: William had not left his palace for several days, there had been rumours of impending arrests and Charnock thought that the king had some knowledge of the conspiracy. It would therefore be too dangerous to try again, for the present at any rate. Furthermore, Charnock said, he thought that enthusiasm for the project was declining. Partly because of the previous Saturday's failure and partly because of the rumours of discovery, 'many people who were hot and forward had now grown cold', and there had been already a number of defections from the band of would-be assassins. On one point, however, Charnock was quite definite: whether or not another attempt were to be made on the life of William, there was no doubt that King James would be landing in England within a very short time.[3] If De La Rue is to be believed, Charnock must have felt very certain of James's imminent arrival, and of the amount of support he would receive from the country as a whole, otherwise he would not have imparted this piece of information with such assurance; he must have thought that it was too late for De La Rue to make much effective use of it, whereas it would have been dangerous for him to know anything of the conspirators' planned second attempt.

De La Rue was clearly not satisfied with the result of his conversation with Charnock. Two days later he sought out Porter at his new lodgings in Berry Street. Porter said he had made the move for reasons of secrecy, but Charnock declared at his trial that he was being pursued by the bailiffs, a more likely reason in view of Porter's general improvidence and spendthrift habits. Porter, as De La Rue must have known, was neither discreet nor cautious and thus was likely to be a much more rewarding source of information. De La Rue was not to be disappointed. Porter at once refuted Charnock's statement that the plan to assassinate King William had been abandoned. He and all the rest were as determined as ever to carry it out and were quite undeterred by the previous Saturday's postponement, which in his opinion was quite coincidental and certainly did not mean that they had been betrayed. Since nobody had been arrested, there could be no truth in the rumours that some news of the plot had leaked out, and they were quite safe from detection. Therefore all had been put in readiness, and the murder would certainly be carried out on the following Saturday as agreed.[4] This of course was just what De La Rue wanted to hear.

The betrayal

Sir William stayed in London over the weekend. Just before he left for Bushey he was obliged to make fresh arrangements for the storage of the 'goods' placed in the care of Charnock's brother-in-law Heywood. Heywood paid a brief visit to London at this time, visited his brother-in-law, and asked him to speak to Sir William about the removal of the property left at his house in Warwickshire. Possibly Heywood had become suspicious about the contents of the wooden chests or, more likely, he needed the space for his own use. Charnock conveyed this message to Sir William, who readily agreed to remove his property as soon as possible. In view of the incriminating contents of the wooden chests, Sir William may well already have felt some uneasiness about their presence in Heywood's house; a curious person, or some other accident, might easily have revealed what they contained. Apart from arousing suspicion of Sir William's subversive activities, this might have incriminated Heywood and Sir William was always careful not to involve innocent persons in the conspiracy. On the next day, 24 February, he despatched Eubanks to Warwickshire with a letter to Richard Evans, the ex-coachman who now acted as caretaker of the manor house at Marston Jabbett. Eubanks must have ridden hard, for he delivered the letter to Evans twenty-four hours later.[5] It contained instructions to remove Sir William's property from Heywood's house with as much secrecy and despatch as possible, and to bury the boxes by night in the garden of the manor house.

Evans obeyed his master's orders without delay. He hired a wagon from one of Sir William's tenants, a man named Whetstone, instructing him to bring it to Heywood's gate that evening after dark. Leaving Whetstone and the wagon at the gate, Evans then went up to the house and asked for immediate delivery of Sir William's property. Heywood was much surprised by this request, coming as it did so suddenly and so late on a February evening. He protested that it was 'an unseasonable time' for a furniture removal, and suggested that Evans come back in the morning. But Evans was insistent, saying that he had hired the wagon and that it was waiting at the gate and so, reluctantly, Heywood consented to hand over the property then and there. The wagon was brought up to the door and the boxes placed in it. Heywood was even prevailed upon to lend an extra horse to help drag the load through the muddy lanes to Marston Jabbett, and obligingly deputed his odd-job man to light the wagon as far as his own gate. It was almost midnight before the wagon arrived at the manor. Here it was unloaded and the bed, tapestries and other perishable odds and ends stored in the house. Then, while Eubanks held a lantern, Evans and Whetstone dug a large hole in the flower-bed beside the house wall and buried the heavy wooden chests.[6] Eubanks later said on oath that he did not know what was in the boxes, and that Evans had told him they contained 'choice goods', an explanation which seems to have satisfied both of them. It would in fact have been perfectly credible. As there were as yet no banks with strong-rooms for the safe-keeping of money or other valuables, it was normal practice to bury such things for security; and to do so at night was a sensible precaution that provided some protection from prying eyes. So it is quite probable that none of the participants in the midnight burial thought it particularly strange or suspicious at the time. Subsequent events, however, were to put the matter in a different light.

Although the principal conspirators had determined to make a second attempt the next Saturday, there was some truth in what Charnock had said to De La Rue about a cooling of enthusiasm on the part of some of the participants. Porter's friend Plowden, for instance, went home to Hampshire on the night of 15 February promising to return in time for next Saturday's expedition. He never came back. Brice Blair met Father Johnson on the evening of 20 February, and Johnson told him that there were warrants out for the arrest of some members of the band, thus confirming the rumours already current amonst the conspirators. Blair had been eager enough to recruit men for Sir John Friend, which had put money in his own pocket, and had at first been willing enough to take part in the assassination. But he now professed disapproval of the business and complained to Father Johnson that he had been involved in it against his will. 'We have brought our hogs to a fine market, and we shall all be ruined now',[7] he said gloomily. Kendrick, who with his comrade Sherborne had been engaged by Porter on 14 February, appeared on the morning of 22 February with his arm in a sling so that he would now be unable to ride. His story that he had broken it falling downstairs was received with some scepticism by his confederates. Sherborne did not appear either, being apparently unwilling to come without his friend. Bertram, who had promised to join but who had been kept at home by his wife on the first Saturday, did not dare to venture forth on the 22 February. Crymes, the spy, who had shown far too much curiosity about the details of the plot and the participants for Bertram's liking, had been put off with some excuse. Several of the others, especially Rookwood, King and Lowick, had little real heart for the enterprise, considering it an unsoldierly, treacherous and ill-advised deed that was likely, even if successful, to bring discredit on their master's cause. But they were soldiers and had no choice but to obey Barkley whatever their private feelings. Even Porter, who could be belligerent enough in the tavern, made some attempt at evasion when it came to taking the field on 22 February. He told Barkley that unfortunately the two horses that Keyes had hired for them had both gone lame. However, if he had hoped by this means to dodge riding to Turnham Green, Porter was to be disappointed. Sir William promptly offered him the use of two of the extra horses which were waiting at the George Inn along with his own three.

At this point we must consider whether or not Porter was an *agent provocateur* in government pay. His behaviour throughout gives some ground for this suspicion. From the beginning of the plot he had been foremost among the conspirators in advocating killing rather than kidnapping King William. It was Porter who said that the best thing would be to put a bullet through the king's head and say that it was a random shot fired at the Guard. It was Porter who persuaded his confederates that it would be quite safe to make a second attempt, and who confidently assured them that they were safe from detection. He seemed indeed to be hell-bent on driving them on, regardless of the hazards of the scheme and the risk to his own and his companions' lives if it should fail, as if intending to involve them all so deeply that the authorities would be able to catch them red-handed. Again, Porter's last-minute attempt to avoid riding out to Turnham Green with the rest of the band looks suspicious – it was no part of an *agent provocateur's* job to run unnecessary risks of maiming or death; having set the would-be assassins in motion, it would of course be much preferable to stay safely at home and wait for them to be caught in his snare. A further consideration of the evidence, however, leads nevertheless to the conclusion that Porter could not have been a government spy. In the first place, his temperament and past history make it plain that Porter could never have had the necessary patience, subtlety and control to sustain so Machiavellian a role over a period of at least three years. He was notoriously violent and aggressive and although he could display a certain cunning, he was (as one of the conspirators remarked) essentially 'fat-brained'. Moreover, as Barkley observed on first meeting him, Porter was no real asset to any cause as he was given to drink and talked much too freely when in his cups, as he frequently was. This propensity, it need hardly be said, is as much a disqualification for a spy as for a conspirator. Then Porter was a spendthrift, chronically in debt, and when the conspiracy was at its height he had to change his lodgings several times to avoid the bailiffs. It is most improbable that he would have been in such dire financial straits if he had been subsidised by the government, for it would have defeated their purpose to have had him imprisoned for debt at the crucial moment.

An even more convincing proof of Porter's innocence is his unquestioning acceptance by his fellow-conspirators. They were shrewd and quick enough to suspect De La Rue and Crymes as traitors. But although Barkley and some of the other conspirators might have had doubts about Porter's discretion, especially when he had been drinking, they never at any time seem to have doubted his *bona fides*. It is most unlikely that some such suspicion would not have arisen during their long and close association had Porter really been a government agent. Further, no evidence had come to light to indicate that Porter had, before the discovery of the plot, held any communication with a government authority such as the Secretary of State's Office that might have been willing to pay for his services. On the contrary, the records all point the other way and indicate that Porter was far too well known as an ill-affected and often riotous disturber of the public peace to have been considered as a possible spy. On the evidence then, Porter must be acquitted at least of this villainy, whatever his other crimes and misdemeanours may have been; but his acquittal depends on his incapacity to play the part of *agent provocateur* rather than on any unwillingness to betray his friends. He turned informer quickly enough when faced with the consequences of his activities, and indeed was probably well aware that should the plot fail and he be caught, this way of escape would always be open to him.

As the week went on, the chief conspirators' confidence that it would be safe to make another attempt was somewhat shaken, partly by the persistent rumours of impending arrests, and also by the defection or evident waning of enthusiasm of several persons. On the evening of Friday 21 February Barkley, Porter, Sir William and Charnock held a conference in the Sun Tavern in the Strand to decide whether or not to carry out the plan next morning as previously arranged. The debate went on for some time as there were varying opinions as to its feasibility and safety. Charnock, who as usual took the cautious view, was for delaying the whole enterprise. He was, he said, convinced that King William's staying at home last Saturday was no accident and that he already had some knowledge of the plot; if they had not all already been arrested, this was simply because the king was biding his time to catch them in the act. Therefore, Charnock held, it would be very dangerous if not fatal to the whole scheme to try again so soon. Once again, it was Porter who finally persuaded the others that there was no foundation for Charnock's pessimistic attitude. He stuck to his view that it was sheer accident that King

The betrayal

William had not gone hunting last Saturday, and that it was impossible that they should have been informed upon – otherwise they would not still be at liberty. What part Sir William took in the discussion is not recorded, but Barkley was clearly inclined to agree with Porter, and besides must have realised that further delay would only increase the risk of discovery. Before the meeting broke up it was finally resolved that the plan should go forward next day, and that the operation should be carried out exactly as planned.[8] Messages were at once sent to the waiting men to hold themselves in readiness to ride out to Turnham Green in the morning. The two spies, Durant and Chambers, augmented this time by Keyes, were ordered to be early at their posts at Kensington Palace to watch for the departure of the hunt. Keyes had at one time served in Lord Oxford's regiment which was on guard duty at Kensington. He was thus a useful spy, for he had several acquaintances among the palace guard and would arouse no suspicion by hanging about the palace yard for a gossip with his old companions-in-arms. So once again the trap was set and the assassins had, as they thought, nothing to do but wait for their victim to fall into it.

Next morning, Chambers and Durant watched the palace unobtrusively, waiting for the king to emerge, while Keyes chatted idly with the guard. Barkley waited nearby in his room over the confectioner's shop, while Rookwood, Porter, Sir William and Charnock assembled at the 'Blue Posts'. The long morning dragged on with no word from the palace. At last, at about eleven o'clock, Durant appeared at the tavern with the welcome news that the royal kitchen and the guard had set out for Richmond, and the king was expected to follow very shortly. But their expectations were short-lived. A few minutes later a breathless Keyes came running to announce that the guard had returned to the palace at the gallop, and the royal coach had returned to the stables, and the courtiers who had assembled for the hunt were already dispersing. Once again, there would be no hunting that day. Keyes brought news even more disquieting – the palace guard was to be doubled and, 'one of My Lord Oxford's regiment had told him that there was something extraordinary muttered among the people' of a mysterious threat to the king's safety.

Keyes's news was alarming indeed, for there could now be no doubt that some word of the plot had leaked out. Barkley, who had hastened to the 'Blue Posts' as soon as he had had Keyes's report, was certain that they had been betrayed and decided at once that the attempt must be abandoned. Charnock and Rookwood were of the same mind, but Porter even now attempted to persuade his companions that all was not lost, and that their danger was not so serious. The king, he argued, might still have been unwell, or he might have been detained by pressure of business. Besides, they had not been arrested, surely a proof that they were undetected. So Porter suggested that they separate for a time and lie low while waiting to see if there were warrants out for their arrest. If not, they could safely meet again and plan another attempt when the present alarms had blown over. This time, however, the conspirators realised that their situation was too serious and the danger too imminent to pay heed to Porter's over-optimistic persuasions. With little further discussion, it was agreed that they must abandon all thoughts of riding to Turnham Green, disperse their men and go into hiding until King James landed in England. Their belief that this event was not many days distant may account for the apparent confidence of the conspirators that they were in no danger of immediate arrest, in spite of clear evidence that the plot had been discovered. Had they thought that the King's Messengers were now upon their tracks, it is unlikely that they would have lingered at the tavern, discussing their plans and drinking many toasts to the success of King James's restoration. And it was confidently believed that even if King William did arrest them, James would arrive long before they could be hanged, so they must have thought that their lives were in no particular danger. Thus it was some hours before the gathering at the 'Blue Posts' dispersed, Barkley and Holmes to make straight for the coast in order to report to King James and the rest to go into hiding. Before they left, Porter proposed a last toast. Picking up an orange and squeezing it until the juice ran out, he drank to 'the downfall of the Rotten Orange'.[9] The squeezed orange was solemnly passed from hand to hand while the toast went round the table, and on this note of bibulous defiance the assembly at last broke up. Had they but known it, the conspirators' confidence that they were in no immediate danger of arrest was much misplaced. The net was closing in upon them.

Early in February William had had at least one warning of the plot. Captain Fisher had then been to the the Earl of Portland with a warning, couched in general terms, that such a scheme was afoot. But Fisher had not named the persons concerned, nor had he been able to give any precise information as to when and where the projected attack on the king's life was to be, for the good reason that thanks to Barkley's discretion, he did not know. William was far too accustomed to vague alarms of this kind to pay much attention to Fisher's story, and so had soon dismissed the matter; it was to be recalled to him in dramatic fashion before many days had passed. It was almost midnight on Friday 14 February when Captain Prendergrass came knocking at the palace gates. He came to deliver a warning that this time could not be lightly dismissed.

Prendergrass, we recall, had been summoned by Porter from his home in Hampshire to join the conspiracy as late as Thursday 13 February, when Porter had revealed to him that he was expected to assist in the murder of King William; he was even supposed to be willing to play a prominent part in it, for Porter had lent him the musketoon, with instructions to fire it at the king through the glass windows of the coach. It was typical of Porter to assume that his friend would feel no scruples about slaughtering a defenceless man, nor did it occur to him that a Jacobite gentleman such as Prendergrass, who was willing to take up arms for the cause, would not immediately and enthusiastically fall in with the conspirators' plans. But Porter had much mistaken his man, and it was his unthinking last-minute recruitment of Prendergrass which in the end was to prove fatal to the whole enterprise. For Prendergrass, when he learnt of the plot, was horrified and privately determined that he must prevent it at all costs by warning the king at the first opportunity. He was, however, unable to do this immediately, because he was not yet in possession of sufficient facts for his warning to be effective. Porter had arranged for him to meet Cranburne, King and Knightley at the Rose Tavern on the evening of Friday 14 February for a final briefing. It was essential for Prendergrass to keep this appointment, first to allay any suspicion of what was in his mind, and secondly to gain more information about the time and place of the intended assassination. He kept the late appointment, therefore, and night was far advanced before the meeting broke up and the other three men had repaired to their several lodgings. Waiting until the coast was clear, Prendergrass hurried through the dark streets to Kensington Palace and asked to see Lord Portland immediately on a matter concerning the king's safety.

King William had no more faithful friend and watchdog than Hans Willem Bentinck, Earl of Portland, who throughout their long association had been as careful of his master's safety as that master had been careless of it. So it is not surprising that Portland, late as it was, had Prendergrass admitted to his private apartments without delay. Prendergrass was now in something of a dilemma. He felt it his duty to give warning of the plot against the king's life, but at the same time honour forbade him to betray the friends who had trusted him with their dark secret. He began by telling Portland quite frankly that he was a Jacobite and a catholic. But, he went on, he did not think that any religion could justify so great a wickedness as taking the king's life, 'and therefore from principles of Christianity and probity, he thought himself obliged, by revealing this matter, to prevent the King's falling into the hands of the conspirators'.[10] Then he told Portland what he knew of the plot, where the attack was to be, and when, and how many persons were concerned in it; he begged the earl to prevent William by any means he could from going to Richmond that morning. More than this, Prendergrass said, he could not do. He had come to Portland with this warning to save the king's life because he felt that it was his duty as a man of honour. But as a man of honour, he could not possibly give the names of the friends who had trusted him, nor would anything induce him to appear as a witness against them in a court of law. From this resolve no arguments or persuasion by Portland could move him, and finally the earl had to let him go with the promise that his confidence would be respected, and that he would not be made the instrument of his companions' destruction. Prendergrass did however agree to return to the palace at a later date if it became necessary to report any further developments.

Prendergrass's story, coming so soon after other vaguer alarms, left no doubt in Portland's mind that the danger to his master's life was both real and imminent and that he must take immediate steps to avert it. As soon as Prendergrass had left the palace, Portland went straight to the king's chamber and reported the whole interview. William, who no doubt was resentful at being wakened in the small hours to hear yet another improbable story of conspiracy, at first refused to believe it was true or that so unlikely a tale could justify his giving up his day's sport. Deaf to the anxious pleadings of Portland, for a while he stuck obstinately to his intention of going to Richmond, refusing to believe that any of his subjects could entertain so monstrous an idea as plotting to murder him. Blackmore says that 'this idea appeared to him so unnatural and incredible that he was with great difficulty, and not until he was overborne with importunities, prevailed upon to lay by his design of going to Richmond on the Saturday, and to remain at home in his palace at Kensington'.[11] So William unwillingly stayed at home and gave up his day's hunting. It is possible that he only gave way to Portland's pleadings at the last moment, too late to countermand the orders for the departure of the kitchen and the advance guard, unless of course this was deliberately intended to put the conspirators off their guard. It may be, too, that even in so well run a Court as William's, someone had simply forgotten to countermand the orders for the hunt. Prendergrass was so obviously an honest man that Portland was convinced of the truth of his story but William, though he heeded the warning, does not seem to have considered it necessary to take any action at that time; this in any case would not have been easy, for the identity of the conspirators was still unknown.

Unsurprisingly, the next informer to appear at the palace was Francis De La Rue. His behaviour throughout indicates that he was a spy, out to get as much information about the plot as he could with a view to profiting by it as soon as the time was ripe. With good reason he was distrusted by most of the conspirators although Porter, with his usual monumental indiscretion, had given him much valuable information. Besides, by frequenting the taverns favoured by the conspirators and chatting with the lesser participants, De La Rue had managed to learn a good deal about the plot and certainly knew the names of most of the persons concerned; and he had none of Prendergrass's honourable scruples about betraying them. Several days after Prendergrass's nocturnal visit, De La Rue also came by night to Kensington Palace and was seen by Brigadier Lewson, one of the officers of the guard, to whom he gave full information of the plot together with the names of most of the conspirators. De La Rue told Lewson that 'he had frequented the company of the conspirators, and made himself intimate with them, on design, when this horrible production was almost ready for birth, by a timely discovery to make it abortive'.[12] He asserted that this was the reason why he had not been to the authorities sooner for, perhaps rightly, he thought that too early a discovery, though it might avert the danger to the king for the time being, would enable the culprits to go free and to plan another attempt. As he was naturally a most garrulous man, with a talent for embellishing his statements with small convincing details, De La Rue's tale lost nothing in the telling and certainly impressed Lewson. He reported it at once to Portland, who passed it on to King William. This latest information agreed so exactly with Prendergrass's account that the king was forced at last to take the conspiracy seriously. He did not, however, take any immediate steps to have the traitors arrested. For one thing, as both Prendergrass and De La Rue had said that there would be no attempt upon him until the next Saturday 22 February, the danger was not immediate; and for another, it was vital according to the law to have two witnesses to an act of treason before a case could be brought to court. Prendergrass, therefore, as the other witness, must be persuaded to give the names of the conspirators before action could be taken against them.

Late in the evening of Friday 21 February, the eve of the projected second attempt, both De La Rue and Prendergrass were summoned secretly to the palace for an interview with the king. Care was taken to see that neither man knew of the other's presence; they were seen separately, and ushered in and out of the palace by different routes. De La Rue was the first to be interviewed by the king in his closet, Portland and Lord Cutts being the only other persons present. He repeated his story, with characteristic wealth of detail, and seems to have convinced his hearers of the truth of it. Thus as on the previous occasion it was midnight before Prendergrass was ushered into the royal presence. At first not even William's persuasions could alter Prendergrass's determination not to betray the names of the conspirators. Respectfully but firmly he told the king that he thought it was enough that he had given warning of the plot. He was, he said, under obligations of friendship to several of the persons involved in the conspiracy, and so he begged His Majesty not to press him to give their names. The king was much impressed with Prendergrass's courage and honesty in bringing this warning. It was indeed an action which required courage for, as a self-confessed Jacobite and a catholic, Prendergrass had, as it were, walked open-eyed into the lion's den. He knew that the information he was withholding was vital to the king's safety, and must have been aware that attempts might be made to wring it from him by forceful means. A less intelligent and far-seeing man than William might well have thrust him into Newgate under a charge of high treason, with the probable result that Prendergrass would have paid with his life for his generous action. Fortunately for Prendergrass, William was far too wise to attempt such barbarous methods, which he no doubt realised were unlikely to succeed with a man of such character. And William, notwithstanding his forbidding public image, could be both charming and persuasive when he chose. He thanked Prendergrass warmly for the care he had taken for his safety, and told him that he had indeed shown himself to be a man of honour and probity by his action. Certainly, the king went on, he would now take what measures he could for his own preservation. But, he continued, that warning would be of no avail and the measures useless if the would-be attackers were still unidentified. If they remained at large and so were able to plan a fresh attack upon him from an unknown quarter, he would be reduced to a permanent state of apprehension and suspicion of all around him; and since it would be impossible to defend himself against unknown assassins, he would be in no less danger of his life than before. Finally the king gave Prendergrass his royal promise that if he would but name the conspirators, his confidence should be respected, and he would never be called upon to give evidence against them without his consent. This promise, together with the king's very reasonable arguments, finally broke down Prendergrass's resistance. Reluctantly, he wrote down the conspirators' names on a piece of paper, which he handed to Lord Portland.[13] In doing so, he had ensured the safety of the monarch against whom, not long before, he had been preparing to fight. And whether he realised it or not he had also ensured the ultimate failure of the cause for which he would willingly have given his own life.

It was Prendergrass's patent integrity and reliability as a witness, rather than the obviously self-interested revelations of De La Rue, that finally convinced King William that the conspiracy against his life must be taken seriously. More serious still was the revelation that this plot was linked to an even graver threat, not only to his life, but to the whole kingdom. Vague rumours of the troop movements across the Channel had already reached the king's ears but, absorbed in preparations for the next campaign in Flanders, William and his government had hitherto paid little heed to them. Now, however, it was evident that prompt action must be taken, not only to arrest the conspirators, but also to put the country into a state of defence against the impending invasion from France. William lost no time. On the afternoon of Saturday 22 February he called an emergency meeting of the Privy Council and informed them of the plot and the invasion plans. On Sunday warrants went out from the Secretary of State's Office for the arrest of the persons named in Prendergrass's list. The first of several proclamations, offering a reward of £1000 for the apprehension of the conspirators, was issued on the same day.[14] By Monday the ports were being watched for escaping traitors, and orders were given that no one might leave the country without a permit signed by the Secretary of State. The Train-Bands were called out, and by Monday evening were under arms throughout the City. Two regiments of troops were immediately ordered home from Flanders to augment the scanty forces left in England. Admiral Russell was sent post-haste to Deal to put the fleet in readiness to repel the invaders. Having taken these immediate steps to deal with the emergency, William's next move was to inform the nation through parliament of the dangers which he and they had so narrowly escaped. On the afternoon of Monday 24 February, commanding the attendance of the Commons, he drove in state to the House of Lords and formally announced the discovery of the Assassination Plot.

9
'Let them see how strictly we are united'

THE KING acquainted the Members of both Houses with the dangers that threatened them all:

My lords and gentlemen; I am come hither this day upon an extraordinary occasion, which might have proved fatal, if it had not been disappointed by the singular mercy and goodness of God . . . I have received several concurring informations of a design to assassinate me; and that our enemies at the same time are very forward, in their preparations for a sudden invasion of this kingdom; and have therefore thought it necessary to lose no time in acquainting my Parliament with those things, in which the safety of the kingdom, and the public welfare, are so nearly concerned.[1]

The king went on to tell the Members what measures had already been taken to deal with the emergency: Admiral Russell had been despatched to put the fleet in readiness to repel the invaders; two regiments had been ordered home from Flanders; search was being made for the conspirators, and some of them were already in custody. He had no doubt that the rest would soon be apprehended. In conclusion, the king said,

having now acquainted you with the danger that hath threatened us, I cannot doubt of your readiness and zeal to do everything which you shall judge proper for our common safety: and I persuade myself, we must all be sensible how necessary it is in the present circumstances that all possible despatch shall be given to the business before you.[2]

William's confidence in parliament's 'readiness and zeal' was more than justified. Indeed, he might well have been astonished by the overwhelming nature of the response to his announcement – and more especially perhaps by the universal and genuine concern express-ed for his personal safety. A joint address was immediately voted, and carried unanimously by both Houses, congratulating His Majesty on his escape and giving devout thanks for the divine goodness in averting so great a calamity from the nation. The address was solemnly delivered to Kensington Palace that same evening. The king was earnestly adjured to take more care of his person in future and was assured that the necessary steps for his own and the nation's preservation would be taken without a moment's delay. Parliament then went on to suspend the Habeas Corpus Act, and made provision for the Five Mile Act, which lately had not been strictly observed, to be put into full operation. A Bill was introduced to provide that parliament should not be dissolved in the event of the sovereign's sudden death by violence. Next, Sir Rowland Gwynne, one of the Members for Devonshire, made a proposal which was to have far-reaching effect. This was that both Houses should enter into an Association pledging themselves to the defence of king and country against popish invaders. Sir Rowland's proposal was received with acclamation, and was at once adopted by a big majority in both Lords and Commons. The Whigs saw that such an Association would greatly strengthen the hand of the government for some time to come; no better way could have been devised for distinguishing the loyal sheep from the supposedly disaffected goats. Thus the discovery of the plot provided a heaven-sent opportunity for the Whigs to triumph over the opposition, an opportunity of which Sir Rowland Gwynne's Association scheme enabled them to take the fullest advantage. That same day an Instrument setting out the terms of the Association was drawn up by the Commons, whereby the signatories were to pledge themselves to defend King William against all his enemies, with particular reference to King James and his adherents, English or foreign; they were also to abide by the Act of Settlement, which excluded James or any other catholic claimant from the succession, and to acknowledge William as 'rightful and lawful' king of England. Finally, in the event of William's death by violence, the signatories were to pledge themselves to avenge him upon his murderers.

The next morning the Association Instrument was laid upon the table of the House of Commons, and one by one the great majority of the Members came up and added their names to it. Between eighty and ninety abstained not, as they were careful to point out, from any disloyalty to King William or the government, but because they felt unable to accept the phrase 'rightful and lawful' as applied to King William. The abstainers were almost without exception Tories who had been content in 1689 to swear allegiance to William as sovereign *de facto*; but even now they felt that they could not, in conscience, go so far as to acknowledge his right as king *de jure* by signing the Instrument as it stood. One of the abstainers, the Tory Sir Edward Seymour, voiced these objections when giving his reasons for not joining the Association:

141

he was not so far abandoned of his reason as to believe that this was not an hereditary kingdom, and that he was very sorry that this test of rightful and lawful was brought in to be applied to K[ing] William; there was a great difference betwixt what was done upon an emergency and in State difficulties, and what was to be done upon deliberation to violate the constitution of the realm; he thought it eno' for him to pay his allegiance, and not to specify upon what head it went, but to define it in that manner was to prejudice the monarchy, and to infringe the laws, which he thought every member of the house was obliged to avoid.[3]

This puts the case for the upholders of hereditary right in a nutshell. To them, the Association was a manoeuvre on the part of the government to establish King William's right to the throne on a more secure basis and, by taking advantage of the upsurge of feeling in his favour, to get him accepted as king *de jure* as well as *de facto*. This was too much for the more convinced Tories and many of them refused to subscribe to the Association. The Lords too, who after all had a vested interest in preserving the sanctity of hereditary right, insisted that the terms of the Association be modified before they would sign it. In the amended form signed by the Lords, the offending phrase 'rightful and lawful' was deleted, King William being said to have 'the right by law to the crown of these realms'. Since the phrase 'right by law' carried no implication of hereditary right, the amendment satisfied the Lords, most of whom signed the Instrument of Association without further ado. Fifteen peers abstained, among them Ailesbury and Montgomery, both well known for their Jacobite sympathies. A similar form was drawn up by the bishops for themselves and the lesser clergy. This, according to Burnet, was 'so universally signed that not above a hundred in all England over refused it'.[4]

By 4 April the Association document was complete, except of course for the signatures of those members who had conscientious objections to its phrasing. On that day the Commons, headed by the Speaker, solemnly presented the Association to the king at Kensington Palace, with the request that together with all the other Association documents signed by his faithful subjects, it be lodged among the records of the Tower to bear witness for all time to the loyalty of the people of England to their Sovereign. After the Association had been presented the king made a brief but sincere speech of thanks:

Gentlemen,
I take this as a most convincing, and most acceptable, Evidence of your Affection; and as you have freely Associated yourselves for Our Common Safety, I do heartily enter into the same Association, and will always be

ready with you and the rest of our good subjects, to venture my life against all who shall endeavour to subvert the Religion, Laws and Liberties of England.[5]

It was a happy as well as a politic gesture on William's part to join on equal terms with all his subjects in subscribing to the Association, and when made public it must have done much to promote the popularity he had so suddenly achieved. Certainly this popularity was soon demonstrated by his people at large in no uncertain way. Copies of the Association were distributed throughout the kingdom to be signed, first by the Lieutenants of the counties, then by the J.P.s and other local office-holders and lastly by private citizens of all ranks. It was subscribed to with enthusiasm by the great majority of the population. Indeed, not to sign the Association was considered as being tantamount to disaffection, and it was not long before those who refused to do so were debarred from holding public office. As a visible indication of loyalty those who had signed wore a red ribbon in their hats, inscribed 'General Association for King William'. Anyone whose hat lacked this adornment was liable to be marched before the nearest magistrate as a suspected Jacobite. Signed copies of the Association poured into Kensington Palace from every city, town and hamlet in England for months to come. Often they were brought in person by deputations of loyal citizens. Among these were the gentlemen of Warwick, who not unnaturally hastened to dissociate themselves from any connection with the activities of the lord of the manor of Marston Jabbett. On 28 March the king received a deputation from that city, who proudly presented him with their Association, unanimously subscribed to by all the inhabitants of Warwick. The king was reported to be well pleased by this and with their accompanying expressions of loyalty.

News of the discovery of the plot, together with copies of the Association, soon reached the colonies, where the Association was subscribed to with equal if not more enthusiasm than in the home country. On 30 May the Governor of New York wrote to the Duke of Shrewsbury: 'I have received the joyful news of the King's deliverance from the base conspiracies of his enemies, and a day of thanksgiving has been appointed. The Association had been signed by me, and copies have been sent to each county to be signed by all officers and inhabitants.'[6]

The Governor of Rhode Island wrote on 30 May, congratulating His Majesty on his escape, and acknowledging the receipt of the Association, 'which has been with alacrity subscribed. There are no dissenters from true loyalty on Rhode Island.'[7] There was, however, at least one dissenter from true loyalty in Boston. A report of 27 April 1697 records that William Vesey, for neglecting to keep a day of thanksgiving for the discovery of the plot, was fined £10 and sentenced to stand in the pillory for one hour. Thus early was Boston the home of contumacious rebels against royal dominion.

The dramatic nature of the king's eleventh-hour escape from assassination, and the equally dramatic revelation of the imminent threat of invasion, had shocked the whole nation and roused it to an unprecedented pitch of loyalty towards the hitherto unpopular William. Thanks to the plot, he gained overnight a popularity which he was never entirely to lose. Hitherto he had been at best tolerated if only because his regime was an insurance against the twin threats of popery and French domination. Now he was seen, not as a foreigner with a dubious right to the throne, but as a king of the English, united with his people in the defence of their religion, laws and liberties; and he had demonstrated this unity by joining with them in the Association. The fervour with which this new-found loyalty was expressed was perhaps due not so much to personal regard for William, but because he represented stability and order, two things which after the tumults of the earlier part of the century the English had at last begun to enjoy. It was inconceivable that they would sacrifice these blessings for the sake of a dynasty that long experience had taught them to distrust. And William, for all his foreign-ness, his dourness and his heavy taxes, had by now shown that he could be trusted not only to govern in accordance with the Constitution, but to join with his people in upholding that Constitution. The red ribbons which his subjects sported in their hats were an outward and visible sign that they were at last united with their foreign king in the defence of their common freedoms.

The discovery of the plot was a godsend not only for William but for his mainly Whig Government, whose failure to cope with the currency crisis was fast losing it popular support. As a correspondent of the day puts it:

I believe of all the sham plots you ever heard or read of, none was so serviceable to the persons that forged and laid them, as this reall one so miraculously discovered will prove to the Government; it will effectually cure all the evils you feared from bad money . . . One told me of a Jacobite rascall that cursed the Plotters that designed to take away his Majesties life; if they would have been quiet, his bad money would have destroyed his Government.[8]

The Whigs were quick to take advantage of this upsurge of popular feeling that for a while quite obscured the problems attendant upon the devaluation of the coinage. Thanks to the Assassination Plot, their ascendancy over the Tories was assured for some years to come. Naturally, they lost no opportunity of vilifying King James and the Jacobites; it was almost universally believed that James, if he had not instigated it, was heavily implicated in the plot. The predictable result was that any sympathy for his plight quickly evaporated; never had anti-Jacobite feeling run so high as in the period immediately following the discovery. Even John Evelyn, himself a non-juror, appears to have believed that James was implicated. Reflecting the general opinion, he writes:

It is certain it had likely to have ben [*sic*] very fatal to the (Danger of the) whole Nation, had it taken Effect; so as I looke on it as a very greate deliverance and Preservation by the Providence of God; for tho many did formerly pitty K. James condition, this designe of Assassination and bringing over a French Army, did much alienate his Friends, and was likely to produce a more perfect establishment of King William.[9]

The king, in the opening words of his speech to parliament at the closing of the session on 7 April, showed that he was well aware of and fully appreciated the unifying effects of the current state of emergency. He was not a man to whom the public expression of his feelings came easily, but it is clear from his brief but sincere expressions of gratitude that he was touched, and perhaps surprised, by his subjects' genuine concern for his personal safety:

My Lords and Gentlemen:
You have shewn so great concern for my person, and zeal for my government, and have done so much for the preservation of the one, and for the strengthening of the other . . . that the late designs of our enemies are, by the blessing of God, like to have no other effect, than to let them see how strictly we are united; and to give me this occasion to acknowledge your kindness, and to assure you of all the returns which a prince can make to his people.[10]

So well had the secret been kept that very little information about the invasion plans had leaked out either in Paris or in London. In a despatch from Paris, dated 2 March and published in the *Postman,* the correspondent writes that 'The unexpected expedition of the late King James is the only subject of discourse here, and never was so great an enterprise managed with so much secrecy.'[11] The first definite information that King William received was a letter from his friend and ally the Duke of Wurtemburg, dated 17 February, warning him of the intended invasion and giving some details of the numbers of men and transports assembled at the Channel ports. The duke remarked regretfully that he wished he could send twenty good regiments to help defend England but, since this was not possible, he was sending instead his A.D.C. Colonel Smettan, with more precise information.[12] On 25 February the captain of an Ostend man-of-war reported that 'more than 300 ships are gone from Dunkirk to Calais in order to take men on board for the intended invasion'.[13] Further confirmation of this report came on 2 March from an unnamed agent in Paris:

The rumours of an important design against England which were thought to be unfounded, prove to be more reliable than one would have ventured to hope. King James left for Calais yesterday morning. Twelve thousand men are there awaiting him, with several hundreds of boats to carry them over, some say direct to England, others to Scotland, where Lord Hamilton is said to have already fifteen to sixteen thousand men at his command. The Marquis of Harcourt will command this expedition. Under him are two quartermasters-general, four brigadiers of infantry, and one of horse. The force is composed of eighteen battalions, three regiments of cavalry and two of dragoons.

The plans have been laid with so much secrecy, that nothing was known till Monday afternoon, when the King went to St. Germains to say goodbye to King James. A chest containing 100,000 *louis d'or* was then sent off, under orders sent but a little while before to the Treasurer-extraordinary for war, who had been directed to keep that amount ready in specie.

That very evening his Majesty referred to the expedition, . . . saying that King James was going to Scotland, that his plans seemed well laid, and that things were in good train in the country itself, but that, nevertheless, it was a matter so difficult that he might easily fail . . .

Others, however, think that he will land in England, near Dover, that he will be joined there by those of his party, and will then advance through the country, whilst Lord Hamilton will march into the north from Scotland. This is deduced from the fact that the majority of the boats to be used are not calculated to make a longer crossing; and, if the actual plan had been to descend upon Scotland, they would have embarked at Dunkirk, not Calais. Also it does not seem that there are sufficient men-of-war to convoy them so far.[14]

From this evidence it would seem that the rumours of a descent on Scotland were put out by Louis as a blind to mask the real destination of the expedition, although the possibility of an internal uprising or an attempt at invasion of Scotland by a secondary expedition could not of course be ignored. On 25 February the Scottish Privy Council was informed of the discovery of the plot and instructed to call out the militia and to take all possible measures to counter a Jacobite rising.[15] On 2 March the king wrote again to the Privy Council with a warning that there was still a danger of a French descent on the coasts and

146

ordering the members to take the necessary measures to repel a landing.[16]

Now the contrary winds that had held the English fleet for so long in port were indeed seen to have been providential. Thanks to this protestant wind the main body of the fleet had been unable earlier to sail for the Mediterranean, and thus within five days Admiral Russell was able to assemble sixty ships, including twelve Dutch men-of-war from the Medway, no mean achievement in days of such slow and difficult communications. A force of sixty ships would certainly be able to repel the invaders for although the transports were said to be about three hundred, the greater part of the French fleet was still in the Mediterranean, and so those that could be spared to convoy the transports were too few to put up a fight against the English. The success of the invasion depended on a surprise descent on the English coast, and now that the secret was out hopes of success were doomed at the outset. Russell lost no time in putting to sea, and by 28 February was able to report to the Commissioners of the Admiralty that the fleet was successfully deployed in the Channel:

I am now at anchor off Graveling (Gravelines), my Lord Berkley half-way between me and Dunkirk. I ordered sir Clow. Shovell into Boulogne Bay, where there was no ship or bark. I sailed close along Calais, which place is crowded with all sorts of embarcations; 'twas impossible to count them, but I cannot judge them less than 300 or 400 sail of all sorts, with their sails to the yards. I saw them very busy on shore removing guns from one place to another, and believe they took the tenders with me to be bomb vessels. I wish two or three had been with me; possibly they might have done some execution on the ships lying so thick, which were hardly to be missed . . . Whether anything can be done upon these ships I cannot inform you. The pilots I have talked with say they cannot be attacked as they lie . . . what can be attempted must be without delay, for this coast at this time of year is no very good place to be upon. I hope the enemies' designs are frustrated seeing such a fleet together. I can never think they will attempt crossing the sea while you are masters of it.[17]

No decisive action was fought off Gravelines, and the enemy transports were safe enough from attack where they lay in Calais harbour. For some weeks the English fleet patrolled the French coast, keeping watch for any attempt at a sortie and effectually preventing the expedition from setting sail. It was not long before observers reported that the men and guns were being disembarked and the whole enterprise in process of being dismantled. Louis, when he learnt of the failure of the Assassination Plot and the discovery of the invasion plan, lost no time in abandoning his last effort to help his ill-starred kinsman to regain his throne. But James, whose capacity for accepting unwelcome facts was never of the best, lingered hopefully at Boulogne for some weeks until the army that was to have swept him back to his throne was completely dispersed. Only then did he realise that he had lost again, and for the last time; and so, turning his back for ever on the waters that separated him from his homeland, he made his way by slow stages back to his melancholy little Court at Saint-Germain. Louis received him with the unfailing kindness that was one of his more pleasing traits, but it was clearly understood between them that there would be no more help forthcoming from him for any future attempt at restoration.

Public criticism of James and his lamentable failure was sternly discouraged by Louis, but in spite of this the people of Paris expressed opinions which left no doubt as to what they thought of the whole affair. There was some popular indignation when the news of the Assassination Plot broke out; the French Court, and the people, had never accorded James the respect and affection that was their king's unfailing attitude towards him, and he was now the object of some uncharitable mockery. There was a demonstration on the Pont Neuf in early March, in the course of which several people were arrested for singing scurrilous songs about him. At about the same time, three gentlemen, for saying that King James would shortly be obliged to return to Saint-Germain 'with his breeches on his head', were committed to the Bastille.[18] But Louis could afford to be kind and generous. Although for James and the Jacobites the expedition was a total loss, it was far from being so from Louis's point of view: it had caused the English to withdraw a substantial number of men from Flanders, thus weakening the allied position in that theatre of war; even more important, the English fleet in the Mediterranean had had to be brought back to prevent the main French fleet, now concentrated at Brest, from making any further attempt at a landing in England. Thus Louis had temporarily succeeded in deflecting some of the forces, naval and military, ranged against him. James had lost all, but the loss to Louis was minimal and the gains large enough to offset a great part of it. William was well aware of the effect that the present situation would have on the progress of the war in Flanders, and was impatient to get there as soon as possible. By 27 April the crisis in England was already well under control, so that he was able, shortly after proroguing parliament on that day, to depart for Flanders, confident in the knowledge that his government and people would effectually carry on the work of making England safe from foreign invasion and popish domination.

'Let them see how strictly we are united'

Meanwhile in England strict and comprehensive measures were taken to suppress any attempt at a Jacobite rising. On 27 February the circuit judges were directed to see that the laws against papists and non-jurors were strictly enforced. The lists of those who had taken the oath of allegiance to King William were to be checked, and the oath tendered again to any who had refused it. Persistent refusers were to be kept under surveillance. On the same day the Duke of Shrewsbury circularised the Deputy Lieutenants of the Counties, informing them that:

> The Lords of the Privy Council have thought it necessary at this time of public danger by the intended invasion from France, and the horrid conspiracy against His Majesties life, to raise the militia in the several counties of this Kingdom, and to cause all horses belonging to papists and other persons disaffected to the Government, or who shall refuse to take the oaths, to be seized.'[19]

These orders were carried out with such thoroughness that travelling, even for the most blameless of citizens, was for some time extremely difficult. Not only were all the ports watched for escaping traitors, but the militia guarded all the roads, and it was for some time illegal for anyone to travel without a pass signed by a Justice of the Peace. The public, however, appear to have suffered this and other inconveniences arising from the state of emergency without complaint, and indeed in general they cooperated with the authorities to a quite unusual degree. A number of towns, on hearing of the discovery of the plot, immediately closed their gates and conducted a house-to-house search for Jacobites. Overnight, Jacobite-hunting had become a popular sport, enthusiasm being stimulated no doubt by the substantial rewards offered for the capture of traitors. 'Tis hoped that none will escape, the people everywhere being very zealous to apprehend them,'[20] the *Postman* reported on 5 March. As in the spy-hunting days of the First World War, many harmless persons must have been subjected to persecution and imprisonment as a result of the prevailing hysteria. It is however very unlikely that any suspects were executed unless there was strong evidence that they had been actually engaged in the conspiracy.

Such was the strength of anti-Jacobite feeling aroused by the discovery of the plot that for some time afterwards it behoved any person, whether in the provinces or in London, who was known or suspected not to be wholeheartedly in sympathy with King William and his government, to lie low. Any publicly expressed sympathy for King James or criticism of the government was liable at best to result in confiscation of the suspect's horse; at worst, in imprisonment. The gaols of London were overflowing with suspected rebels, and soon extra guards were posted at night round the walls of Newgate and the other prisons to prevent a break-out or a rescue attempt. Those Jacobites not already in prison were everywhere compelled to go to ground; it would have been a more than usually foolhardy Jacobite who ventured at this time to drink King James's health at the Dog Tavern, or to light a bonfire in his honour. Such subversive demonstrations had in the past been a source of annoyance rather than alarm to the more law-abiding citizenry. A typical expression of the general satisfaction at the instant removal from the scene of this nuisance is that of a Whig gentleman, Thomas Tash: 'I was yesterday at the Fleet, and I think there are above 300 (Jacobites) there. But I ne'er see the town so pleasant in all my life, for now they are all of a side, for it is the hardest matter in the world to find a Jacobite.'[21] Most of those arrested on suspicion were however released in late May for want of evidence.[22]

For obvious reasons, much emphasis was laid on the necessity of immobilising suspected rebels by impounding their horses. The luckless owners, in addition to being deprived of their means of transport, were obliged to pay for the animals' keep. The horses were generally placed in the charge of an inn-keeper, who must often have made a substantial profit. The additional clause to the Bill empowering the king to apprehend suspected persons states that: 'The Lieutenants of all counties or their agents, may, until Sept. 1 1696, seize the horses of such persons as they shall judge to be dangerous to the Peace of this Kingdom; and that, if such horses be left with an Inn keeper, the owner shall pay for their meat not exceeding four shillings per week'.[23] Four shillings a week over a period of six months represented quite an outlay, especially if a suspect had several animals. The regulations were for some time strictly enforced, and the Justices of the Peace must have been kept busy administering this and the numerous other orders sent down from Whitehall. They carried out their duties conscientiously, for on 5 March the *Postman* gleefully reports that:

Guards are placed in all the roads of this Kingdom, and no persons suffered to travel without passes, and all horses fit for service are seized, and the Inn-keepers and stablers forbid to part with them without orders of the next Justice of the Peace. About 300 belonging to suspected owners are already seized in the outparts of the City, by which method the Jacobites will not only be frustrated of their design, but also deprived of the means of conferring

'The Villanous Plot', from *Ballads, vol. 5* in the Pepys Library

God Preserve
from all his

KING *William*

ENEMIES.

The Villanous PLOT:

Being a Contrivance of several Villanous Papists

To Kill King WILLIAM.

To the Tune of, *Liggan Water*, &c.

WHat means this grumbletonian Crew!
  Oh! what is it they fain would do?
Sure mischief on themselves they bring,
Who Plots againſt our gracious King.

What is it more these Men would have,
Then what there is a Prince most brave,
Who for his Nation thinks it good,
To venture still his dearest Blood?

To Flanders yearly he does go,
To fight brave England's greatest Foe,
And yet the Jacobites, they say,
Are plotting Mischief e'ry day.

For Knights and Majors, Captains too,
And others of his hellish Crew,
Who all did Plot up on one day,
To take the King's dear Life away.

Forty or fifty were the Gang,
I time at Tybourn they may hang,
And then their Quarters separate,
For to be set upon each Gate,

For wickedly thus to combine
In this same hellish base design,
That is to give the fatal Blow,
When the King should to his Chappel go.

But thanks to Heaven, which o're rules
These Jacobites and plotting Fools,
And put it in the Heart of one,
For to discover the whole Gang.

Who did a Letter send away,
For to prevent this bloody Day,
Which notice gave of e'ry thing,
And why they were to Kill the King.

Oh! Traitors, Traytors, full of Blood,
You're can act for England's Good,
Who ſtrives for to deſtroy our King,
And bring a foolish Papist in.

Besides the bloody French must come,
Oh! where are we then e'ry one?
For Father, Mother, Son and Wench,
Must all be Slaves unto the French.

Our Liberty, Religion, and
All that's dear unto this Land,
Must by a Papist Power be
Inslaved then in Misery.

But Heaven, who does Power give,
Does still preserve our King alive,
In spite of Plotters wicked hand,
Who would deſtroy our King and Land.

As by this wicked bloody Plot
Of Papists, who together got,
Some Irish, French and English, who
Would hands in Royal Blood imbrew.

At Richmond they design'd to act
This villanous and bloody Fact;
But by a Letter that was sent,
It did (thank God) the same prevent.

Another time they had pitc'd on,
When the King was a Hunti g gone,
Two or three hundred had agreed
To make our Royal King to bleed.

But now comes all their discontent,
For sev'ral are to Newgate sent,
And must remain in Goal each one
Till try'd, then Tybourn is thir doom.

London: Printed for M. Carew, in Old-Bedlam.

notes, or consulting how to avoid the gallows, which has groaned for them ever since the discovery of their horrid conspiracy.[24]

Although many innocent persons must have suffered the deprivation of their horses and other inconveniences imposed by the state of national emergency, there was apparently some justification for these stringent regulations. Vague reports of bodies of horsemen on the move in the remoter parts of the countryside began to come in to the Secretary of State's Office; the reports are not very well substantiated, and the numbers of horsemen involved were no doubt exaggerated, but taken together and considered in the light of Abraham Sweet's evidence about the journey to Leicester made by Sir William Parkyns and Scudamore earlier in the year they are credible. It may well have been that a number of the more active and enthusiastic Jacobite gentlemen, especially in the Midlands, were acting on instructions and riding to meet King James or to join a rising in the north. Thus on 21 February Dr Richard Kinston wrote to Sir William Trumbull informing him that 'In Nottinghamshire at this present are more than 100 Jacobites well horsed and armed that in small companies traverse that county in expectation to be joined by a stronger party and to march nothwards. In Rutlandshire are 40 men dispersed in like manner and a greater number far north. They are buying horses everywhere and in expectation of some sudden enterprise.'[25] Again, on 23 February, this more detailed account was sent to Trumbull by Henry Baker, a King's Messenger:

On Thursday night last Mr. Huet of Nottinghamshire told me he had received two letters the last post that gave him an account of a sort of persons that lay lurking about the little villages in that county bordering upon the Forest of Sherwood to the number of about 50. They were gentlemen-like men, well mounted and in companies of about 8, 10 or 12 . . . and at Worksop there were 12 of them. The country people . . . took them for highwaymen. A friend of his had letters that they were about 80 . . . There have been like accounts from Lincolnshire.[26]

Vague as they are, these reports must have had some truth in them; significantly they were made before the news of the plot broke out and the whole country was on the watch for Jacobites; the fact that the country people took the mysterious riders for highwaymen indicates that there was at the time no general suspicion of a Jacobite rising. The most likely explanation of these movements of small mounted groups is that they were part of the force of 2000 men who were to meet King James on his landing, and that they were acting on instructions received from Sir William, Scudamore and other agents. Some at least were thought to be marching northwards; if this were so it could mean either that King James was after all intending to land somewhere in Scotland, or that a simultaneous rising had been planned there. At any rate it certainly looks as if the Jacobite gentlemen were obeying orders, and that some of these orders had been conveyed to them by Sir William. He had then good cause to remark to Sweet on his return from Leicester that 'all things had gone well' and that 'The Gentlemen of the North were as well inclined as the Gentlemen of the West'. Unfortunately for these gentlemen, however, everything soon went very wrong. How long they lurked under the dripping trees of Sherwood Forest and elsewhere, waiting with fading hopes for directions that never came, it is not of course possible to know; they must have dispersed in haste when the news of the discovery of the plot broke out, for there were no more stories of mysterious riders on the move in the Midlands. It would not in any case have been possible for these men to make any further attempt to ride out again in support of King James, for their absence from home at so critical a time cannot have gone unremarked by the local officials who at best would have promptly impounded their horses. For these gentlemen the adventure was over before it had begun. They were more fortunate than they knew: an infinitely worse fate was soon to overtake some of the more prominent actors in the conspiracy.

10
The hunters hunted

SOME OF THE WANTED MEN managed to escape to France, but most of the rest were captured within a few weeks. Barkley had prudently secured his own retreat and made haste to depart as soon as it was apparent that the conspiracy had been betrayed. Taking Captain Holmes with him, he rode straight to Romney Marsh to the house of Hunt the smuggler. Here Captain Gill and his owler were waiting, as Barkley had told them to stand by until needed. Thanks to this foresight, he and Holmes were able to cross safely to France before the pursuit had properly started. According to Ailesbury, Barkley had a frigid reception from King James, who signified his disapproval of the attempt to murder his nephew, and of Barkley's part in the affair, by banishing him forthwith from the royal presence. 'I know for certain', Ailesbury writes, 'that King James detested that action, and Berkley [sic] never after appeared before him, and by order.'[1] But Ailesbury was mistaken about the permanency of Barkley's banishment. The envoys who came to Paris in 1697 to discuss the Treaty of Rijswijk were much affronted to see him and several others of the conspirators about the French Court, and apparently still welcome at Saint-Germain. Among them was Father Johnson, who had vanished from London at the same time as Barkley and Holmes by an unrecorded escape route. He and the other two were fortunate, for by 5 March Hunt was under arrest, and was giving full information to the government about his illegal cargoes in exchange for a pardon.[2] The Fleming, Durant, one of the spies appointed to watch at Kensington Palace for the king's setting forth for the hunt, also vanished and was not heard of again in England.

No time was lost in hunting out the traitors. Warrants for their arrest, and orders to search the houses of suspects, poured out of the Secretary of State's Office. The Messengers, supported by detachments of soldiery and zealously assisted by the public, worked fast and efficiently. Charnock was the first to be arrested. Strangely he, who had throughout been the one to express doubts and fears of betrayal,

154

seems not to have thought it necessary to take measures for his own safety. On the evening of 22 February, after the final gathering of the conspirators at the 'Blue Posts' had broken up, Charnock had gone quietly home to his lodgings at Mrs Conant's in Norfolk Street. He seems to have had no premonition of danger, for he made no attempt to go into hiding, or even to change his lodgings. It was almost midnight on the following day, Sunday, when a Messenger with a posse of dragoons at his back appeared in Norfolk Street with a warrant for Charnock's arrest. The Messenger found him peacefully asleep in his bed. It was a rude awakening for Charnock, who was hurried through the dark streets to finish the night in a Newgate cell.[3]

Porter, Prendergrass and Keyes were arrested together on 27 February. Porter, when the last toast had been drunk at the 'Blue Posts', announced that he intended to go into the country and stay in hiding until the alarm had blown over, and invited Prendergrass to go with him. Prendergrass, although he knew he stood in no real danger, agreed willingly. He may have done this in part out of friendship for Porter for whom, surprisingly in a man of such upright character, he seems to have had some regard; it is more likely though that he feared that a refusal might arouse suspicions of his loyalty. This consideration was certainly in his mind, for before leaving London he managed to scribble a brief note to Portland, telling him that he would not be able to keep in touch with him for the present, because he was going into the country with some of the conspirators (whom he is careful not to name). 'I dare not refuse for feare of suspision', he tells Portland, adding that his lordship should be 'very careful here in the meantime'.[4] Keyes, naturally, was ordered to accompany and attend upon his master, who was evidently not intending to travel in haste or discomfort. He despatched Keyes to his lodgings to collect clean shirts and other necessities for the journey, with orders to bring them on the following day to him and Prendergrass at their first hiding-place, the house of two counterfeiters, Carter and Davis. These were two of Porter's old acquaintances, whom he had met in Newgate when committed there at the time of the Dog Tavern riot. Almost certainly Carter and Davis were Jacobites as well as counterfeiters. They must have been trustworthy as Porter and Prendergrass remained safely hidden in their house until Wednesday when Keyes, who for some reason had been delayed, finally appeared with the clean linen. Perhaps because they expected King James would be landing in England very soon, the fugitives seem to have felt no sense of urgency. If does not seem to have occurred to them that a speedy departure should perhaps have taken priority over clean shirts.

It was not until the next morning, Thursday 27 February, that Porter, Prendergrass and Keyes set out for the country. Porter makes no mention of their destination, but they may have been making for the south coast. By midday they were about five miles beyond Kingston and they stopped for refreshment at a roadside ale house. It was their undoing, for by this time news of the conspiracy had spread far and wide and people everwhere were on the look-out for escaping Jacobites. The landlord and patrons of the ale house naturally viewed the three strangers with suspicion, and no doubt with thoughts of a reward in mind determined to arrest them. Seizing whatever weapons they could lay hands on, the landlord and countrymen surrounded the inn and secured all three men, tied them up and marched them before the nearest Justice of the Peace. They were soon identified as persons named in the proclamation and despatched under guard to Newgate that same day.[5] The fortunate captors later claimed and received the full reward, amounting to £3000. The apportioning of this considerable sum between the claimants is interesting; it looks as if payment was made with due regard to the social status of both captives and captors. Thus, for apprehending Porter and Prendergrass, Mr Combes and Thomas Trevor each received £1000. Porter and Prendergrass were 'gentry', and Porter, as one of the principals in the plot, was a valuable prize. For the capture of the servant Keyes, the reward was divided between seven persons, six of whom are listed without any prefix to their names, indicating that they had no particular social status; they were no doubt the 'band of countrymen well armed' reported by the *Postman* as having captured all three fugitives. The seventh claimant for the capture of Keyes was Sir Francis Vincent.[6]

The prompt capture of Porter was a piece of great good fortune for the government for, since he had been one of the leaders of the conspiracy, he would be a key witness if he could be persuaded or frightened into turning King's evidence. Porter could be bold and bloodthirsty enough in a tavern but, faced with the prospect of hanging, his courage rapidly evaporated. As Burnet acidly remarks, he was 'a man of pleasure, who loved not the hardships of a gaol, and much less the solemnities of an execution'. It is not surprising then that Porter, without a sign of compunction for the friends whom he knew he would be condemning to death, at once set about saving his own skin. He must have made a move in this direction immediately after his capture, for he relates that on the very next morning Lord Cutts visited him in prison (probably at the request of Portland). Cutts, according to Porter, 'used many arguments to persuade me to serve the government'; it may safely be assumed that Porter did not need a great deal of persuading. He knew just how valuable a witness he would be and was determined to make the government pay for his services, not only by granting him life, but also by making that life more comfortable. This was to be an essential part of the bargain, for Porter knew that even if he escaped condemnation for his part in the plot, his creditors, who were legion, would see to it that he remained in a debtor's prison for an indefinite period if not for life. He told Lord Cutts that he was 'mightily in debt, that my life was not the thing I valued, but that I had rather a thousand times die than lead a miserable life in prison for debt'.

Cutts realised that Porter's information was not to be bought cheaply, but he could not of course make any definite undertaking as regards its price. However, he promised him that if he served His Majesty faithfully, he would use his influence with the king to see that he was 'taken care of'. Cutts seems to have done this to some effect, for a few days later William wrote to Portland, agreeing to grant Porter a pardon on condition he told all he knew.[7] Financial reward was not mentioned at this stage; that came later, when the government was satisfied that it had got full value for its money. The promise of present pardon and future reward was enough for Porter; he at once 'entered into his majesty's service and served him with zeal'.[8] His zealous service was to bring nine of his erstwhile companions to Tyburn.

Prendergrass, it will be remembered, had hitherto steadfastly refused to give evidence in court on the grounds that this would be a betrayal of Porter and his friends. But when he learned of Porter's treachery, which shocked him profoundly, Prendergrass realised that there was no longer any point in refusing to appear as a witness, and withdrew his objections. He was released from Newgate shortly after his arrest and duly appeared in court, to provide useful supporting evidence for the crown case. But unlike Porter, he neither asked nor expected any reward.

Two more arrests, of King and Knightley, were made on 27 February. John Belbin must have caught King single-handed, for he got the full reward of £1000. Knightley, making a desperate attempt to escape in women's clothes, was recognised, chased and caught by ten persons, who in due course shared the reward.[9] The *Postman* reports that Cardell Goodman was also captured on 27 February. Since Goodman had been a successful actor, his face must have been well known to many Londoners, so it is not surprising that thirteen persons claimed the reward for his arrest. Among these claimants was Matthew Smith, Sir William Parkyns's nephew, whose share was

£60.[10] Smith must have had hopes of doing better out of the hunt, for he probably knew who most of the conspirators were and looked forward to claiming the full reward for at least one of them. But since he had never been admitted to their councils he did not know enough to betray their whereabouts, not even those of his uncle William, who had prudently disappeared.

Crymes, the government spy, was still hot on the trail. To lull the suspicions of the conspirators, he had had himself arrested along with one of the men from Saint-Germain, Edward Lee. In this way he hoped to obtain more evidence against Lee and, even more important, the names of those of his confederates who were still at large. 'I am thoughtful how to do further service', he assures Trumbull on 25 February, and suggests that if an escape for himself and Lee can be contrived, 'this will so rivet me with the party that I do not doubt but to secure several that are obnoxious'.[11] Ever anxious to impress Trumbull with his devotion to duty he adds, 'if I am jealoused by the party, I can expect no other fate than to be murdered'; he hopes that in the event, the government will take care of his family. Whether Crymes's plan was ever acted upon, and how many arrests he was responsible for, is uncertain. It may have been following information from him that Lowick and Cranburne, Porter's armourer, were caught on 28 February, and Bertram, against whom Crymes had plenty of evidence, on 2 March.

Bertram, who was no hero, soon turned King's evidence. But he was an insignificant conspirator, having mostly confined his activities to helping Brice Blair recruit for Sir John Friend's regiment. Thanks to the forceful intervention of his wife, who had stopped him from going to the final meetings, he had had little or nothing to do with the Assassination Plot. He was, however, a useful witness for the prosecution at several of the trials, especially that of Lowick. His life was spared and he was eventually released, but unlike Porter he was in no position to claim a financial reward for his services.

Brice Blair was arrested on or about 10 March and confined in the Gatehouse Prison. Like Porter and Bertram, Blair lost no time in turning King's evidence and so saved his own neck. It is clear from his numerous and detailed testimonies that he was concerned to earn a full pardon by implicating as many persons as possible. He recounts his recruiting activities on behalf of Sir John Friend in great detail, and it is from Blair's depositions that much valuable information can be gained about the amount of support the party was counting on, not only in London, but in other parts of England. Blair was not involved in the Assassination Plot, although he knew a good deal about it, and in his efforts to clear himself of any suspicion of participation in it he spared no one. His statements, in which he eagerly produces name after name, are couched in self-pitying and sycophantic terms and make unpleasant reading. There is a threatening note in his remarks about Captain Fisher who, unknown to Blair, had already absolved himself from a charge of high treason by being the first person to give information about the plot:

As to Captain Fisher, I leave that to his own relation . . . and if his memory fail him, I will endeavour to refresh it; only, by the way, I have made both him and Bertram so sick of this villainy that they were at that time ready to vomit it up, if they have not already done so, for I hear they are both in custody.

As a further proof of his own innocence Blair quotes another conversation with Fisher, which must have taken place shortly before the discovery of the plot, and which looks as if Blair knew or suspected that Fisher was intending to betray it: 'And now, dear Fisher, says I, if you should come to be examined on this account, you will not deny, but I had an abhorrence of this damned business all along: Ay, that I will says he again, readily, for I can do it with a good conscience.'

Most of Blair's statements were written from the Gatehouse, a prison less rigorous than Newgate, and where the inmates were not confined to their cells during the daytime. Even so, it seems to have been a miserable place, and Blair's complaints of the discomforts and privations under which he was writing are frequent and long-winded; he evidently thought he deserved better treatment in return for his services:

I had expected more accommodation to write, or else I had begun sooner this day; for yesterday I was detained till ten o'clock at night in a crowd before I could get to my lodgings, in a cold hole, without fire, table, or so much as a chair . . . I thought the best way was to send you what I have done at present, and to beg time and some better accomodation for the rest; for I have a great deal more to say.[12]

He had indeed a great deal more to say and said it at great length, with many more complaints of his harsh treatment and of the illness brought on by his privations in the Gatehouse. His evidence told heavily against his former benefactor, Sir John Friend, who was arrested shortly afterwards; according to Macaulay, Sir John was discovered hiding in the house of a Quaker. He was not charged with complicity in the Assassination Plot, for even the treacherous Blair testified that he had had nothing to do with it. But it was chiefly on Blair's testimony that Sir John was charged with high treason in attempting to make war against the king. Like most of the accused, he was committed to Newgate and placed in solitary confinement.

THE PLOT

'That Grand Incendiary Ferguson,' as the historian Richard Kingston calls him, was hunted for some time before the discovery of the plot. As well as taking an active part in the plans for a rising, Ferguson had given great help to the Jacobite cause by his inflammatory pamphlets, most of which were printed in France and secretly distributed about the country from such centres as Sir William Parkyns's house at Bushey. One such pamphlet, vilifying King William and the Earl of Portland and calling on all true Englishmen to rise and rid themselves of the Dutch yoke, came into the hands of the historian Kingston; it so incensed him that he told Trumbull he would 'give the world to bring the wretched Scot to condign punishment'. Ferguson's friends in London managed to keep him hidden until 12 March when he was finally run to earth by the Messengers and confined to Newgate.[13] There was, however, insufficient evidence to bring him to trial and he was eventually set free. He went to France, where he spent the rest of his long life indefatigably pouring out pamphlets against King William, and after the king's death against Queen Anne.

On 27 February Messengers with warrants for the arrest of Sir William Parkyns were despatched to Bushey and to Marston Jabbett. The Messenger who went to Bushey spent several days searching the house and several others in the neighbourhood without finding a sign of Sir William. This is not surprising, since he must have known that he would be searched for there, and Sir William was always careful not to involve his immediate family in his dangerous activities; he would have been especially careful now, as it was a capital offence to harbour a traitor. The Messenger who went to Warwickshire, although he did not find Sir William, had better luck. Some person or persons unknown, on hearing the news of the plot, must have become suspicious and informed the parish constable at Marston Jabbett of the nocturnal removal of the 'goods' from Heywood's house and of their burial in the manor house garden. The constable searched the garden and soon found the boxes where they had been buried in the flower bed by the house wall. Assisted by the tenant Whetstone, he dug them up and took them to his own house. When the lids were prised off the 'choice goods' were revealed – the four dozen swords, with their hilts in a separate box, the thirty-two carbines and the twenty-five brace of pistols; all, the constable reported to the Messenger when he arrived, very bright and fit for service, and sufficient to equip a troop of Horse.[14]

So sensational a discovery was unlikely to remain a secret for long in a small rural community. The villagers of Marston Jabbett soon got wind of it and proceeded to demonstrate their loyalty to King William and their disapproval of the lord of the manor's traitorous activities by banding together and looting the house under pretext of searching for more arms; they also uprooted everything in the orchard and garden. This incident is reported in the *Postman* on 5 March; the report states that 'the country people got together and pulled down his house, that it might no longer be a nest of traytors'.[15] But as the house was still standing when the inventory of Sir William's possessions was taken two years after his execution, the *Postman*'s report must have been an exaggeration. The manor house, apparently intact, was included in the inventory, but the usual accompanying list of its contents is missing, and there is a significant reference in the document to 'goods and chattels feloniously removed'.[16] From this is would seem that the villagers had rewarded themselves for their loyalty by removing everything they could carry; there is no record of them having been brought to book for this piece of lawless behaviour.

The Lieutenant of the County, Sir Richard Newdigate, sent an official report of the discovery to Shrewsbury, who replied on 5 March:

I . . . wish your zeal for His Majesty's service may be imitated by others . . . seeing there is reason to believe that a great many arms lie concealed in the country, which were designed to be made use of in the intended invasion; as to those you have recovered in Sir William Parkyns's garden, the Board of Ordnance will send an order about them.[17]

A search for more hidden arms, in the course of which a good many quite innocent gentlemen's gardens must have suffered damage, was diligently made throughout the county, but nothing was found. If any Warwickshire gentlemen had ridden out to join the little bands of Jacobites lurking about the Midlands and waiting for King James to land, they had concealed both the fact and their arms with greater skill than had Sir William.

Evans the caretaker, Heywood, Whetstone and even the odd-job man Hipwell, naturally fell under suspicion of knowing something about the contents of the boxes. Since Evans had prudently disappeared, he must almost certainly have been in the secret. The other three, after interrogation by Sir Richard Newdigate, were arrested and taken to London by the Messengers. Watts, the parish constable, was also taken along as a witness but unlike his less fortunate travelling companions he must have had quite an enjoyable trip, for his expenses were paid and he was certainly not lodged in Newgate on arrival.[18]

There can be no doubt that the weapons found in his garden were the property of Sir William, and that they were the weapons reported to be hidden in his house in 1694 by Matthew Smith. And they were certainly buried on his instructions – that much came out clearly at his trial. But who was to use them, and when, remains a mystery. As has been said, they cannot have been intended for the use of the troop Sir William had raised in London, for that was armed and ready for action by January 1696, and his men could not in any case have been dependent on arms hidden as far away as Warwickshire. The most likely explanation seems to be that they had been bought two years previously at the time of the Lancashire Plot, and since there had been no opportunity to use them they had been left hidden to await some future rising. It is even possible that the arms were Sir William's contribution for a troop to be raised by one of the mysterious persons who met him and Scudamore in Leicester in January. His careful concealment of these weapons was to be one of the most damning pieces of evidence at his trial, but neither he nor anyone else ever gave any clue as to their intended use.

The King's Messengers need not have searched so far afield for Sir William, for he had gone to ground almost on their doorstep, in the Temple. According to Brice Blair, there were a good many 'pretty brisk men' in the Temple ready to fight for King James when he landed,[19] so Sir William must have had friends and sympathisers there who could be trusted not to betray him. He would have been safer in the Temple than in either of his houses as he knew that both would be searched and his family and dependants penalised if they were found to be harbouring him. And there was of course always the risk that someone, either in Bushey or Marston Jabbett, would be tempted by the £1000 reward to inform upon him. No doubt also Sir William thought it better to stay in London, for like his confederates he confidently expected King James to land in England very soon. He should therefore be at hand to rally his troop and ride to meet his king. These expectations must have faded as time went by and no news of a landing came, while with every day that passed the danger of discovery increased. The search for him in Hertfordshire went on, but Sir William managed to remain safely concealed in the Temple until 10 March. He might have stayed hidden indefinitely had it not been for the indiscretion of Richard Smith, the rector of Bushey. The rector appears to have been a crypto-Jacobite, and was certainly a crony of Sir William, for he was so far in his confidence that he knew where he was sheltered. He inadvertently let fall this piece of information, which came to the ears of the Messenger. Naturally, Richard Smith fell under suspicion of knowing more than he should about the conspiracy, and was carried up to London for interrogation; it was presumably his information that led to Sir William's arrest.[20]

The *Flying Post* for 10–12 March reports that 'On Tuesday in the evening, an Officer in the Guards seized Sir William Parkyns, mentioned in the Proclamation, in a Gentleman's chamber over the Crown Office in the Temple, with another in his Company, but the student who owned the Chamber was absent.'[21] It has not been possible to trace the identity of Sir William's companion, who may have been one of the 'pretty brisk men' abounding in the Temple. It is clear that there must have been persons able and willing to help him; someone must have known that the student's room was unoccupied, and that it would be a safe, if temporary, hiding-place. Someone too, perhaps his unidentified companion, must have provided him with food and drink and other necessaries, for Sir William was too well known in the Temple to have been able to do this himself. But who this person or persons were never came to light. His captors, however, are identifiable, because they claimed and received the reward of £1000, which was divided among them as follows: £630 to Sir Nathaniel Powell; £200 to Captain Leonard Powell; £20 to four soldiers of the guard; £50 to Matt. Johnson and Edward Jones; £100 to a safe nominee for Robert Maddiston, who was presumably the absent owner of the room.

As in the case of Porter, Prendergrass and Keyes the rewards seem to have been apportioned with a nice regard for the social status of the recipients. Sir Nathaniel Powell, who got the largest share, may have been the person most concerned with Sir William's discovery and capture. Captain Powell, the officer of the guards mentioned in the *Flying Post,* could have been a relative of Sir Nathaniel. £5 was considered adequate reward for the four soldiers, who in fact must have earned it easily enough by marching the captive from the Temple to Newgate, a distance of a few hundred yards.[22] What part the other persons mentioned played in Sir William's capture in not recorded, but no doubt their reward was carefully calculated in accordance with their deserts. The prisoner was loaded with heavy chains and placed in solitary confinement in Newgate, and for some time was allowed no contact with his family or his lawyers. On 12 March he was taken to the Duke of Shrewsbury's office for the first of several interrogations by a committee of the Privy Council.

Meanwhile, the evidence against Sir William was piling up. On 10 March the Secretary of State was informed that one of his servants, whose name is not given, but who may have been the groom James

163

Eubanks, was in custody in Bedford gaol. Shrewsbury wrote at once to the governor of the gaol, instructing him to tell the prisoner that his master was in Newgate, and that he should tell all he knew of Sir William's recent activities. As Eubanks was kept in custody in order to give evidence at Sir William's trial, it was probably he who was in Bedford gaol. He was not charged with complicity in the plot, and was released soon afterwards. The Messengers who went to Hertfordshire had orders to search for Abraham Sweet, who was soon discovered and arrested on suspicion of high treason. Sweet had been the recipient of many of Sir William's confidences about the raising of the troop and other matters, and even if he had played no active part in it he certainly knew a good deal about the intended assassination. He was therefore highly suspect, but as he gave important evidence against Sir William as one of the two vital crown witnesses, he was not charged and like Eubanks was released soon after the trial.

Among the last to be arrested were Ambrose Rookwood and his friend John Bernardi. Rookwood's fate was an unhappy one, for he had taken part in the Assassination Plot only with the utmost reluctance. The plight of Bernardi was even worse, for he had been drawn in only through his friendship with Rookwood and knew nothing of the plans for the assassination, although there is evidence that he would have been willing to join the general rising; it was his presence at one of the later tavern meetings that led to the inclusion of his name in the second proclamation of 22 March. But poor Bernardi was born under an unlucky star, as his autobiography, from which the following details are derived, shows.[23]

Major John Bernardi was descended from an ancient and noble Genoese family. His father, Francis Bernardi, had been Genoese Agent at the Court of Charles II and had settled in England after the termination of his appointment. Francis Bernardi was, even in those days, thought to be an excessively stern father. He treated his son John with great severity, beating him unmercifully for the slightest real or imagined fault, and keeping the boy locked up in his room for long periods. At last John Bernardi, at the age of eighteen, ran away from home and took refuge with kindly and sympathetic friends, who helped him to join the army. He became a professional soldier, serving first in the Netherlands under William of Orange, later to become William III. In the course of his campaigns on the Continent Bernardi sustained a severe injury to his right arm and lost one of his eyes, but these injuries did not hinder his military career, and he gained a reputation as a brave soldier and competent commander, rising eventually to the rank of Major. In 1685, shortly after the accession of James II, he left the service of the Prince of Orange and came to England to serve under King James until the Revolution. Bernardi was a catholic and a loyal supporter of James in 1688. After the Revolution, like so many of his fellow-officers, he refused to subscribe to the oath of allegiance to William and Mary in 1689. Taking his wife and six children with him, he followed his old master to France, where he lived quietly for several years. Bernardi's harsh upbringing had not soured his nature, and he was a loyal and generous friend to his fellow-refugees. Although he was far from wealthy, he spent considerable sums in helping the less fortunate among them to establish themselves in exile, and was a notable benefactor to their wives and children.

Bernardi's wife died while he was living in France, and in or about 1691 he obtained permission from King William to return to England with his children. He settled in Essex where he lived quietly and devoted himself to gardening. So far as is known he took no part in Jacobite activities. In December 1695 the owner of the house that Bernardi had rented in Essex gave him notice to quit, as he required it for his own use. Bernardi therefore had to leave his home and garden and moved with his family to live in London. It was an unlucky move for him as early in February 1696 he met Ambrose Rookwood, an old friend and comrade-in-arms. They met and dined together several times over the next two weeks. According to Bernardi, Rookwood explained that he had left King James's service and intended to settle and live quietly in England. But for the present it was necessary for him to keep out of sight of the authorities, as he had come over without waiting for the necessary official permit, without which it was a criminal offence to travel from France. However, Rookwood assured his friend that all would soon be well as his brother, who lived in England, was going to use his influence to obtain a permit for him. Rookwood's story was only true in so far as it was necessary for him to conceal his presence in London, and Bernardi, in order to establish his own innocence and perhaps that of his friend, denies that he knew of any more sinister reason for Rookwood's need for concealment. Here Bernardi cannot have been telling the truth, because it emerged later that he did know something of an intended rebellion, and was quite willing to take part in it.

On the evening of Saturday 22 February, when it had become clear that the Assassination Plot had been betrayed and that the conspirators must scatter at once, Rookwood sought out Bernardi at the latter's lodgings and asked if he might spend the evening with him. Bernardi, observing that his friend seemed agitated, asked if 'any evil had befallen him?'. Rookwood, anxious to keep from Bernardi any knowledge of the Assassination Plot and of his own part in it, told him that a proclamation had come out that very evening for the apprehension of certain traitors, and that his, Rookwood's, name was unfortunately included among them. If, therefore, 'any person should be so malicious as to give information of his being come over at that time, he should certainly be taken up' – the implication here being that Rookwood's only offence was to have come over from France without a permit. Even at this late date no rumours of the intended assassination seem to have reached Bernardi's ears, and he trustingly accepted this rather thin explanation, and very willingly agreed to bear Rookwood company that evening. But, he told Rookwood, he was already engaged to spend the evening at a tavern on Tower Hill with two friends, and if Rookwood agreed, they would, he was sure, have no objection to his joining the party. Rookwood probably knew that Bernardi's friends were trustworthy and made no objection to the meeting, which duly took place. After the other two men had left, Rookwood and Bernardi sat on over their wine; Rookwood no doubt knew that he was safe from arrest in a private room in an obscure tavern, but it would have been dangerous to go home to his lodgings, or even out into the street. So they hired a room in the tavern and slept there that night, Rookwood no doubt hoping to make his escape in the morning.

During the evening, it happened that a maidservant from a near-by house came into the tavern to fetch a pot of ale for her master. She was evidently an inquisitive girl and probably knew that there was a reward for the apprehension of suspected Jacobite traitors. Seeing two strange gentlemen in the tavern, she asked the potman if he knew who they were. The potman gave the girl 'a rude and surly answer', whereupon she flounced out of the tavern and went straight to the local constable, informing him that 'some evil-minded men were at the tavern and the people of the house refused to say who they were'. Early next morning, with several more constables and supported by a posse of dragoons, the constable appeared at the tavern and arrested Rookwood, Bernardi and the tavern-keeper, together with his entire family and servants. As it was Sunday the Recorder was at church and so both prisoners and guards had to wait at the tavern until the service was over.

Rookwood's situation was now desperate, and he had involved Bernardi to such an extent that he too might be charged with high treason, or at best with the capital offence of assisting a person charged with high treason. There was, however, still the hope that they would both be able to conceal their identities. Rookwood took advantage of the time gained by the wait in the tavern to confess to Bernardi that he was heavily involved in the plot to kill King William, and that this was the real reason for his name having been included in the proclamation. He would therefore inevitably be charged with high treason if his identity were known and, since they had been arrested together, Bernardi would be liable to the same charge. Their only hope, Rookwood said, was to give false names to the Recorder. He would call himself 'Felton', and Bernardi's not very original alias should be 'Smith'. Whatever Bernardi may have thought of the murder plot and of his friend's part in it, he was far too loyal and generous a man to betray a companion; he agreed without hesitation to help Rookwood to the best of his ability and at whatever cost to himself. When 'Felton' and 'Smith' were interrogated they must have given a satisfactory account of themselves, for the Recorder found no evidence to support the maidservant's accusation. Nevertheless he told them, not unkindly, that in view of the disturbed time and of the accusation laid against them, he would have to detain them for the time being. He did not however consider that the charge warranted committal to Newgate, and sent them instead to the Poultry Counter, a near-by prison for lesser offenders. The Recorder can have had no suspicion of the true identity of his prisoners, because he told them that he was sending them to the Poultry Counter so that from thence 'they might with less difficulty and expense obtain their liberty when the storm had blown over'. As to the tavern-keeper and his entourage, they were released on bail and suffered no further inconvenience.

Rookwood and Bernardi spent a whole month in the Poultry Counter without any suspicion being aroused as to their true identities. As each was in solitary confinement and so unable to communicate with the other, it would have been easy for Bernardi to gain his own liberty and establish his innocence by betraying his friend, but it was not in his nature to contemplate so dishonourable an action. Rookwood's only contact with the outside world was his subordinate, Harris, who had come over from Saint-Germain at about the same time as himself, and in whose fidelity he had complete but, as it turned out, mistaken confidence. Harris, because he had not been named in the first proclamation, was still at liberty. Under the assumed name of 'Jenkins' he was able to come and go with little fear of arrest, and visited Rookwood several times in the Counter. Then on 23 March a second proclamation was issued, and this time Harris's name was included, as well as that of Bernardi. There was in fact no evidence to connect Bernardi with the murder plot, but he had been seen at least once in company with Rookwood and Barkley, so that one or other of the informers must have assumed that he had been enlisted for the expedition to Turnham Green. Also Bernardi, through no fault of his own, had disappeared; this looked suspiciously as though he had gone into hiding or fled the country. And so the unfortunate man now found himself wanted for high treason, with a price of £1000 on his head.

Since Harris was also named in the second proclamation his own immunity from arrest and probably hanging could not last much longer if he stayed in London. But he could save his own neck and earn £2000 by informing on Rookwood and Bernardi. The double temptation was too much for him. The day after the second proclamation appeared he went to the Secretary of State's office and informed Sir William Trumbull that Rookwood and Bernardi were in the Poultry Counter, having been committed there a month ago under the false names of Felton and Smith. That same evening a detachment of guards arrived at the Poultry Counter. Their officer bore a letter from Sir William Trumbull to the Lord Mayor of London, who had jurisdiction over the Counter. Trumbull wrote: 'I am informed that two men committed to the Poultry Counter by your lordship's order under the names of Felton and Smith, are two of the persons named in the Proclamation of the 22nd. inst., as engaged in the detestable conspiracy against the King, the supposed Felton being Rookwood, and Smith, Bernardi. I desire you will deliver the men to the bearer, one of the Officers of the Guards.'[24]

The prisoners were duly handed over and taken before the Privy Council for interrogation. Thanks to the treachery of Harris, their true identities were quickly established. Rookwood stolidly denied all the allegations made against him by his betrayer but Bernardi, perhaps because he was relatively more innocent, was a little more forthcoming. He admitted knowing something of a plan for a rising, and did not deny that he would have taken part in it. He also admitted that he had been on a few occasions in the company of the conspirators, but clearly he had no detailed knowledge of their plans, for he had asked Barkley on one occasion, 'what was to be done?', and all Barkley and Charnock, who was also present, had told him was that there would be 'a rising all England over'. It certainly looks as if Bernardi intended to join the rebels, for he said that Barkley had promised him a pair of pistols, and that he had recently bought a horse 'which stood at the Red Lion in Eagle Street'.[25] In view of this confession, it seems that Bernardi was not quite as innocent as he would have the readers of his autobiography believe. After interrogation both prisoners were committed to Newgate, where they were 'loaded with heavy chains, and put into dismal, dark and stinking apartments'. They never saw each other again.

Harris, in addition to earning a pardon and £2000 for informing on Bernardi and Rookwood, shortly afterwards made himself another £1000 by informing on Counter, another of King James's soldiers sent over from Saint-Germain. Two more of these soldiers, Chambers and Meldrum, were arrested at about the same time. The subsequent histories of these three men are linked with that of Bernardi, with whom they were confined in Newgate. Their fate was the saddest of all those who suffered for their implication in the conspiracy, as we shall see in a later chapter.

The Earl of Ailesbury's Jacobite leanings and his personal devotion to King James were too well known for him not to come under suspicion of conspiring against King William. As far as the Assassination Plot was concerned, however, he was generally admitted to be blameless. Indeed, it is certain that he never knew of it until after the discovery as the conspirators would have been careful to let no rumour of it come to his ears, knowing that he would have done his utmost to prevent it. Although Ailesbury had been active in King James's cause in 1692–3, it is difficult to say how far he was involved in the plans for a general rebellion in 1696; but there can be little doubt that he at least knew a good deal about them. On his own admission, he had been present at the two meetings of the previous summer when it had been agreed between all those present to send Charnock to Saint-Germain with messages urging James to seek French help for another attempt to regain the throne. Ailesbury himself, writing twenty years afterwards, and for obvious reasons still wishing to minimise his part in the affair, emphatically denied that he knew of the real purpose of those meetings. But his name appears among the signatories of the document that Charnock took to France, and all the witnesses at the trials declared that the earl had been present when the plan was discussed and the terms of the message to James agreed upon. He must too have known a good deal of what was going on when he met Berwick in London in January 1696, because he certainly knew why Berwick had come to London, and it was he who urged him to get back to France while there was still time. Taking all this into account, and in spite of his protestations of innocence, it is clear that Ailesbury had seriously compromised himself even if he were not guilty of high treason.

By the end of February Ailesbury realised that he was in imminent danger of arrest. His friends, fearful for his safety, urged him to flee the country, but knowing that flight would invitably be construed as an admission of guilt, he stayed on uneasily in London, hoping that the storm would soon blow over. Unhappily for him the storm did not abate; rather, it gathered momentum as fresh evidence of conspiracy and danger came to light, and Ailesbury found that his situation *vis-à-vis* the government was becoming daily more precarious. Finally, acting on the advice of his friend Sir Phillip Meadows, he took the bull by the horns and went on 21 March to see Shrewsbury, the Secretary of State, in order to clarify his position.

Ailesbury and the Duke of Shrewsbury were old friends and hitherto had been on the best of terms, in spite of Ailesbury's embarrassing Jacobite tendencies. He was, therefore, astonished and disquieted by his chilly reception. 'I repaired forthwith to the Duke of Shrewsbury', he writes; 'I told him I came here to offer myself. He received me with the last coldness and reservedness, perhaps out of policy; he answered me with a grave countenance that he had heard nothing of me, and so I went to my old acquaintance, Sir William Trumbull.'[26] Trumbull had no ties of old friendship with Ailesbury, and probably had had his instructions from Shrewsbury. He promptly signed a warrant for the earl's arrest and sent him to the Tower.

Ailesbury says in his memoirs that he never knew why, or on whose evidence, he had been arrested. He thought himself safe from Porter, because the latter was still enjoying the income from the annuity that Ailesbury had sold him in 1688; it would cease if Ailesbury died, and so he did not expect that Porter would want to kill the goose that laid the golden eggs. Unhappily, Ailesbury underestimated Porter's cunning; he already had the assurance of a royal pardon, and knew that his life was safe; but he had more evidence to sell, and determined to get as much as he could for it. And, as he did not neglect to point out, by informing on Ailesbury, Porter was sacrificing an assured income – a proof that he was 'entirely in His Majesty's service without reserve'.[27] The annuity, in fact, was the sprat to catch a mackerel in the form of a much larger government reward. On 14 March Porter appeared again before the Privy Council and gave a full account of the two fateful dinner parties of the previous summer. He also told the Privy Council that Charnock had brought back letters from King James to all those present.[28] There was quite enough evidence here to arrest Ailesbury, and it must have been known to both Shrewsbury and Trumbull by 21 March, when the unsuspecting Ailesbury walked straight into the trap set by Porter. It was not surprising that Shrewsbury received him with 'coldness and reservedness' and that Trumbull arrested him on the spot.

Ailesbury spent the best part of a year in the Tower in close confinement under extremely rigorous conditions. During his imprisonment his wife, to whom he was devoted, and whose health had been seriously undermined by anxiety about her husband, died in childbirth. The baby also died a few days later. It was not until February 1697 that the government decided that there was insufficient evidence to bring him to trial, and he was released on bail. Ailesbury's release, incidentally, meant that Porter, in addition to a handsome government reward, was able to continue in enjoyment of the annuity for the rest of his life. Shortly after his release Ailesbury obtained King William's permission to leave the country on condition that he remained abroad permanently. He went first to France and finally settled in Brussels, where he married again and lived quietly for many years. His exile was a reasonably happy one, for he lived in some state, collected works of art, delighted in entertaining English visitors and was much respected by the Bruxellois. For various reasons, mainly political, but later by his own choice, he never returned to England. He died in 1741, aged eighty-five.

The last man to be arrested was Sir John Fenwick, who had managed to stay in hiding until June 1696. By that time the invasion scare was over, the forces intended for it being fully occupied in Flanders, where the long war was at last drawing to a close. Most of the conspirators had been tried and condemned. The Assassination Plot was beginning to recede into history. But Fenwick's trial by Attainder raised issues that for some time divided both government and nation; and he, who in life had never been highly regarded, became in death a figure of national importance. It is Sir John Fenwick's name that is most often recalled in connection with the Assassination Plot, although ironically it was never proved that he had any part in it.

PART III

Retribution

11
'The highest crime'

'HIGH TREASON', said Solicitor-General Sir John Hawles at the trial of Charnock, King and Keyes, 'is the highest crime that our law takes notice of: and it very well deserves to go under that name, for it tends to subvert the very foundations of government, and to bring all into confusion and desolation, by taking away the life of the King, which life the law makes sacred above all others, because without that be safe, there can be no safety to any particular person.'[1]

This view of high treason is not of course peculiar to the seventeenth century. It has obtained whenever and wherever the safety of a community is threatened by subversion, and is still the only crime that can carry the death penalty in England. But since for almost two centuries after the seventeenth century death was the penalty for a great number of petty offences besides murder, it followed that a more spectacular punishment was fitting for the gravest crime of all. This opinion was almost universally held at the time. Even that most just and merciful of judges, Sir John Holt, said of treason that it should be punished 'not only *cum ultimo supplicio*, but with an Aggravation of Corporal pain, because it is a crime committed against the Body Politic, in the person of the King, who is head of the Kingdom'.[2]

If, in that smaller and less highly organised society, high treason was punished with terrible ferocity, it was mainly because that ferocity was bred of fear and insecurity. The government's means of maintaining public security were far from efficient, and public order tended to be chronically precarious. The police force was still rudimentary; communications were slow and unreliable; the standing army, frequently called in to quell disturbances, was small and often mutinous or disaffected. Such traitors as did not escape capture, then, had to be made examples of at all costs, for it was essential for the government to demonstrate that it could protect itself and the kingdom from the menace of treachery from within. Thus the swift and horrible punishment for treachery was intended both as a reassurance to the law-abiding and a deterrent to traitors. Further, there was another

175

aspect of high treason that loomed larger in the seventeenth-century mind than it generally does today: the offence was not only a political one; it was also sacrilege. Because a crowned and anointed king was invested by the Church with spiritual as well as temporal powers, his person was 'sacred above all others'. Therefore whoever threatened the king's life was doubly guilty, for he had committed a crime against God as well as against man. The doctrine of divine kingship is as old as kingship itself, but while a seventeenth-century monarch could hardly be treated as a sacred being in the same way as, for instance, an Egyptian Pharaoh, nevertheless his person was in a very real sense sacrosanct. This concept is implicit in the grim formula used for the indictment of traitors:

that you, not having the fear of God in your heart, not weighing the duty of your allegiance, but being moved and seduced by the instigation of the devil, as a false traitor against the said most serene most clement and most excellent Prince . . . your supreme, true, natural and rightful lord.[3]

Thus the crime of high treason was considered to be doubly heinous, and for this reason was punished with 'Aggravation of Corporal pain' and ignominy. Indeed the barbaric sentence reads more like an account of a primitive sacrifice than a judgement that was often carried out until well into the eighteenth century:

that you go back to the place from whence you came, and from thence be drawn upon a hurdle to the place of execution, where you shall be hanged up by the neck, and cut down alive; your body shall be ripped open, your privy members cut off, your bowels taken out and burnt before your face; your head shall be severed from your body, your body to be divided into four quarters, and your head and quarters are to be at the disposal of the king; and the Lord have mercy on your soul.

How far this punishment was deliberately designed to fit the crime is a matter for speculation. Certainly there seems to be a strong element of symbolism in it. The body of a person who has threatened the body politic must be utterly destroyed in a ritual way that bears a significant relation to the nature of the offence. Thus the head that menaced the head of state is cut off. The generative and other organs controlling the bodily functions are consumed by fire, an element held from time immemorial to have the power of destroying or neutralising evil. As the victim had threatened to break up the body politic, so is his body dismembered and broken up. And there could be no question of Christian burial. God might have mercy on the criminal's soul. Neither Church nor State would show mercy for his body.

The wording of the sentence was medieval, but was still pronounced in full over the condemned person. By the end of the seventeenth century however, there were some mitigations, albeit slight, of its full horrors. The practice of dragging the victim to the place of execution on a hurdle was discontinued; a sledge, often with small wheels, was substituted, in which the condemned man was able to sit upright. This modification may not in fact have been made from motives of humanity. The victim had often arrived in too battered a state to take a conscious part in the rest of the proceedings. Again, the body was allowed to remain on the gallows until life was extinct. Even so, this must often have been only a partial mitigation of suffering, for hanging at that time was not always carried out efficiently; if the drop was too short to break the neck and thus make death almost instantaneous, the victim died by slow strangulation. But at least the subsequent butchering was carried out on a corpse and not on a still-breathing body. Afterwards, the dismembered corpse was loaded onto a cart and taken back to Newgate. Here, in a remote back room, commonly called 'Jack Ketch's Kitchen', the remains were par-boiled in a solution of bay salt and cumin seed. The first was a preservative, the second was supposed to render the flesh obnoxious to birds. When this process was completed the head, trunk and limbs were impaled on spikes and displayed in prominent places about London. Temple Bar was at this time the most favoured site, but it was not unusual to distribute the exhibits for greater effect, or even to send a limb to the deceased's native town as a warning to his fellow-citizens. For instance, the remains of Sir Thomas Armstrong, executed in 1683 for his alleged part in the Rye House Plot, were widely scattered. The head was put on Westminster Hall, one limb on Temple Bar, another on Aldgate, a third on Aldersgate, while a fourth quarter was despatched for display in Stafford, which Sir Thomas had represented in King Charles II's last parliament.

This sentence was never carried out on the bodies of women. For them the punishment for high treason was burning alive, a fate quite as dreadful, if less ignominious. But it had not been carried out since Elizabeth Gaunt was burnt alive in 1685 for harbouring rebels. Lady Alice Lisle was condemned for the same offence in 1685, but her sentence was commuted by King James to beheading. In 1693 Mrs Ann Merryweather was convicted of high treason for publishing King James's Declaration and other treasonable pamphlets. She was sentenced to be burnt alive, but was five times reprieved and finally pardoned. Although accustomed to scenes of execution, the savagery of this sentence was clearly too much for the populace; there had been some public oucry at the burning of Elizabeth Gaunt, a harmless old lady of over seventy years who had done no more than give shelter to two exhausted refugees from the battle of Sedgemoor.

Between the execution of Sir Thomas Armstrong in 1683 and 1696, the full sentence for high treason was rarely carried out. In 1691 John Ashton, condemned for high treason, was granted the unusual privilege of going to Tyburn in a carriage; he was not beheaded and his body was delivered to his friends for burial. When Anderton, the printer of seditious pamphlets, was condemned in 1693, Queen Mary remitted the quartering of his body, and it too was delivered to his family for burial. Why the sentence was partially remitted in these and several other cases during those years is a matter for conjecture. Certainly it was out of keeping with the spirit if not the letter of the Bill of Rights, which expressly mentions 'cruel and unusual punishments' as being contrary to the laws and liberties of Englishmen. Possibly the growth of the educated middle class may have influenced public opinion. Executions, it is true, were still a popular form of entertainment, but perhaps in an age of increasing refinement, even the crowds who flocked to such spectacles found the butchery practised on the corpse of the traitor offensive.

Trials for high treason were regulated by the Statute of 25 Edward III, passed in 1351. Under it the accused's chances of defending himself were minimal. He was not allowed counsel to defend him in court, although he might have legal advice on points of law before the trial. Witnesses for the defence could not be subpoenaed or put on oath. Hearsay evidence was accepted, as was that of accomplices, who were often the chief witnesses for the crown. Since the prisoner was not allowed a copy of the indictment, he would have only a general idea of the charges before coming into court. The judge could, and often did, act in a limited sense as counsel for him, in so far as he could advise him on points of law during the trial. The prisoner had no other help. His one slender chance lay in detecting a mistake or omission in the indictment or the sentence. If he could do this, the trial would be nullified and he would go free. Very few, however, slipped through the meshes of the law in this way, for great care was taken to see that the wording was precise. Thus, as J. P. Kenyon says, 'a seventeenth-century treason trial was not an attempt to ascertain the truth or adminster justice, except in the punitive sense. It was a morality play, staged as a demonstration of government power, an affirmation of kingly authority, and a warning to the unwary.'[4]

As the century advanced, some minor amendments to the medieval law were enacted, but its main provisons remained in force until 1696. It was however felt increasingly that even a person accused of high treason should have the same opportunity of defending himself as lesser offenders. Thus Lord Jeffreys, who was certainly not noted for leniency towards traitors, said in 1684:

I think it a hard case, that a man should have counsel to defend himself for a twopenny trespass, and his witnesses examined on oath, but if he steal, commit murder . . . nay, high treason, where life, estate, honour, and all are concerned, he shall have neither counsel, nor his witnesses examined on oath.[5]

Jeffreys was expressing an opinion commonly held by his colleagues on the bench; thus it was that some of the reforms to be embodied in the new Act had become common practice. The prisoner had a week's notice of his trial, and his counsel was allowed to help him prepare his case. He was also allowed a copy of the jury panel at least two days before the trial. These concessions, however, continued to be regarded as a favour rather than a right. Time was very much on the side of the crown; complaints by the accused that he had been given no time to prepare his case are a common feature of all late seventeenth-century treason trials. But the law was uncompromising on this point. 'Persons that will venture upon such sort of things', said Justice Pollexfen in 1691, 'are not to condemn the law if it be a little hard on them; for it is the common preservation that is aimed at in such things; and if this accusation be true, it is just and reasonable that all speed should be used to enquire into, and prevent it.'[6] Trials, by modern standards, were certainly speedy, and seldom occupied more than a day. The court opened between seven and eight o'clock in the morning, and would sit without a break until three or four o'clock in the afternoon. If necessary, it would assemble after a break of two hours or so for the final stages.

A Bill to bring the treason law more into conformity with the spirit of the Bill of Rights was brought in in 1689, but did not become law until 1696. The long delay was mainly due to opposition from the Lords, who insisted on the inclusion of a clause providing for their right to be tried by an assembly of peers. The Commons refused, and the Bill went to and fro between the two Houses for six years. Opposition also came from the Whigs, who maintained that reform was unnecessary in view of the many amendments to the old statute. Moreover, they thought that any relaxation would have the effect of encouraging the ever-present fifth column in their midst; one Whig member even went so far as to describe the Bill as a licence for king-killing. The main support for it came from the Tories. It was not until January 1696 that the newly elected Whig Parliament finally gave way to the Lords' insistence on their ancient right. The Bill was passed by a coalition of Tories and more liberally minded Whigs. It received royal assent on 12 January, but did not take effect until 25 March 1696.

The preamble to the Treasons Act or, to give it its full title, the Act for Regulating of Trials in Cases of Treason and Misprision of Treason, voices the more humane attitude towards those accused of this crime that had at last prevailed:

> Whereas nothing is more just and reasonable than that Persons prosecuted for High Treason and Misprision of Treason, whereby the Liberties, Lives, Honour, Estates, Blood and Posterity of the Subject may be lost and destroyed, should be justly and equally tried and that Persons accused as offenders therein should not be debarred of all just and equal Means for Defence of their Innocencies in such cases.[7]

The main provisions of the Act were: the accused was to have a copy of the indictment not less than five days and a copy of the jury panel two days before the trial; witnesses for the defence as well as the prosecution could be subpoenaed and put on oath; the accused's counsel could plead for him in court; as under the old statute, two witnesses were necessary before the case could be brought but they need not be witnesses to the same act of treason; no person could be prosecuted for treason if three years had elapsed between the alleged offence and a prosecution therefor. An exception to this ruling was made in the case of persons 'designing or attempting any Assassination on the Body of the King'.

Thus, with the passing of the Treasons Act, the person accused of this crime at last gained the same right to defend himself as was granted to lesser malefactors. Although the justice of this was generally acknowledged, those who had opposed the measure on the grounds that it endangered the safety of the throne enjoyed a certain belated triumph when the news of the Assassination Plot broke out. Here, it was said, were assassins preparing to take advantage of the 'licence for king-killing' that they hoped the Act would give them, even before it had become law. And here too was justification for arguments in favour of retaining the old statute in all its severity. In part at least, it may have been this attitude of the opponents of the Act that influenced the government's decision to hurry on the trials, so that the conspirators already captured could be dealt with under the old statute. There were besides strong practical reasons for making an example of them as quickly as possible. The public alarm caused by the twin threats of invasion and a Jacobite rising was still at fever pitch; prompt punishment of the offenders would reassure the populace and strengthen their confidence in the government's ability to deal with those threats. Moreover, the evidence against the accused was so strong that there can be little doubt that the verdict would have gone against them even had they enjoyed the advantages of the new Act. King William too was anxious to have the trials over and the country settled before he embarked for Flanders, where his presence was urgently needed. The decision to try the prisoners as soon as possible was supported by the Whigs and Tories alike; the Whigs were naturally anxious to take full advantage of the upsurge of popular feeling in King William's favour while it was still at its height; the Tories, even the more moderate among them, were all for silencing the conspirators quickly. Rumours of the involvement in the conspiracy of several highly placed Tories were rife, and no one knew, though many feared, what further interrogation of the prisoners might reveal. Thus political expediency and the exigencies of the current state of national emergency dictated the government decision that the prisoners must be brought to trial with all speed.

Most of the conspirators were in prison by the first week of March, and already had been several times interrogated by the Privy Council, and Porter and various other informers had made their statements, so that the government had sufficient evidence to set up the trials without further delay. It was hoped that the accused would be persuaded to name more of their confederates, but there is no indication that undue pressure was put upon them to do so. Torture had not been used in England since the 1640s, but there were still those who regretted its discontinuance. An anonymous correspondent writing to Sir William Trumbull says, 'Job Hewet removed arms and horses and carried letters for Sir William Perkins; had he been kept a close prisoner or put a little to the torture, he would have discovered some persons that were never yet spoken of.'[8] Dr Leopold Finch of All Souls College informs Trumbull that 'Charnock's acquaintance in Magdalen College say that as he is a desperate fellow, so he is of no great courage when hard pressed, and . . . they apprehend he may be brought by rough means to confession of things within his knowledge.'[9]

In spite of the government's anxiety to discover which persons of note had been implicated in the plot, no 'rough means' were used on Charnock. According to Burnet, his brother was sent to him in Newgate to persuade him to give information in exchange for his life. At first Charnock seemed inclined to accept the offer, but at his brother's next visit he told him that 'he could not save his own life without doing that, which would take away the lives of so many, that he did not think his own life worth it'.[10] If this is true, it seems to belie

Dr Finch's estimate of Charnock's courage; and even Burnet remarks that 'this shewed a greatness of mind that had been very valuable, had it been better directed'. Burnet, however, goes on to give a different and less creditable account of Charnock's behaviour. Several years after the trial, he says, Lord Somers told him that Charnock had offered the king a full discovery of the plot in exchange not for a pardon, but for an easy life imprisonment. William was said to have refused the offer, foreseeing that Charnock would implicate many persons who would make no more trouble now that the plot was discovered, so long as they were not persecuted. He wisely decided to let the matter rest and to leave Charnock to stand trial. Which of these accounts is true it is impossible to say, but Charnock's behaviour at his trial and execution rather point to the first as being correct, for he showed great courage and never betrayed his friends. The lesser conspirators, such as King and Keyes, had nothing of importance to add to the evidence already collected, and were given no chance of escaping the consequence of their misdeeds. The case for the crown was soon complete, and as usual in cases of political importance, a Special Commission of Oyer and Terminer composed of six eminent judges was set up to try the prisoners.

Judges, then as now, were appointed by the monarch. During most of the Stuart period these appointments were made *durante beneplacito,* that is, 'during the King's pleasure'. This meant that the king had the power of summary dismissal, and could use it to get rid of judges who brought in verdicts unpleasing to him, and to pack the bench with persons whose judgements would be sympathetic to his own wishes. James had notoriously over-used this power, dismissing at least six of his judges in the course of his short reign, and even appointing a catholic, Sir James Allibone, to the bench in 1688. There can be few more notable instances of the sound sense and political wisdom of William III than his prompt abandonment of the ancient formula *durante beneplacito.* Although the change was not made statutory until 1701, from 1689 onwards his judges were appointed *quamdiu bene se gesserint,* during good behaviour, and could only be dismissed by the king for misbehaviour, or on a petition from both Houses of Parliament. Thus no longer could a judge be summarily removed if he failed to please a royal master, and the independence of the bench from the vagaries of kingly favour was assured. The effect of this reform was immediately apparent. William's judges were selected, after careful enquiry into their credentials, for their ability, probity and learning and not, as under James, for their religious persuasion and political subservience. No one who has read and compared the reports of treason trials before and after this change can fail to be impressed by the improvement in their conduct, and no one can express it more quotably than Macaulay:

The whole spirit of the tribunal had undergone in a few months a change so complete that it might seem to have been the work of ages. Twelve years earlier, unhappy Roman Catholics, accused of wickedness which had never entered into their thoughts, had stood in that dock. The witnesses for the Crown had repeated their hideous fictions amidst the applauding hums of the audience. The judges had shared, or had pretended to share, the stupid credulity and the savage passions of the populace, had exchanged smiles and compliments with the perjured performers, had roared down the arguments feebly stammered forth by the prisoners, and had not been ashamed, in passing the sentence of death, to make ribald jests on purgatory and the mass . . . To these scandals the Revolution put an end.[11]

Among the judicial appointments made by King William, there were few more able or respected lawyers than the six who composed the Special Commission. The presiding judge was Lord Chief Justice Sir John Holt, famed for his integrity, learning and scrupulously fair attitude towards the prisoner at the bar. Holt was a moderate Whig, and had been a member of the Convention Parliament that had set William and Mary on the throne. Appointed Lord Chief Justice in 1689, he held that office until his death in 1710. In his obituary of Holt, Richard Steele said of him: 'He was a man of profound knowledge of the Laws of his Country, and as just an Observer of them in his own Person. He considered Justice as a cardinal Virtue, not as a Trade for Maintenance. Whenever he was Judge, he never forgot that he was also Counsel. The Criminal before him was always sure he stood before his Country, and, in a sort, a Parent of it.'[12] Of the other five members of the commission, Sir George Treby had like Holt been a member of the Convention Parliament, and had strongly supported the view that James, by flying the country, had abdicated. From 1692 until his death in 1701, Treby was Lord Chief Justice of the Court of Common Pleas. He was commemorated in a lengthy ode which concludes:

> Great without Pride, and without Wrinkles wise,
> Obliging without Art, and just without Disguise,
> Wise in his Counsels, humble in Discourse,
> Good without Noise, and pleasant without Force,
> Easy of Access, willing to bestow,
> Regarded Vertue, and forgot his Foe.[13]

Sir Edward Ward, Lord Chief Baron of the Exchequer, was a

Chancery lawyer, a member of the Inner Temple and a near-contemporary of Sir William Parkyns, whom he probably knew. He was made Attorney-General in 1693 and knighted in 1695. Foss, in his *Lives of the Judges,* remarks that Ward was 'an honest and intelligent judge . . . but his name is not distinguished by any prominence of character'.[14] Justice Sir Edward Nevil had been dismissed from his post as Baron of the Exchequer in 1685 for his refusal to support James's assumption of the dispensing power. He was reinstated by William in 1689 and two years later was made a Judge in the Court of Common Pleas. Justice John Powell was noted for his profound knowledge of the law. He was one of the judges at the trial of the seven bishops in 1688 who gave a verdict in their favour. James signified his displeasure by dismissing Powell forthwith; King William restored him to the bench, where he sat until his death in June 1696. Justice Thomas Rokeby's fervent support of William dated from before the Revolution; he had been a member of the party opposed to King James and his misuse of the dispensing power. He was made a Judge of the King's Bench in 1695.

The judges appointed to the special commission were all Whigs and were firm adherents of King William and his government. All had suffered some loss of office for refusing to comply with the policies of King James, and were not therefore likely to be favourably inclined towards the conspirators who had tried to restore him. Still less could they be expected to feel sympathy for those who had planned to murder the king to whom they owed their positions, and under whose rule they enjoyed independence and security of tenure. Nevertheless, this would be no Bloody Assizes. The prisoners tried by this assemblage would have as fair a trial and as patient a hearing as the existing law allowed. With Holt as presiding judge there would be no bullying or intimidation from the bench, nor would the accused suffer any curtailment of the customary relaxations of the ancient Statute of 25 Edward III, even though those concessions were not yet made legal. The statute imposed many hardships upon them, but justice would be done in strict accordance with the law. Although the commission had, almost to a man, opposed the passing of the new treason law, it should be emphasised that the decision to bring on the trials before it came into force was made by the government, and not by the judiciary. Their function was simply to implement the decree by trying the prisoners at once.

Charnock, King and Keyes were the first of the prisoners to be tried at the Old Bailey on Wednesday 11 March. Since their arrest they had been kept in strict solitary confinement. It was not until Thursday 5

March that permits were issued from the Secretary of State's Office for counsel to see them in order to prepare them for their trial.[15] Two lawyers, Vavasour and Jones, had permits to see Charnock. The third person named in the permit was Mrs Charnock, the unfortunate lady to whom he had been married only a few weeks. Vavasour also saw King, together with two more lawyers, Copley and Waldegrave. King was unmarried and lived with his mother, who was permitted to visit him at the same time. Keyes repeatedly said at his trial that he had had no legal advice, because he had no money to pay for it. But this cannot have been altogether true, for there is a permit for a Mr Munday to see him with a view to preparing him for his trial. Keyes's wife Elizabeth had been named in the first warrant for his arrest, and must have been suspected of some involvement in the plot; she seems, however, to have exculpated herself, since she was able to visit her husband in prison.

The five days between 5 and 11 March left little enough time to prepare cases for the defence, and the difficulties were much increased for Charnock and King by the withdrawal on 7 March of three of their legal advisers. These gentlemen may have feared suspicion of Jacobitism through association with so politically dangerous a trial, and they withdrew after one interview with the prisoners. Vavasour, the counsel who was to have acted for both Charnock and King, announced that he was sick or out of town, and was replaced by a Mr Thornbury. Charnock's solicitor Jones gave the same reasons for being unable to act for him and his place was taken by another solicitor, Webber. King's solicitor Copley also withdrew at the same time.[16] All the prisoners asked in court for a postponement of the trial on the grounds that they had not had time to summon their witnesses or to consult properly with their lawyers. But the bench disallowed their pleas, maintaining that they had had the maximum time allowed by law. 'We think you have had convenient notice', Holt told Charnock after making careful enquiry into the matter. 'If you have neglected opportunity of consulting them [the lawyers], you must blame yourself and nobody else; we must go on according to the law.'[17]

12
The trial of Charnock, King and Keyes

MANY RUMOURS OF THE IMPLICATION in the plot of an unknown number of eminent persons were current in London. So far, however, no arrests other than of those directly involved in the conspiracy had been made and, to the chagrin of the government, no attempts to persuade the prisoners to name even one prominent suspect had been successful. So the trials naturally attracted great public interest, not only because of the sensational nature of the plot, but also because there was much speculation, and in some quarters apprehension, as to what the prisoners might reveal in court. On the morning of 11 March the Old Bailey was packed to capacity with 'a great many of the nobility, members of Parliament, and other persons of Quality', together with as many others of lesser status as could find standing room. The six judges composing the Special Commission of Oyer and Terminer were on the bench. Below them sat the officials of the court and the counsel who would conduct the prosecution. The Statute of 25 Edward III being still in force, there was no counsel for the defence; this function was fulfilled in part by the judge. It was for this reason that Holt, as presiding judge, took a much greater part in the proceedings than would his modern counter-part. It was not his duty to defend the prisoner, but he could and did see to it that he suffered no undue hardship from ignorance of the law, nor would he allow the prosecution to put forward inadmissible evidence or otherwise harass him. Most importantly perhaps Holt, as every prisoner who came before him knew, would ensure that the prisoner would be allowed to conduct his own defence to the best of his ability. That justice might be seen to be done, trials were always recorded verbatim in shorthand and subsequently published in full.[1]

The court assembled at ten o'clock. Charnock, King and Keyes were brought in and set to the Bar. The proceedings were opened by the Clerk of the Arraignments, who read the indictment, a long and wordy document. The main charges against the prisoners were that as 'false traitors to their supreme true lawful and undoubted sovereign King

William' they had conspired with other traitors unknown to subvert the king's government, had planned to assassinate the king and had attempted to bring His Majesty's faithful subjects and the freemen of the kingdom of England into 'intolerable and miserable slavery to Lewis the French King'. Each of these charges carried the death penalty for high treason, but in fact the second, that of planning the 'execrable, horrid and detestable assassination' of King William was the one with which the prosecution was mainly concerned at this, the first trial. As the indictment went on, it was clear that the crown had quite enough evidence to condemn the prisoners on this charge alone, thanks to Porter and the other informers. The planning of the plot, the various meetings and consultations, the procuring of horses and arms and the recruitment of the band of murderers were all described in telling detail. The informers had done their work well and thoroughly, and when the long indictment at last came to an end there seemed little chance of an acquittal.

Charnock was first asked whether he would plead 'Guilty' or 'Not Guilty' to the charges laid against him. But Charnock, instead of answering this question, made the opening move in the day-long battle for his own and his fellow prisoners' lives. Pitted against the most able lawyers of his time, with little but an educated layman's knowledge of the law and with the weight of the evidence overwhelmingly against him, Charnock had no real chance of acquittal. But he never gave up hope, and conducted the defence with a skill, intelligence and persistence that excited admiration even in those who had formerly spoken of him with contempt. 'Never a man defended so well a base as he did at his trial', was Ailesbury's comment,[2] while even Burnet admitted that 'Charnock shewed great presence of mind, with temper and good judgement, and made as good a defence as the matter could bear.'[3]

The shuffling and murmuring in the crowded court made it impossible for the bench to hear Charnock, and he had to be asked to repeat his request for a copy of the indictment and counsel to help him during the trial. These things, he said, he would be entitled to under the provisions of the new Act. But Holt pointed out that the new Act had not yet become law, and therefore he could not grant these requests. To do otherwise than to conduct the trial under the existing Statute of 25 Edward III, said Holt, would be to act contrary to the law. It was in vain that Charnock pleaded that, since the Act had already been passed by parliament, he ought in equity to have the benefit of it; especially, he maintained, since most of its provisions had already become common practice. Holt and Treby consulted together on this point, and both agreed that counsel in court and a copy of the

187

indictment had never been allowed in the past and certainly could not be so now. Some relaxations of the old statute had indeed become customary, and Holt was at pains to ascertain that Charnock had had the benefit of them, that is, he had had due notice of his trial and counsel to help him prepare for it. Since this was not a court of equity, Holt told the prisoner, he had no right to any further privileges and the trial must proceed according to the law. Charnock was asked once again whether he wished to plead 'Guilty' or 'Not Guilty'. But he ignored this question, knowing that if he once entered his plea the trial must go on. He knew full well that his one slender chance was to delay the trial long enough for the new Act to come into force. So, with an obstinacy born of desperation, he fought for time. Again and again he pleaded for the benefits that the Act would give him, seeming not to hear Holt's repeated statements that this was not possible. Furthermore, he complained that he had not been given enough time to consult with his counsel or to summon his own witnesses. Holt dealt patiently and at some length with these objections, until at last even his patience began to wear out: 'The time of the Court must not be taken up in this manner', he told Charnock, and asked once more that Charnock enter his plea so that the trial could proceed. Realising that there was now no hope of delaying the trial, Charnock abandoned his position, but only temporarily. He was to return to his arguments and pleas for more time at intervals throughout the day. He now changed his tactics and threw himself on the mercy of the court. Addressing his judges, he said: 'My Lord, I was never instructed in the quirks of the law . . . and I hope your lordships will take care that I be not hurt for want of knowledge of the forms of the law.' To which Holt replied: 'You may assure yourself, Mr. Charnock, you shall not be hurt by your ignorance of the law. All the harm you will receive will be for having done contrary to the law, and there is none of your counsel, if they have been faithful to you, but must tell you the same things as we tell you now.'

At last Charnock consented to plead, and the Clerk of the Arraignments went through the time-honoured formula:

Clerk: 'How sayest thou, Robert Charnock. Art thou Guilty of this treason whereof thou standest indicted, or Not Guilty?'
Charnock: 'Not Guilty.'
Clerk: 'Culprit, how wilt thou be tried?'
Charnock: 'By God and my Country.'
Clerk: 'God send thee good deliverance.'

King was now asked to plead. He too asked for a copy of the indictment and for counsel to represent him in court, but was told that since these things had already been refused to Charnock, they could not be allowed in his case. King was a man of few words and evidently realised that he could never succeed in argument where Charnock had failed. He accepted the court's ruling with characteristic stoicism and pleaded 'Not Guilty'. As for Keyes, he was clearly too ignorant and too bewildered to put forward anything but his servile status and his poverty. Perhaps he hoped that his evident helplessness would excite the mercy of his judges. 'My Lord', he said when asked to plead, 'I was a servant to Captain Porter; I was not able to fee any counsel.' He too pleaded 'Not Guilty'.

Charnock asked for pen, ink and paper, so that he might take notes of the evidence. This, as was usual, was readily granted by the court. Holt then made him an offer which showed his real sense of justice and consideration for the prisoner at the Bar. He asked Charnock if he would like to have the indictment read again, this time in Latin. Charnock accepted the offer, and so the long document was gone through again in Latin. At the end of the reading Charnock complained that he had not been able to hear it properly or to take full notes, 'for there is so great a noise in the Court, and that gentleman hath not the most perfect delivery'. Holt commanded silence in the court whilst the Clerk of Arraignments read the indictment once more. This time Charnock was able to take fuller notes and so get a clearer idea of the details of the charges; it was in fact almost tantamount to letting him have a copy of the indictment. The extra time taken up by these two readings was not begrudged by Holt and the bench. Clearly, it was felt that although the law compelled the judges to refuse to let the accused have a copy of the indictment, he had in equity some right to a fuller knowledge of its details. Thus Holt, whilst strictly adhering to the letter of the old law, took this opportunity to act in accordance with the spirit of the new one. He knew too that Charnock was a scholar and would have no difficulty in understanding the Latin.

Before the jury could be selected and sworn, it was necessary for the court to ascertain whether the prisoners wished to exercise their right to separate trials, or if they preferred to be tried together. King and Keyes were well aware that Charnock was by far the best equipped to conduct the defence and both elected, with Charnock's agreement, to be tried together. Charnock thereupon undertook to act as spokesman for his fellows, but not before he had made fresh and still unavailing demands for a solicitor and counsel to help him. The prisoners' decision pleased the court, for much time and expense would be saved by having one trial instead of three. The jury was empanelled and at last the trial proper could begin.

The Attorney-General, Sir Thomas Trevor, opened the case for the crown with a long speech to the jury, outlining the evidence against the prisoners and covering much the same ground as the indictment. He did not neglect to dwell on the heinousness of their crime, and spoke most feelingly of the merciful providence of the Almighty in preventing the dreadful consequences of it to the king and to the whole nation:

Gentlemen, this offence is in its nature so horrid and barbarous, that as it needs no aggravation, so it is incapable of having any, by any words that can be used; for the very naming of an assassination of a king, carries such horror and detestation in itself, to all honest people, that it is impossible to aggravate it.

If anything could make the offence worse, the Attorney-General went on, it was the immeasurable debt that all loyal Englishmen owed to King William. 'A king, who everybody knows first ventured his own life, to restore our religion, laws and liberties, when they were just expiring under the oppression of popery and tyranny.' This last piece of political propaganda was well calculated to impress the jury of honest Whig gentlemen with the gravity of the prisoners' crime and the narrowness of their own escape from the horrors that would have followed the murder of their liberator.

When the Attorney-General at last finished his speech, the witnesses were called. Porter was the first to give evidence. Before he could be sworn in, however, Charnock pointed out that there were several more of the witnesses, including De La Rue, in the court. He asked for their removal; he did not think it fair that they should hear each other's testimonies. Holt and the judges allowed this, and De La Rue and the rest of the witnesses were taken out. Next Charnock tried to get the court to disallow any evidence not relating to 10 February, the date mentioned in the indictment as that on which the plans for the plot had been finalised. This objection was overruled by Holt, who pointed out that although 10 February was the only date spoken of, the wording of the indictment covered a period of time both before and after it. Porter then proceeded to give his evidence. He was a good witness, clear, succinct and deadly. Since he had been one of the leaders of the conspiracy from the very beginning, he was able to give the court a full account of all the meetings and the plans made to carry out the assassination. Charnock, as was to be expected, figured largely in the story and by the time Porter had finished there could be no doubt about the former's having taken a prominent part in the affair. The chief part of the evidence against King was concerned with the

190

journey which he, Porter and Knightley, had taken to Richmond to choose the best place for the intended attack on King William. Porter also assured the court that Keyes knew all about the conspiracy and that he had procured horses and arms for his master and himself knowing full well for what purpose they were intended. Keyes had also been present at most of the meetings, and although he was a servant, had often been allowed to sit down with the rest of the conspirators. He added, by way of confirmation, that Keyes on these occasions, 'used sometimes to entertain us with his trumpet'.

Beyond remarking at the beginning of his testimony that he had been 'unfortunately engaged in this affair', Porter showed no sign of repentance, and certainly displayed no compunction for his ertswhile friends and fellow-conspirators. Indeed, his determination to secure their condemnation was evident throughout and especially so in the case of his servant Keyes, towards whom he might have been expected to show some sense of responsibility. Possibly he feared reprisals if his victims should, after all, escape the law, and was therefore determined to see as many of them as possible brought to the gallows. Nor was Porter the man to jeopardise his own pardon by withholding any evidence, and it is also probable that he hoped to gain not only his own freedom, but also some substantial reward if he did his work thoroughly enough to satisfy his new masters.

When Porter had finished his testimony, Charnock was invited to question him. But he objected at some length that Porter could not be either a legal or a credible witness, and that therefore his evidence was not valid. He gave three reasons for this: firstly, Porter was by his own confession a criminal, and criminals could not legally give evidence. Secondly, Porter had turned informer to save his own skin at the expense of the lives of others, and therefore could not be credible. Lastly, Porter had wasted his patrimony and as Charnock knew well was desperately in need of money; he was hoping to barter the lives of his friends for the sake of the £1000 reward. Holt countered these objections with his usual patience. He told Charnock that Porter was a legal witness; as far as the law was concerned he was not a criminal because he had never been formally charged with a crime. Moreover he was not entitled to any reward, as he had not come in voluntarily but had confessed after his arrest. As to Porter's evidence being inadmissible because he was an accomplice, Holt declared that the law had never objected to this, for the evidence of accomplices was often the only means available to the crown of obtaining evidence of treachery. 'It is certainly a very hard matter, if not impossible', Holt remarked, 'to discover crimes of this nature, if the accomplices in those crimes shall not be allowed to be good witnesses against their fellow conspirators.' In view of the rudimentary means of detecting criminals available in the seventeenth century, Holt's argument was incontrovertible. So Charnock was forced to accept it as far as the legality of Porter's evidence was concerned. He continued, however, to maintain that in view of Porter's behaviour and the circumstances under which he was giving evidence, his testimony could not be reliable. Holt's tart reply was that it was for the jury to judge this.

Charnock could not shake Porter's evidence. He tried to trip him up over details of time and place, and attempted to make the jury believe that the whole story was a figment of Porter's imagination. Charnock was clever enough not to deny everything. He knew, he said, of the impending descent of King James upon England, and had discussed this in a general way at the meetings; but this was common knowledge, and he did not think it a crime to talk of it. He admitted too that he had been present on some of the occasions talked of by Porter, but denied that he had been aware of any criminal purpose in those gatherings. He was especially concerned to deny that he knew of the real purpose of the reconnoitering expedition to Richmond. It was true, Charnock said, that Porter, King and Knightley had come into his lodgings that evening. Porter had told him that they had been to Mortlake to see a friend, and that was all Charnock knew of the matter. He appealed directly to Porter to confirm this: 'and if you do remember, captain, you could not pull your boots off well, and complained of the gout, and was very peevish'. But Porter, totally unmoved by this poignant reminder of their former intimacy, merely repeated his statement that he and his two companions had returned to Charnock's lodgings in order to report the results of their expedition, and that he knew where and why they had been. This was sufficient indication to Charnock that he could expect no mercy from Porter and he made no further appeals to him.

Porter had alleged that he and Charnock had discussed King James's Commission, although neither of them had ever seen it. The prosecution laid great stress on this document, for the obvious reason that it implicated James in the Assassination Plot. Charnock, who was well aware of the importance of exonerating his exiled king from any complicity in the plot, did his best to convince the jury that there had never been any such Commission, and that even had it existed it had certainly not been 'writ in the king's own hand'. The king, he said, had ministers to do this for him, and therefore it was most unlikely that he would have written the whole document himself. It was, as he was sure the jury would see, yet another of Porter's fabrications. That James would have sent a general Commission for waging war, Charnock admitted, was not unlikely, although he had never seen such a document. He maintained, however, that there had never been any royal authorisation for a murder attempt.

This concluded Charnock's questioning of the first witness. It was now King's turn, but he could do little except deny that the purpose of his journey to Mortlake and Richmond had been for the purpose alleged by Porter. They had merely gone to 'take the air', he said, but this was at once corrected by Porter. Keyes, asked if he would like to question the witness, could do nothing but repeat his helpless cry, 'My Lord, I have nobody to advise me, no counsel, I was only a servant to Captain Porter.' He was obviously quite unequal to asking any questions of his former master, so Porter was stood down and the next witness, Francis De La Rue, was called.

De La Rue's evidence was typically verbose and full of incidental but not always relevant detail. He said that he had been present at a number of meetings when the plot had been discussed, and confirmed that Charnock and Keyes, and on occasion King, had been present. But because he had never been fully trusted by the conspirators much of what De La Rue had to say was hearsay, at least as far as it related to Charnock; this part of his evidence was very properly disallowed by Holt. De La Rue then told the court how Charnock had enticed several of the Earl of Oxford's regiment into his lodgings, where they had indulged in seditious talk and drunk traitorous healths. Upon being questioned by the Attorney-General, he also described the abortive plans of the previous winter, when he had invited Charnock to go with him to Deal to hire a vessel to carry the captive King William to France.

The next witness was the Earl of Portland, who was ushered to the witness stand with almost as much deference as if he had been King William himself: 'We must humbly pray that my Lord Portland will be pleased to be sworn', said the Attorney-General, evidently much impressed by his lordship's condescension in favouring the court with his presence. The ruling that witnesses should not hear each other's testimony did not seem to apply to so grand a personage as Portland, for he was asked whether he had heard De La Rue's account of how he came to Kensington to give information about the plot, and was requested to be so good as to confirm it. Portland told the court how De La Rue had been brought to him on the night in question and that he, Portland, had taken him to see the king. The account of the plot which De La Rue had given on that occasion was substantially the same as that which the court had just heard. Prendergrass was then called, and told how Porter had involved him in the conspiracy, and how he had resolved to frustrate the design, if possible without betraying Porter. He explained that his determination to shield him and the other conspirators had been overcome by the king's persuasions, and that when he learned that Porter had turned informer, he had felt absolved from any obligation to protect him. Lord Cutts, who had also been present at Prendergrass's inverview with the king, confirmed this account. The last two witnesses, Bertram and Boyse, gave their relatively brief and confirmatory testimonies, and the case for the crown was complete. Charnock was then called upon to speak in defence of himself and his fellow-accused.

Considering the circumstances under which he was forced to give it, Charnock's speech for the defence was a remarkable *tour de force*. Until he came into the court that morning, he had had only the most general idea of what the charges would be; he had no means of knowing, until the indictment was read, how much evidence, or what witnesses, the crown had been able to assemble. He had, it is true, been able to take notes during the three readings of the indictment, and of the evidence as it was given. But as the trial proceeded without any break, there had been no time or opportunity to study those notes and to make adequate preparation for a speech upon which might depend the lives of three men. In spite of being thus handicapped (and he did not omit to point out to their lordships that he was at a severe disadvantage) Charnock made a very long, skilful and almost convincing defence. He dealt with each item of evidence in proper sequence, and took full advantage of the weaker points in the case for the crown. He first stressed the circumstantial nature of the evidence, as he saw it, maintaining that there was no real proof of an overt act of treachery. Dealing first with Porter's evidence, he repeated what he had previously said about the unreliability and venality of this witness, from which if followed that the jury should not believe anything that Porter had said. He also denied once more that he had ever seen or discussed with Porter a Commission from King James. As to the troop that Porter alleged he was to have commanded for the attack at Turnham Green, Charnock declared that this troop had never had any existence outside Porter's imagination. Porter had not been able to name any of the members of it and this, to Charnock's mind, was sufficient proof that it had never existed. Next, he attempted to demolish Porter's story of the buying of arms and horses. Charnock said he had never bought a horse in his life; it was all 'moonshine' made up by that criminal in order to escape from the consequences of his own treachery.

De La Rue's evidence was treated in much the same way for he too, Charnock told the jury, was an accomplice, and hoped besides to gain a reward. As to De La Rue's account of the previous winter's plan to kidnap William and carry him off to France, this, he said contemptuously, was such a nonsensical tale that surely no sensible person could believe it. 'I cannot but think', he remarked scathingly, 'that anyone would believe us madmen to entertain such a chimera in our heads.' Prendergrass's evidence was treated similarly, and was, he thought, far too vague to condemn anyone. Moreover, he asserted that Prendergrass's arrest was a put-up job, arranged in order to divert suspicion from him as an informer. In order to confirm his contention that the witnesses' stories of the planning of the plot were malicious inventions, Charnock next tried to convince the jury that those plans were so ill-laid, so haphazard and so impractical that it was not possible there could be any truth in them. This argument, though cunning, was not very convincing, for although it was well known that the king's guard consisted of twenty-five men, Charnock asserted that there would have been three times that number, and pointed out that to attack them with only forty men would have been suicidal folly. Furthermore, he continued, even had the attack been successful and the king murdered, no proper arrangements had been made for the retreat and concealment of the murderers; unless they had hidden themselves at once, they would have risked being torn in pieces by an outraged populace. No sensible persons could have concocted such a wild scheme, Charnock contended, adding that even if they had been so foolish, the jury would surely think that 'we ought rather to have been confined to Bedlam, than any other place, if we could have been thought guilty of so much rashness and folly'.

Having dealt with the statements of the witnesses, Charnock returned to his previous argument, which indeed was the main bulwark of his defence. While admitting that there might have been some vaguely seditious talk, he declared that the prosecution had been unable to prove that there had been any overt act of treachery. Without this proof, as the court well knew, there could be no condemnation. He must have had some legal advice on this all-important point, for he was able to quote two great legal authorities, Hales and Coke. Both had ruled that 'bare words' and loose talk of treachery unsupported by proof of treasonable action were not in themselves sufficient to condemn a man. The distinction between words and action was therefore a vital one, and Charnock appealed to Holt to make sure that the jury fully understood it: 'My Lord, you are always presumed to be of counsel for the prisoners; and I look upon it as assured, that you will do that justice to persons in our circumstances, as truly to instruct the jury . . . particularly, my Lord, I desire that they may be told plainly and truly, what is proof of an overt act and what is not.' He dwelt on this at some length, insisting over and over again that there was no 'plain and manifest proof of any overt act, but only presentations of the whole scene of the thing'. In support of his contention that the evidence was insufficient and circumstantial, he made a further attempt to discredit the witnesses who, he said, were manifestly out to mend their fortunes as well as to save their own necks at the expense of innocent lives. Towards the end of this long speech, he complained yet again that the trial had not been fair, because none of the defendants had been allowed counsel in court or time to prepare their case. Since he had been deprived of these benefits, Charnock said, he had been forced to make a hasty and unskilled effort to refute the charges laid against him and his fellow-prisoners. He had done the best he could under these disadvantages, and he hoped the jury would make allowances for them when considering their verdict. He came to an end at last, with a final plea to Holt to make plain to the jury what constituted an overt act of treason. 'This is all the favour I have to beg of the Court', he said, 'and I hope I need not doubt the justice of the jury.' A final remark perhaps not calculated to incline them in his favour.

King was asked if he had anything to say in his own defence. But he was not an articulate man, and merely said that he thought that Charnock had put the case for all three of them much better than he could have done; he must rely on the jury's being persuaded by those arguments. King did, however, go on to deny all the accusations of complicity in the plot made by Porter and the other witnesses. He admitted going to Mortlake with Porter and Knightley, but again assured the court that it was merely to 'take the air' and that no treasonable schemes had been discussed then or at any other time. The wretched Keyes was quite unable to say anything coherent in his defence. His only response to an invitation to do so was to repeat once more that he was only a servant and had done nothing but obey his master's orders. This lame excuse provoked a severe reply from Holt. He told Keyes that 'No man is so much under the command of his master, as that he ought to obey him, if he command him to commit high treason.' Since none of the defendants had anything further to add, the case for the defence was concluded. It was now the turn of the prosecution to sum up the evidence and put the case for the crown.

The Solicitor-General, Sir John Hawles, led the case for the crown.

He began by reminding the jury of the plans for the invasion and insurrection, which had figured in the indictment but had not been referred to since. Although there was a strong probability that the prisoners had been involved in these plans, they were not being charged with participating in them; these matters would be dealt with at later trials. He then summed up the evidence against the prisoners, pointing out that it was very full and detailed, and that all the witnesses agreed that the three accused had been fully involved in the plot to murder the king. This was clear legal proof of an overt act, or acts, of treachery. It was clear too that the plot had been planned over a long period of time. So Charnock's argument that these plans were too impractical to gain credence was not valid, for his statements about them were incorrect. The witnesses had told how the scheme had been worked out at the many meetings and consultations, and it was clear from their accounts that 'the horrid and detestable conspiracy' had stood a much better chance of success than Charnock would have the jury believe. There was besides ample proof that Charnock had not only been present at these meetings but had been one of the moving spirits in the whole scheme. The Solicitor-General's speech was followed by that of Mr Conyers, one of the supporting counsel. This was in the main a commentary on that of his predecessor. He laid particular stress on the fact that the evidence which the court had heard was clear and valid in law. Mr Cooper, the second supporting counsel, then spoke in a similar strain. He too refuted Charnock's argument that the evidence against him was all hearsay, and told the jury that Porter's evidence in particular left no doubt that Charnock had been one of the principal agents in the conspiracy, if not the leader of it. In confirmation of this, he pointed out that it was Charnock who had first introduced Sir George Barkley to Porter and the rest, and that it was with the arrival of Barkley that the plot really began to take shape. There could also be no doubt of King's involvement, the chief evidence for this being his journey to Richmond, the purpose of which had been made quite clear by Porter.

Holt's summing up now followed. It was long, scrupulously exact, and, as might have been expected, very fair. He used no emotive adjectives when referring to the conspiracy, such as 'horrid', 'execrable', or 'traitorous' that had been employed with telling effect by the prosecution. He took the jury once more through the evidence, as given by the various witnesses, in meticulous detail. He was interrupted during this part of the summing up by a disturbance in the body of the court. This was occasioned by Mrs King, mother of the prisoner, who, as laconically reported in *State Trials*, 'in a very

197

outrageous violent manner, got into the Court, but being removed, the Lord Chief Justice proceeded'. What piteous outcry or protestations this poor woman made is not recorded. She was hustled out of the court, and when the hubbub had subsided the judge continued. Having dealt with the evidence of Porter and the other witnesses, Holt dicussed the arguments put forward by Charnock in his speech for the defence. What Charnock had said about 'bare words' being insufficient evidence for a condemnation for high treason was, he said, perfectly true,

for loose words spoken, without relevance to any act or design, are not treason or an overt act of·treason; but arguments and words of persuasion, to engage in such design or resolution, and directing or proposing the best way for effecting it, are overt acts of high treason, though the argument be verbal only and not reduced to writing . . . and it was never yet doubted, but to meet and consult how to kill the king, was an overt act of high treason.

Now, the evidence before the court, Holt continued, could leave the jury in no doubt but that a great deal more than bare words and loose talk had passed between the accused and their fellow conspirators; it was perfectly clear that preparation had been made to carry out a murderous attack on the king, and that all three of the accused men had taken an active part in those plans.

Holt went on to deal with Charnock's contention that the trial had not been a fair one because the witnesses, being accomplices and self-interested into the bargain, were neither legal nor credible. The law said nothing, Holt told the jury, about disallowing the evidence of accomplices. Indeed, such evidence had to be allowed because it was often the only means of detecting treachery, for

traitorous conspiracies are deeds of darkness as well as wickedness, the discovery whereof can only come from the conspirators themselves; such evidence has always been allowed as good proof in all ages, and they are the most proper witnesses, for otherwise it is hardly possible, if not altogether impossible, to have a full proof of such secret contrivances.

As to the honesty of the witnesses, that, Holt said, was a matter that must be left to the consideration of the jury. The question of self-interest did not in any case arise in the case of Prendergrass or of De La Rue. These two had given warning of the plot before there had been any danger of their own arrests and therefore it was manifest that their motive had been solely to avert danger from the king. Moreover, their honesty and disinterestedness was vouched for by Lord Portland and Lord Cutts. Clearly then, whatever conclusions the jury might come to about the other witnesses, there could be no doubt about the credibility of Prendergrass and De La Rue. At last Holt came to the end of his summing up with a few words of advice to the jury:

Gentlemen . . . I leave it to you, you have heard what the prisoners say for themselves, you are the judges of this fact; if you are not satisfied that there has been given sufficient evidence to prove them guilty, you will acquit them; but if you are satisfied, that upon the evidence and all the circumstances of this case, that they are guilty, I suppose you will discharge your consciences, and give your verdict accordingly.

The jury now retired to consider their verdict. They were absent for about half an hour. On their return they pronounced all three prisoners guilty. It was the expected and inevitable verdict; it was, according to Macaulay, received with acclamation by the waiting crowd both within and without the courtroom.[4]

The trial had gone on without a break since ten o'clock that morning, and it must by now have been well into the afternoon. It was adjourned until seven o'clock in the evening when it re-opened for the sentencing of the prisoners. Holt and the senior judges did not return when the court re-assembled, the bench being manned by the Common Sergeant, the Lord Mayor and as many of the court as would make up a quorum. The prisoners were brought back to the Bar. Charnock was the first to be aked if he had anything to say before sentence was pronounced upon him. Predictably, he replied that he had a great deal to say and proceeded to repeat at some length the arguments that he had already put forward in his speech for the defence. The court listened to all this patiently enough, considering that they had already heard it a number of times. The Common Sergeant countered each of Charnock's objections in turn, in much the same terms as had Holt. That is to say he told Charnock yet again that he had been granted all the privileges and help that the current law allowed. More the court could not do, the trial had been a fair one and the witnesses and the evidence good in law. And it was useless for Charnock to plead for the benefits of the new Act, because it was not in the power of the court to grant them. His objections therefore were not relevant and could not be allowed, but if he had anything further to say he could rest assured that the court would give any valid objections their full consideration. Charnock, as he said, was now 'upon my last legs', but he fought desperately to the end. Much time was taken up by attempts to upset the indictment, which he maintained was incorrect 'because it is laid for assassinating the King and all that is proved against me, that I was in company where such a thing was discoursed of'. This point had already been dealt with by Holt and

199

was dismissed briefly by the Common Sergeant. In a final despairing attempt Charnock then brought up a number of trifling objections to the indictment, all of them concerned with the Latin wording, which he declared was incorrect in several places. Each in turn, and with growing impatience, was rejected as irrelevant by the Common Sergeant. At last Charnock gave up, remarking bitterly, 'I see it is impossible for me to offer anything that the court will think material; therefore it is in vain for me to speak, and trouble myself and the court with what will be of no use to me.'

The Clerk of the Arraignments asked King if he had anything to say before sentence was passed. King, however, was clearly resigned to his fate; he had said very little throughout the trial, and all he could say now was that since Charnock's arguments were not to be heard, there was no point in his putting them forward again. Keyes, as was to be expected, could only repeat for the last time that he had had no counsel at all to help him, and that he was only a servant and had done no more than obey his master's orders. He was told once more that that was no excuse for committing high treason, to which rebuke the wretched man replied pathetically, 'I cannot help it, Sir, I have done; I hope you will take care of my wife and children when I am gone.'

The Common Sergeant, whose duty it was to pronounce sentence, now seated himself upon the bench and the court was commanded to be silent. He first addressed the accused in a short speech, telling them that they had a fair and legal trial and that they had been found guilty upon good evidence of the most heinous of crimes that a man could commit. 'You are gentlemen of liberal education', he said at the end of it, 'and I hope this will bring you to some reflection both upon the state of your own case, and the blackness of your offence, in the time you have to live, which I fear is but short.' Then followed the dreadful sentence for high treason.

When the clamour of approbation from the crowded courtroom had subsided, Charnock asked if they might have their friends and relations to come to them in prison. This was freely granted, as always in such cases, with the usual proviso that due care be taken for the security of the prisoners. Then Charnock, perhaps remembering the injustices and cruelties practised upon condemned catholics in the not-so-distant past added, 'And I hope we shall have no hard usage when we are in prison.' The Common Sergeant appeared genuinely shocked that Charnock should have felt it necessary to ask this: 'No! God forbid that you should. You may assure yourself that you shall have none.' The court was adjourned and the prisoners taken back to Newgate. The execution was fixed for 18 March, a week after the trial.

The trial of Charnock, King and Keyes

During the few days between the trial and the execution, the wife whom Charnock had so recently married made a last-minute attempt to save his life. On 12 March, the day after the trial, she went to see Lord Cutts, possibly at her husband's instigation, and begged him 'most earnestly' to visit him in Newgate. Cutts, no doubt hoping to extract some further information from Charnock, duly went to see him the next day and on his return reported to Secretary Trumbull that the prisoner had offered to tell all he knew in exchange, not for a reprieve, but for an easy imprisonment for the rest of his life. At Trumbull's request, Cutts went again to Charnock, and told him that if he would write a full statement of all he knew, it would be put immediately before the king, who would then decide whether or not to reprieve him.[5] Whether Charnock accepted the offer, wrote a confession and was refused a reprieve by William, or whether he changed his mind at the last moment and decided to take the nobler course and keep silent, may never be known, but certainly no reprieve came from the king. As there is no record of a written confession by Charnock, a document which would almost certainly have been preserved along with the others in the case, it looks as if the latter explanation is the more likely one, and that Charnock's final decision to let the law take its course rather than betray his friends frustrated his wife's attempt to save him. If Burnet's very similar story of Charnock's brother's having made a previous attempt to get him to confess in exchange for his life is true, then this decision, made in spite of having been twice tempted to save himself at the expense of others, is much to his credit. And he stood by it to the end. Just as at his trial Charnock was most careful not to implicate any of his confederates so, in his last statement, was he particularly concerned to exonerate all but those directly engaged in it from any knowledge of the conspiracy.

On 18 March the three condemned men were brought out of their cells and placed in the sledges waiting in the prison yard; then the procession, escorted by mounted soldiers, made its slow way to Tyburn. Charnock faced death with a courage and dignity that belied his opponents' reports of his pusillanimity. He wore a fine new coat and was most particular that morning about the powdering and curling of his wig. King, though he probably could not afford a new coat, behaved with the quiet courage that might have been expected from a man of his soldierly training and stoical nature; not so poor Keyes. He may have had some hopes of a last-minute reprieve, for Macaulay says that 'his tears and prayers excited the pity of the spectators . . . it was said at the time . . . that a servant drawn into crime by his master was a proper object for royal clemency'.[6] But the time for royal clemency had not yet come, and so Keyes's cries were unavailing.

It was some years since the populace had witnessed so spectacular an execution. It was a wintry day; the 'protestant wind' that blew from the north-east had turned February's rain to frost and snow,[7] but in spite of the cold a huge crowd collected at Tyburn and filled the seats on the scaffolding erected for the spectators, while hundreds more stood tight-packed in the space between the seats and the gallows. The sledges and their mounted escort drew up beneath the gallows, the men were unbound and placed in the waiting cart. If those of the spectators who were near enough to hear had hoped for edifying speeches from the condemned they were disappointed. Instead they each handed a written paper containing their last words to the Sheriff. The prison chaplain, who had accompanied the procession from Newgate, then approached the cart to hear the prisoners' last prayers. But Charnock, on behalf of himself and his companions, refused the chaplain's ministrations. They would die, as they had lived, in their own faith. Charnock performed the last offices for himself and his fellows according to the rites of the Catholic Church.[8] When the last prayers were said the executioner tied their hands, placed the ropes round their necks and covered their heads with black hoods. The cart was driven from beneath their feet and the rest of the sentence was carried out in all its grisly detail.

As was customary, the last statements of Charnock, King and Keyes were published a few days after their execution. Keyes's paper is very short, consisting of a few lines only, and reads as if it had been composed for him by the prison chaplain, or perhaps by some better-educated catholic who had paid him a last visit. It is a pathetic little document, in which he admits his guilt and asks for divine forgiveness:

God is just in all his judgements, and I accept of this death as a just punishment of all my iniquities . . . I forgive all my enemies . . . Have mercy on me, O Father of Mercy, and through thy only Son forgive all my sins. Thomas Keyes.

Behind the brief and formal phrases one can sense the bewilderment and despair of this simple man, caught up by his unscrupulous master in events which he cannot properly have understood. Since he so freely admits it, there can be no doubt that Keyes was guilty according to the law, but one could wish that in this case William had seen fit to temper justice with mercy and to reprieve him.

King, being a 'gentleman of liberal education', must have written his own statement. Like Keyes, he begins by confessing his guilt, and he hopes, through repentance, to obtain divine forgiveness:

I am . . . brought to this place by the just hand of God, in punishment of all my crimes, but particularly that of which I have been lately arraigned . . . but I hope that goodness of God, which has given me a sense of my own wickedness, will accept my repentance and show mercy on me.

He is particularly careful to exonerate King James from any knowledge or approbation of the plot, declaring solemnly that he never saw or heard of any commission from the king authorising an attack on King William. Neither was the scheme entered into with the knowledge or approval of 'any body of men, either catholic or protestant'. He was drawn into it, 'by my own rashness and passion', and therefore, he hopes, no others will suffer on his account. If any have been injured through his actions, he begs their forgiveness, as he 'freely and heartily' forgives all mankind:

In this disposition of a sincere repentance, and true charity, I commend my soul into the hands of God, and hope to find mercy from him. And for this I beg all your prayers. Edward King.

King's slightly abject expressions of repentance might give rise to a suspicion that he had been subjected in prison to some 'brain-washing' or other form of compulsion to confess. But this cannot have been so, for two reasons. In the first place, he would undoubtedly have been 'persuaded' to incriminate others besides himself, and this he is most careful not to do, taking full responsibility for his actions, particularly as regards King James. Secondly, torture had been discontinued in England for more than half a century, and there is no evidence whatsoever to show that undue pressure was put on any of the prisoners to implicate their confederates. Conditions in Newgate might be appalling and the punishment for wrongdoers savage, but at least the claim of Celia Fiennes that 'here are no wrackes or tortures used'[9] was quite justifiable, and King's confession must have been made of his own free will.

Charnock's paper[10] is the longest and most interesting of the three, and is so characteristic of the man that it deserves to be quoted in full:

That I might avoid distractions, and be composed as much as is possible at the time of my execution, I thought it much more proper to communicate this to the sherriffs, than to give myself the uneasiness of speaking, leaving it to them to publish (if they should think convenient) for the satisfaction of the world; and in what I have to say, I have taken as much care as I could to be short, that I might not lose time in my greatest concern.

RETRIBUTION

As concerning an invasion intended by king James upon England, there was certain intelligence of it from abroad, I presume everybody was satisfied, and to the facilitating of which, I own that myself and some others did agree upon the undertaking to attack the prince of Orange and his guards, for which I am now to suffer; but I think myself obliged, by all the ties imaginable both of conscience and honour, to declare, that as for any order or commission of king James's for assassinating the prince of Orange, I never saw or knew of any, but have had frequent assurances of his having rejected such proposals when they have been offered.

I confess, I did hear that there was a commission arrived for levying of war; and which was natural to believe, if the king was in such a readiness to come over as was reported; but if there was any such authority as that, I declare I never saw it.

As to what regards the body of the Roman Catholics, I must do them this justice, and which I dare to positive in, that they had no manner of knowledge of this design; nor do I believe it was communicated to any other party of such as are reputed the king's friends, but carried on merely by a small. number, without the advice, consent, or privity of any parties whatsoever.

I ask forgiveness of all the world for what offences or injuries I have done to them; and I am (I bless Almighty God) in perfect charity with all mankind.

ROBERT CHARNOCK

Charnock was intelligent and imaginative, but not naturally brave. He was clearly concerned lest he should not be 'composed as much as possible' at the time of his execution. Like King and Keyes, he does not deny having taken part in the conspiracy, and is careful to exonerate King James and 'any body of Roman Catholics' from any complicity in it. But, unlike his fellow-sufferers, Charnock does not appear to think it necessary to ask forgiveness for his crime either from God or man; his asking forgiveness 'of all the world' is in general terms, and clearly does not include his part in the plot. It is rather, he seems to imply, for him to forgive mankind, and he thanks God he is able to do so. There is a certain arrogance in this, as if Charnock did not think himself in need of either divine or human forgiveness.

Nor did he. While awaiting execution he wrote, in the form of a letter to an anonymous friend, a long vindication of his actions. This document was intended for private circulation among the faithful, 'when it may be done without drawing more persecution upon those honest men wholly under the jealousy and suspition of the present government'. The letter is an ingeniously argued exposition of the more extreme Jacobite views, and is printed in full as appendix 1. It leaves the reader in no doubt as to the sincerity of Charnock's belief in the rightness of the cause for which he died, nor can there be any doubt about the truth of the evidence against him and his fellow-conspirators. He says at the outset that everything that Porter said at the trial was true, except in one important particular: there never was, nor could have been, a commission from King James to levy war on the *person* of the Prince of Orange. As to the assassination attempt, he bluntly asserts that since to all honest men the Prince of Orange was no better than a robber, or even a 'wolf or wild beast', it was justifiable, even meritorious, for private citizens to take the law into their own hands and rid the world of him.

Charnock was reputed not to be sincerely religious, but he was, as Ailesbury said, 'of a dark, close temper', and so it may be doing him an injustice to think that because he made no public profession of faith or humility in the face of eternity, he felt neither of these things. But whatever sustained him at the end, whether pride, faith or the conviction that he was a martyr in a just cause, Charnock went to his death in his new coat and curled wig as bravely as the best of King James's soldiers.

13
The trials of Sir John Friend and
Sir William Parkyns

SIR JOHN FRIEND was tried on Monday 23 March.[1] Once again
the Old Bailey was crowded with a 'great confluence of the nobility
and gentry', many of whom must have been personally acquainted
with the prisoner. Sir John was not accused of complicity in the
Assassination Plot, for there was no evidence that he had anything to do with it. He was to be tried for conspiring with the
king's enemies abroad and fostering rebellion at home. Although both
of these were capital offences, the weight of evidence against him was
much less heavy than in the cases of Charnock, King and Keyes. In
addition, grave though Sir John's offences were, his crime was not
quite so heinous as the attempted murder of an anointed king. It is
therefore quite possible that if the trial had been postponed for a few
days so that he could have had counsel to defend him in court, or even
if he had been able to put up a better case himself, he might have
escaped the death penalty; it is very doubtful whether he would have
been acquitted. But poor Sir John was no Charnock. His ignorance,
ineptitude and obstinate insistence on irrelevant arguments made the
outcome inevitable. Indeed, there was more truth than he realised in
his repeated assertion that he was as innocent as a baby for, if not as
innocent, he was certainly as helpless as a baby when faced with the
might and majesty of the law. To add to his disabilities Sir John was
hard of hearing; Holt several times ordered silence in the court and
repeated the substance of the evidence for his benefit. Although Sir
John Friend was a peripheral figure in the story of the Assassination
Plot a brief account of his trial is included here because it is a glaring
example of the hardships suffered by persons tried for high treason
under the statute of 1351.

The court assembled at ten o'clock with Justices Holt, Rokeby and
Treby on the bench. The prisoner was brought in and set to the Bar
and the indictment was read. Sir John pleaded 'Not Guilty'. 'I don't
know anything of it, I am as innocent as the child unborn', he cried.
His request for counsel to plead for him in court was inevitably

refused, but he was allowed pen, ink and paper so that he could take notes of the evidence. The first and principal crown witness was George Porter. Sir John had sense enough to know that Porter's evidence would be central to the case for the prosecution, and therefore tried hard to get his testimony invalidated on the grounds that he was reputed to be a papist. Papists, he asserted, could not legally give evidence against protestants, because they would think it no sin to lie in order to defame or injure anyone who was not of their faith. Moreover, their priests would willingly absolve them from the sin of perjury in such circumstances. He demanded that Holt ascertain whether or not Porter was a papist: if he was, he could not be sworn. The argument that all catholics, being liars and perjurers, were disqualified by law from giving evidence against protestants was Sir John's main line of defence. Quite apart from the fact that it had no foundation in law this was a curious plea for him to put forward, since he had risked life and fortune to restore a catholic king.

Repeatedly, but in vain, Holt and the other two judges tried to convince Sir John that there was no law debarring catholics from giving evidence against protestants. So ignorant was he that it had to be explained to him that this could not possibly be so, because when the great Statute of Treasons was made in 1351 everybody was catholic. Even a reading of this and a later regulation failed to shake his conviction, but in spite of his protests Porter was at last sworn and gave his evidence. This was mainly concerned with the first part of the indictment and related to the meetings in June and July 1695, when Charnock had been sent to France to ask King James to borrow troops from King Louis to assist in an invasion. Porter swore to Sir John's presence at these meetings, and told the court that he had been among those who had undertaken to raise 2000 Horse to meet King James when he landed in England. To do him justice, Porter exonerated Sir John from any part in the Assassination Plot, quoting him as having said that he had heard of it and was sorry for it, for he thought it would be very harmful to King James's cause.

The evidence of Brice Blair, the second witness, concerned the second part of the indictment, that is, raising and financing troops for the rebellion and accepting a Commission from King James. The sanctimonious Blair prefaced his testimony by saying several times over that he was, 'sorry, very sorry indeed, to come on such an account as I do now against him', and was brusquely cut short by Holt, who told him to get on with his evidence. Clearly that most upright of judges had little liking for this hypocrite, although forced to make use of him in order to get at the facts. Under meticulous cross-examination from the Attorney-General, Blair succeeded in thoroughly compromising Sir John. He told how he himself had been appointed adjutant to the regiment, and how he had recruited a number of officers and men for it, and had spent a good deal of Sir John's money to buy drinks for them. He also swore to having seen the Commission from King James empowering Sir John to raise the regiment and naming him as colonel. Sir John was invited to question the witness, but his only response to this opportunity was: 'I say he is a Roman Catholic, and I have witnesses to swear that he is so; and desire that I may prove he is Roman Catholic, and therefore he is not to be heard against a Protestant.' He then produced his first witness, William Courtney, who had been in the Gatehouse with Blair, and who had had some previous acquaintance with him. Courtney was either unable or unwilling to say that Blair was a catholic, but before he was stood down he made it plain to the court that Blair was giving evidence against Sir John to save his own skin. This, in the hands of skilled counsel, might have turned to Sir John's advantage; but he, poor foolish man, seemed quite unaware that he could have helped himself by throwing discredit on a witness for reasons other than religious. The last witness for the prosecution was Bertram, who was called to corroborate the testimony of Blair. His evidence was brief and closed the case for the crown. Sir John was called upon to defend himself and to produce the rest of his witnesses.

As the trial went on it seemed that Sir John was under the impression that all that was necessary to establish his innocence was to prove himself a good protestant. To this end he now summoned no fewer than eight witnesses to testify to his loyalty to Church and Crown. Unhappily for him, none of these gentlemen had seen him for some time past, a circumstance that rendered their encomiums less helpful than they might have been. They all declared that during the time they had known him, that is, up till four or five years ago, Sir John had regularly attended church and had joined in prayers for King William and, during her life, for Queen Mary. He had often told these persons that although his conscience prevented him from taking the oath of allegiance to the new monarchs he intended to live peaceably under their government, and would never join in any plots or conspiracies against them. 'Catch me in the corn and put me in the pound', he would say when talking with his friends. Questioned about Sir John's conversation and church-going in more recent times, however, all the witnesses became suspiciously evasive, and none could swear that he had been seen at church over the past two years or so. This, naturally, was taken to indicate that he had been attending the services of the proscribed non-juring church, where he would be able to pray for King James, meet other Jacobites and talk, if not plan, sedition. In effect, then, Sir John's eight witnesses had done nothing to establish his innocence and indeed tended rather to tell against him, since it was evident that he had been avoiding his former friends for some time past.

'I could bring a thousand more to prove me a Protestant', said Sir John when the last witness had been stood down. Holt told him in a kindly way that he could bring as many as he chose, and the court would hear them all. But, no doubt to the relief of the whole court, it appeared that there were only two more, and that even they had not appeared. So far, the prisoner had not been able to produce any real evidence of his innocence, nor had he made any sensible attempt to counter the allegations of the crown witnesses. Holt clearly thought that, in fairness, he should be given another chance to clear himself. He therefore asked Sir John whether he could furnish any proof that either Porter or Blair had any reason for making false accusations against him. This only provoked a long and involved complaint that he had not been given time to summon more witnesses; that various people had failed to help him, and that he had been 'disappointed in everything'. But even had Sir John been able to bring in more witnesses, it is doubtful whether they would have been any help to him, for when Treby asked him again if he could give a reason why the crown witnesses should have been lying he could give no answer – except, needless to say, that they were all lying papists. He had nothing more to offer in his own defence, and so Holt asked the Solicitor-General to sum up the case for the crown.

The opportunity to draw a favourable comparison between the conduct of this trial and that of similar ones held under the previous regime was not to be missed, and the Solicitor-General made the most of it. He told the jury:

I am sure both he, and you, and all of us, very well remember, when persons of as good quality as he is, or better, had not the same usage or liberty of defence, in such cases, as this gentleman has had: and though all things are very well now, yet the time was, within all our memories, when innocency was no safety for a man's life, much less his liberty.

He dwelt briefly on the ingratitude of conspiring against a king who had risked his own life to bring about this happier state of things and concluded by saying, 'And it is a melancholy thing to consider, that there should be a sort of people among us, so in love with what we then dreaded, as to be continually endeavouring to bring it about

again.' The Solicitor-General's remarks were not altogether unjustified, for the trial had been conducted as fairly as the existing law
allowed. Sir John's feeble and unreasonable arguments had been
listened to with great patience and Holt, in his capacity as counsel for
the prisoner, had given him what opportunities he could to defend
himself. Reading the report of the trial, it is impossible not to think
that the judges, and indeed the whole court, felt some pity for the
foolish and bewildered old gentleman before them. The verdict could
never have been in doubt, but it seems to have been given in a spirit
more of sorrow than of anger or revenge. The jury, after an absence of
less than a quarter of an hour, declared the prisoner 'Guilty'. The
court adjourned and Sir John was taken back to Newgate. He would
be brought to the Old Bailey again next day to hear his sentence.

Like the rest of the accused, Sir William Parkyns had been kept in
close confinement in Newgate, no one being allowed to see him
without an official permit. There had been very little time to prepare
the defence, for it was not until 19 March that his solicitor, Ferdi-
nando Burleigh, was issued with the necessary permit.[2] On the same
day another permit was issued from the Secretary of State's Office for
Lady Parkyns and her daughter Suzanna. It was rumoured that Sir
William was wavering in his resolve never to purchase his life by
betraying the men he had brought in to the conspiracy. His daughter
Suzanna was said to have persuaded her father to take the nobler
course and to refuse to name his accomplices, even though this would
almost inevitably cost him his life.[3] No confirmation of this story has
so far come to light, and since a similar rumour had been current
about Charnock, it is probable that both were put about to denigrate
the characters of the accused. Certainly Sir William, both before and
after his trial, gave no sign of weakening in his resolve not to betray his
associates.

Lady Parkyns, although she later professed to be an adherent of
King William, was loyal to her husband while he lived. She came at
once to London with her daughter and lost no time in doing what she
could to mitigate the hardships of his imprisonment. Not the least of
these hardships, which afflicted the whole family of a person under an
accusation of high treason, was sudden and complete destitution.
Since the property of such a person would, in the event of conviction,
be forfeit to the crown, no rents, dues or other monies would be paid
to him. His credit was destroyed from the moment of his arrest. Thus,
with his liberty Sir William lost his income. 'All things have been torn
from me, since I was apprehended . . . for no money can I get from

anybody, nobody will pay us a farthing', he told Holt at the trial. Apart from having to maintain his wife and four children, Sir William needed cash to subsist in Newgate. Without money he would have been reduced to the starvation diet doled out to indigent prisoners, and he would have been unable to pay the fees demanded by the gaolers for firing, laundry and sundry other small services that mitigated the hardships of prison. In this extremity Sir William was forced to raise money by selling his plate and other valuables. On his instructions, Lady Parkyns packed a trunk with their best silver and linen, together with some clothes and other small items intended for personal use, and despatched it to her husband in Newgate. In the circumstances, it is scarcely surprising that the prison authorities refused to deliver the trunk to Sir William. The Sheriff, notified of its arrival, promptly impounded it and had it taken to the Secretary of State's Office, where it was opened and searched for incriminating papers. It was probably owing to the proverbial slowness of the bureaucratic machine than to any deliberate intention of depriving the prisoner of his property that the trunk was not handed over to its owner until he had made a poignant plea for it in court. 'My Lord, I have nothing to subsist upon, unless I can make something of what is there', he told Holt. 'I have a wife and four children, and nothing to subsist upon.' Holt, careful to see that no prisoner was deprived of his just rights, looked into the matter and told the Sheriff that the trunk was to be delivered to Sir William immediately, for, 'he must have wherewithal to subsist and buy him bread while he is in prison'.

No incriminating papers were found in Sir William's trunk. A careful inventory was made of the contents, which fortunately has survived. It is an interesting document and gives a good idea of the quality and quantity of the more treasured possessions of a person of Sir William's social status.

Contents of a trunk open'd at Mr Secretary Trumball's office, supposed to belong to Sr. William Perkins. The 18 March 1696[4]

> 1 Silver munteith marke W P S[5]
> 1 large salver with a coat of Arms
> 1 large tankard, arms
> 1 pr. lge. candlesticks
> 1 sett of casters, 3 in number
> 4 table salts, small
> 1 saucepan or skillet with cover
> 1 porringer
> 1 cup with two handles
> 1 snuff dish with snuffers

211

1 case cont. 6 forks 6 spoons 6 knives, guilt
1 black velvet gown
1 green embroidered carpet on ye edging
3 pieces of embroidery
20 pieces of linen supposed to be table cloths and sheets
4 dozen and eight napkins of sundry sorts
2 bundles of rags, linnen, old
2 silk mantles, 1 tufted holland ditto
1 pillow case
1 old silk gown
2 keyes on small silver chain

receipt for 1 black trunk, signed by Ed. Willis.

The sale of the plate and linen would have realised a good sum, sufficient to maintain Sir William and his family for some time. The less valuable articles, such as the 'saucepan or skillet with cover', the pillow-case and, one hopes, some of the linen, must have been kept for the comfort of the prisoner in his cell. There is something particularly pathetic about the housewifely inclusion of '2 bundles of rags, linnen, old'. The use to which these could be put in a Newgate cell are perhaps best left to the imagination. Sir William must have had a handsome collection of plate, for the Sheriff estimated its weight as between two and three hundred ounces. The linen, too, must have been of good quality, for it was described as 'damask and diaper', a patterned weave with a silky finish. Clearly, by the standards of their time, Sir William and his lady lived in some luxury; had the gravity of his present situation not obscured this minor woe, it would have been hard for both of them to part with their most prized possessions.

The only other persons with warrants to see Sir William were an unnamed clergyman, described as 'the rector of the Poultry' (possibly Jeremy Collier, the well-known non-juring divine) and Richard Parkyns.[6] This may have been the son of Sir William's uncle, Nathaniel Parkyns, and hence a cousin. Richard and Nathaniel held a mortgage on the Bushey estate, which would therefore be exempt from forfeiture to the crown in the event of Sir William's conviction. Whether from financial necessity, or as an insurance for his son in case the plans for King James's restoration should fail, Sir William had taken out this mortgage some years previously.[7] Richard and Nathaniel Parkyns seem to have acted as trustees for Sir William's eldest son, Blackwell, for in due course he came into possession of the Bushey estate. It was a wise provision, in view of the dangers of Jacobite plotting; no doubt Richard Parkyns was able to assure Sir William that, if the worst happened and he was condemned, his son would not suffer too heavily for the sins of his father.

For almost three and a half centuries an uncounted number of people, guilty and innocent alike, had been sent to their deaths under the ancient Statute of Treasons. That the law was at last modified and humanised was due as much to the efforts of the legal profession as to the politicians. There is thus an unkind irony in the fact that it was a lawyer who was to have the unenviable distinction of being the last Englishman to be tried and condemned under the old Statute.[8] Sir William Parkyns's trial was held on 24 March, twenty-four hours before the new Act came into force; and, as a lawyer, he must have known better than most what advantages a short delay would have given him. Not that he would have had much chance of acquittal even under the new Act, for the case against him was black indeed, but he would at least have been able to put up a better fight for his life. As it was, like Charnock he made 'as good a defence as the matter would bear', basing his arguments on the law, or rather on his own interpretation of it. He knew too much to waste the court's time on useless attempts to discredit the witnesses on grounds of religion or venality; it was the substance of the evidence that he strove hard to disprove. But the odds against him were too great, and he must have known from the start that it was a losing battle.

The court re-assembled at ten o'clock on the morning of 24 March.[9] Lord Chief Justice Holt, Chief Justice Treby and Justice Rokeby were on the bench. The prisoner was brought into the crowded court and set to the Bar. Before trial could begin Sir William raised the matter of his trunk, which caused some delay. Then the jury was selected and sworn and the indictment read. Sir William was accused of high treason on three principal counts: of conspiring with Robert Charnock and others to procure French forces to assist in the overthrow of King William and the restoration of the late King James; of planning the assassination of King William and of procuring horses and arms to that end; and of enlisting men and gathering together arms for an insurrection. The prisoner pleaded 'Not Guilty'. He asked immediately for a postponement of the trial on the grounds that he had not been given time to make arrangements for his defence. He said he had been kept so close a prisoner that there had been no opportunity to summon his witnesses or to confer properly with his solicitor. He ought, he argued, to be tried under the new Act, since it had already been passed by parliament and so had become law. That law, he pointed out, expressly stated that it was just and reasonable that a prisoners should have the benefits that it conferred, such as counsel to

213

plead for him, and sworn witnesses. 'And my Lord, what is just and reasonable tomorrow, sure is just and reasonable today; and your lordship may indulge me in this case, especially when you see how streight notice I have had, and what little time has been allowed me, that I am not able to make my defence.'

Holt agreed that this argument might hold in a Court of Equity, but pointed out that this was a Court of Criminal Justice, and that the judges had no choice but to administer the law: 'We cannot alter the law, we are bound by our oaths to proceed according to the law as it is at present.' Moreover, he went on, Sir William had had as much notice of his trial as the law allowed, and would not have had more under the new Act. Besides, he had known at the time of his arrest a fortnight earlier what he would be accused of, and therefore should have had ample time to summon his witnesses. It was his own fault if he had neglected to do this. As there is no record of any permit to see Sir William in Newgate before 19 March this seems a little severe, for it is clear that he had indeed very little time to make arrangements for his defence. But whatever Sir William might say, the judges had no power to alter the date of the trial which had been fixed by government decree, and in spite of the prisoner's last despairing plea, 'But, My Lord, it wants but one day!' Holt ordered the trial to proceed.

The Attorney-General, Sir Thomas Trevor, set out the case for the crown at considerable length. The first and principal witness for the crown was, as before, George Porter. If Porter felt any compunction for the man who had been for so long a close companion and confederate, he gave no sign of it. For the third but not the last time, he recited the story of the conspiracy and of his own and Parkyns's part in it. He swore to Sir William's presence at the two meetings at the 'King's Head' and Mrs Mountjoy's tavern and that he had been active in the proceedings. Next he told how he had come to lodge with Charnock and Sir William at Mrs Conant's house in Norfolk Street, making it plain that the three of them had lived together on close and convivial terms: 'We used frequently to visit a tavern in the evenings, or drink a bottle of wine in our chambers.' Here Barkley had been brought to be introduced to Porter and Sir William, at a time when the former was confined to his room with the gout. Here too, 'one evening when we were smoking our pipes by the fireside', he had asked Sir William about James's Commission, and Sir William had told him that he had seen it and had described it to him. He left no doubt in the jury's minds that Sir William had been one of the principal actors in the conspiracy, and that he had promised to supply five horses and sundry accoutrements for the attack on the king. Although Sir

William had been prominent in the planning of the Assassination attempt, Porter said, he had not intended to ride out with the others to Turnham Green, giving as his reason that he was too busy preparing his troop of Horse to meet James on his landing in England. Porter had little of note to say of this troop and its personnel. For evidence as to this, the crown relied on the next witness, Abraham Sweet, the Excise Officer.

Sweet was himself under arrest on suspicion of high treason, and it was clear that he knew a good deal about the conspiracy, even if he took no active part in it. Had he refused to give evidence against his patron he would have risked death, or at best long imprisonment. He was not a heroic character, and besides was a poor man with a large family to support. So although he may not have been as willing a witness as Porter, he turned King's evidence and saved his own life at the expense of that of his former friend and patron. Under protracted cross-examination by the Attorney-General, Sweet told the court of the conversations he had had with Sir William about King James's return and how, since Christmas, Sir William had been increasingly positive that this long-looked-for event would take place in the near future. Sir William had told him at that time that he had bought thirty saddles and other accoutrements for the troop he was raising; that it consisted 'all of old soldiers' and that some gentlemen officers were to ride with it. He also gave evidence about bringing the horses up from Bushey at Sir William's orders, and related the conversations they had then, from which it seemed that Sir William had had thoughts of getting him to ride to Turnham Green. Finally, Sweet was minutely cross-examined on Sir William's remarks to him about the journey into Leicestershire. Sweet was a very important, indeed a vital, second witness, because his evidence related to that part of the indictment not covered by Porter's testimony. For this reason the Attorney-General was particularly careful to get from him the details as to time and place of his talks with Sir William, and to make him repeat his words exactly. It was, for instance, important to establish that Sir William had said that his troop *consisted of*, rather than that it *was* to consist of, old soldiers. The first would indicate that it was already in being, the second that it was still a future prospect, and hence not so indictable an offence. Sweet's evidence was clear and consistent under the long questioning, both from the prosecution and from Sir William himself. At the end of it the jury could have been left in no doubt but that the troop had been enlisted and armed, and that the accused had been actively conspiring to raise a rebellion.

The next witness, James Eubanks the groom, was called mainly to corroborate the testimony of Sweet. He told of the ride to Leicester and what he knew, which was not much, of the transactions there. He had also been the bearer of messages, both on 15 and 22 February, from Sir William to a person whose name he did not know, but who was identified as Barkley. Eubanks was also questioned closely about his ride to Marston Jabbett, where he had been sent by his master in February to arrange for the removal of the boxes of arms from Heywood's house to the manor garden. He strenuously denied that he knew what the boxes contained before he saw them opened. The discovery of the buried arms was one of the key points in the case for the crown. Incontrovertible evidence was produced to prove that these were the property of Sir William, that he had concealed the nature of their contents and had caused them to be hidden at a crucial time.

The countrymen from Warwickshire were brought into court to testify to this. First came Hipwell, the odd-job man. Hipwell seems to have been an independent character who 'lived of himself', but worked for Heywood 'when he chooses to employ me'. He told how he had, at Heywood's behest, opened the gate for the wagon late at night, and how he had been sent to borrow a neighbour's mare as an extra horse for the return journey. Then he had helped Sir William's man Richard Evans and the tenant Whetstone, who had come with him, to load the wagon and, taking his lantern, had lighted the party as far as his master's gate. Heywood was interrogated next. He gave an apparently innocent account of how, to oblige Sir William, he had taken the boxes of 'choice goods' and other items into his own house, and of how through Charnock he had later asked Sir William to arrange for their removal. He had been astonished when Evans arrived late at night to fetch them away, but since the wagon was already at his gate he had unwillingly agreed to the removal. He swore that he knew nothing of the contents of the boxes or of what happened to them after they left his house. Heywood, as Charnock's brother-in-law, naturally fell under suspicion of collusion, but since there was no evidence that he knew anything of the conspiracy, no charges were ever preferred against him.

The tale was then taken up by Whetstone, who had returned to the manor with the wagon and had helped Evans to bury the boxes in the garden. The last witness was Watts, the parish constable, who had first searched the house and then had found and dug up the boxes in the flower-bed. Whetstone was present at the exhumation and must have shown Watts where to dig. They took the boxes back to Watts's house and broke them open, 'and there we saw them . . . four dozen of swords, thirty-two carbines, twenty-five brace of pistols'. Asked about the swords, Watts said that they were 'broad swords, two-edged swords', that is cavalry swords. All the weapons were new and in excellent condition. Had Richard Evans been in court, he could have given full confirmation of this evidence. But a warrant was out for his arrest, and the most likely explanation of his non-appearance is that he had prudently concealed himself when he learned of his own and his master's peril.

The rest of the evidence dealt with the movements of the five horses that Sir William was alleged to have supplied for the assassination attempts on 15 and 22 February, with particular reference to the second date. An ostler from the George Inn stated that on the night of Friday 21 February, five of Sir William's horses had been brought into the stables by Sir William's groom and another servant. The horses were all saddled. Four of the saddles were equipped with holsters and pistols; there were also two pairs of jack-boots and some other gear. The next morning two men had called for the horses and had taken them out. They brought them back two hours later and had evidently ridden them hard, for they arrived in a sweat. Later that day the horses were taken away, the ostler did not know where, nor could he say who took them. He knew they belonged to Sir William, as he had been stabling his horses at the 'George' for some years past and as he knew his equine guests as well as the landlord knew his human ones, he had no difficulty in recognising them. When questioned about the movements of these or any other strange horses during the week preceding 22 February, the ostler was less definite. Some horses, how many he could not remember, had been brought in, among them a roan gelding which he had been told belonged to Lord Feversham. This horse had remained in the stable of the 'George' until Monday 24 February, when a very fat man, later identified as 'Old England' Holmes, had ridden it away in company with Sir William Parkyns. A second ostler confirmed this story, adding that the roan gelding had been brought in by Mr Lewis, Lord Feversham's gentleman of horse. This concluded the evidence for the crown. Sir William was now called upon to make what defence he could.

Sir William relied for his defence mainly on attempting to prove that the evidence against him was insufficient according to the law. He began, with a conspicuous lack of tact, by admonishing Chief Justice Holt to be fair in his interpretation of the evidence to the jury. 'My Lord, I rely on your lordship for my defence; for I am ignorant of these proceedings; ... I hope your lordship is so just, that you will repeat the evidence to the jury as it is, and no otherwise.' Adopting an authoritative tone, Sir William attempted to demolish the case for the prosecution:

But I do not observe, that as to the assassination, there is more than one witness, and that is Captain Porter; there is not a tittle more! and as to that, I suppose your lordship will declare to the jury, that I was not concerned in it; and Captain Porter declares, I was to have no hand in it, only I was to furnish five horses, and accidentally I was at some meetings, but he does not declare that I was to do anything in particular.

Though ingeniously argued, this was not very convincing in view of Porter's precise and damning evidence. Only an impossibly credulous jury could believe that the presence of the accused at the conspirators' meetings was 'accidental' or that he had no hand in the plans laid at them. What Porter said about his supposed troop or regiment, Sir William went on, was nothing but hearsay and therefore ought not to be taken into consideration. Neither, in his opinion, should any weight be given to the testimony of the other witnesses as to his troop. He insisted, again and again, that Porter was the only good witness and that he only testified to one overt act of treason, whereas the law required that there should be two witnesses to each act. This, if it had been correct, would have invalidated the case against the accused; for without two witnesses the case could not be brought to court. Unfortunately for Sir William he had misinterpreted the law, either from ignorance or more probably with deliberate intent. As Holt told him, both the old Statute and the new Act made it plain that no case could be brought without two witnesses, but they need not be witnesses to the same act of treason. In the present case the first witness, Porter, had given clear evidence that Sir William had taken an active part in the plans for the assassination. The second witness, Sweet, had given equally clear testimony as to the other act of treason, namely the recruitment and arming of a troop. Therefore the case was good in law, whatever Sir William might say.

At Sir William's request, Sweet was recalled and his evidence gone through again. Particular attention was given to Sweet's report of the journey to Leicester and to his account of what Sir William had said on his return. It was evident from this, as Holt said, that he had gone there for no good purpose: 'He [Sweet] says that which makes it plain . . . and upon your return, you did give an account that all was well, and the west as well inclined to King James's interest as the north.' Sir William did not deny that he had been to Leicester to meet some friends, as he put it, and that he had said that they were all 'well inclined'. 'And I hope', he added piously, 'that is no evidence against me; everybody ought to be well inclined.' But this, in the opinion of Holt and the court, depended on what they were inclined to. Sweet was recalled again to testify that the gentlemen's inclination was specific and was towards the restoration of King James. He was also interrogated once more on the conversations with Sir William about the raising of the troop, but could only repeat what he had said before, that he had been told that the troop consisted entirely of old soldiers. Sir William tried hard to make him alter this statement and to put a less damning construction on his words: 'Pray recollect yourself, Mr Sweet, and think of what you say . . . I am upon my life, and pray speak nothing but the truth.' But Sweet, in spite of these pleadings, stuck to his story. It was in fact likely that he was telling the truth, for if he had not been doing so some inconsistencies in his account must have come out under the severe cross-examination to which he was subjected. Abandoning at last the attempt to make Sweet alter his testimony, Sir William now tried to counter it. There was not a shred of evidence, he said, to prove the existence of this troop, or that it was anything but a product of his own boastful imagination. How could it be otherwise, since 'none of these men do appear. Does this troop consist of men in the air? That I should list men *in nubibus,* and not one of them to be known. Suppose I should tell him a lye, or make some brags, is this treason?'

It was an ingenious argument, for it was never discovered who were to be the recruits for Sir William's troop. It might have been more convincing had it not been for the discovery of the arms buried in his garden. This, in the eyes of the court, was evidence enough of intended treachery. It was true as Sir William had said that there was no evidence as to when or for what purpose the arms were bought but this, in the circumstances, was hardly necessary. The mere fact that they had been concealed was proof that they were to be used for no legal purpose. At this point Sir William made a fatal mistake, and one which was to throw doubt on his credibility throughout the rest of the trial. He declared that he had never bought the weapons; they were found, old and rusty, in the house when he inherited it two years ago. Why, then, had he concealed them? Because, Sir William replied, 'it did not do to be found with any quantity of arms during these troubled times'; a very lame excuse and patently untrue, since the constable had declared that the weapons were new. Sir William's attempt to explain away the suspicious comings and goings of his horses was equally unconvincing, so that in view of his having just produced one foolish falsehood the court was understandably not impressed. He asserted that there was nothing suspicious or unusual in his bringing so many horses to town – it was his usual practice. 'I never kept less than six or seven horses these twenty years; sometimes a great many more; and they were very little horses, pads, no way fit for the service they were presumed to be for.' He failed, however, to give a convincing reason for their presence in the stable of the George Inn at the very time when they were to have been used for the assassination attempt. As to their small size and general unsuitability for such an enterprise the prosecution, after much technical argument with their owner, ascertained that they were average-sized animals of about 14 hands, and could quite well have been used for the expedition. Moreover, the pistols and jack-boots that had arrived with them looked extremely suspicious.

Sir William was losing his confidence. One by one, his excuses and arguments had been disproved or overborne, and it was now clear that his case was desperate. He changed his tactics. Abandoning the legalistic and slightly authoritative tone which he had hitherto adopted he fell back on a personal appeal to Holt and the court. He admitted that there was indeed some slight evidence that he was 'inclined to King James' and that he had sometimes talked in private of his possible return. But, he insisted, there was insufficient proof that he had ever done more than this. He ought therefore to be given the benefit of the doubt: 'Then I hope, my Lord, you will not strain the law to take away my life; according to the rule, That it is better five guilty men should escape, than one innocent man should suffer: for the blood of a man may lie upon everybody, if it be causelessly shed.' Holt acknowledged the truth and justice of this in cases where guilt could not be proven to the satisfaction of the court. But in this case, whatever Sir William might say to the contrary, there was ample evidence of his guilt supplied, as the law required, by two witnesses and corroborated by a number of other testimonies. By his actions he had endangered not only the life of the king but the peace and safety of the kingdom; it was the duty of the court to ensure that justice be done between the king and his subjects. And he added, especially at this time, 'the government ought to take care to preserve itself'.

Sir William tried once more to enlist the sympathy, not of the court, but of Holt himself, speaking to him as a colleague of many years' standing: 'Besides, your lordship has known me this many years, and you know that my education was not to war and fighting, but to the gown, and your lordship knows how peacably I have lived.' But Holt made it clear that he was not to be influenced or deflected from his duty by a personal appeal. He replied severely: 'I have known you heretofore, Sir William, while you kept your profession and your gown.' Clearly Sir William, by his late activities, had lost any claim to sympathy or pity from Holt and his erstwhile fellow-lawyers. Nevertheless, he tried one last plea for mercy:

The trials of Sir John Friend and Sir William Parkyns

And now in my old age, my lord, I am grown lame, and have lost the use of my hands with the gout, and scarce able almost to go on my feet. Therefore it cannot in reason be thought probable that I should engage in such a business as this; and therefore I hope you will interpret all things in a milder sense, in favour of life, rather than for the destruction of it, and the ruin of a man's fortune and family.

It was a moving appeal, but all the same it is impossible not to suspect that Sir William had somewhat exaggerated his age and infirmity in order to excite the pity of his judges. He was forty-nine years old and had very recently ridden to Leicester and back within the space of three days, as Holt and the court well knew. Neither did his frequent journeys on horseback to and from Bushey indicate that he was as decrepit as he would have the court think.

If Holt felt any pity for his ageing and erring erstwhile colleague, he could not show it. The offence was too grave and the evidence too strong for so upright a judge to bend the law in favour of the prisoner. He merely repeated once more that he had given his opinion concerning the number of witnesses, and could say no more. Perhaps to convince the prisoner of his impartiality, or more likely as routine procedure, he called upon his fellow-judges to give their opinion. Lord Chief Justice Treby spoke first. He confirmed in some detail, and not without frequent interruptions and protests from the prisoner, that the evidence was more than sufficient to prove his guilt. That is, two overt acts of high treason had been proved by two good witnesses, according to the requirements of the law. Justice Rokeby spoke in the same strain, supporting the judgement of Holt and Treby as to the evidence. Sir William Parkyns, he went on, had made an appeal for pity; he knew that the jury would consider this, for it was right that justice should be tempered with mercy. But the jury must also reflect that Sir William had shown no pity either for the king whose murder he had helped to plan or for his countrymen, who by his actions would have been plunged into war and desolation. He left it to the jury to judge whether so great a criminal was worthy of mercy.

The trial was drawing towards a close. Sir William, asked if he had anything further to say, made a last attempt to persuade his accusers that the evidence against him was neither convincing nor legal. Sweet's evidence, he said, and not without some justification, was nothing but hearsay, while that of Porter was much exaggerated. He laid himself open to contradiction on this last point for, as Treby told him, the testimony of Porter had already been sufficiently confirmed, 'by the acknowledgement of dying persons'. This was unanswerable, for there could be no reason to doubt that Charnock, King and Keyes were speaking the truth when they confessed their treasonable activities in their last statements. It was unfortunate for Sir William, and indeed for several who came to trial after him, that those who suffered first had, in asserting their undiminished loyalty to the cause for which they died, unwittingly helped to condemn their fellows. Sir William now realised that his case was hopeless. He had nothing more to say in his own defence, and threw himself on the mercy of the court. The Solicitor-General summed up the case for the crown. Holt gave his directions to the jury. They retired for less than half an hour, and brought in a verdict of 'Guilty'.

Sir John Friend was brought into the court to be sentenced along with Sir William. Both men were asked if they had anything further to say before sentence was passed. Sir John made a futile appeal for a re-hearing of his case, which predictably was refused. Sir William made no further effort in his own defence. He was realist enough, and lawyer enough, to know it was hopeless. He merely asked that he might be allowed to have his friends and relations and a minister to visit him in private, without the restraining presence of a gaoler. Knowing full well that even a Chief Justice's assent to such a request needed written confirmation, he asked Holt for an order for this, 'otherwise I shall not have the benefit of it'. Holt willingly granted the order, and made out a similar one for Sir John. The trial had gone on until well into the afternoon without a break, as was customary. There now followed a short adjournment before the pronouncement of the sentence on the two prisoners.

At six o'clock the court re-assembled and Sir John and Sir William were set for the last time to the Bar. They were asked if they had anything further to say before judgement was passed. Sir John said that all he had to say had been said already; Sir William, that he had nothing more to offer. Silence was ordered in the court, and the Common Sergeant, whose duty it was to read the sentence, took his place on the bench beside the three judges. First, he addressed the prisoners in a short speech. They had been found guilty, he told them, after a fair trial, of the most heinous of offences: 'for robbery and murder are injuries to private persons, but compassing the death of the king, is compassing the destruction of the father of your country, and letting in rapine, death and desolation upon thousands of people'. But though the fairness of the trial and the justice of the punishment for so atrocious a crime were firmly asserted by the Common Sergeant, there is in his concluding remarks some indication that he regretted the barbarity of the sentence he was about to pronounce:

The trials of Sir John Friend and Sir William Parkyns

I would not add to your affliction; I am sensible of the severe judgement that is to follow, and which you have brought upon yourselves, and cannot but pity you for the severe burden of guilt that you have laid yourselves under. I only say this to offer it to your serious consideration, in the few moments you have to prepare yourselves for another world, and another judgement. All that remains for me, is to pronounce the judgement of the law in these cases, and the court does award it.

He pronounced the sentence. The condemned men were carried back to Newgate. The execution was to be on Thursday 2 April.

14
An execution and its aftermath

THE TWO PRISONERS IN NEWGATE had nine more days to live. For most of this time the judicial order was observed and they were allowed to see their families and friends in private. Sir John Friend had no surviving wife or children, but he had two nephews who must have been Jacobite sympathisers, even if they were not active in the cause. They must also have had frequent contact with their uncle, whose heirs they probably were. Some months after Sir John's execution a government Agent reported that the elder nephew, an Excise official in Kent, had told him that he had helped several refugees over to France and that he would have done the same for his uncle, had not the latter with characteristic unwisdom, refused to go. At some point, probably shortly after Sir John's arrest, these two nephews had managed to conceal his money, plate and jewels to the value of £4000.[1] The government was thereby cheated of this sum when the estate was assessed for forfeiture to the crown after Sir John's execution. Presumably his nephews were among the relatives permitted to visit him in Newgate, when the concealment of his treasure was arranged with his agreement. For spiritual comfort and guidance Sir John naturally turned to the pastors of the non-juring Church. Two non-juring clergymen were constantly with him up to the last two days before he died. One was William Snatt, the son of John Evelyn's old schoolmaster, and the other was Shadrach Cook. They were allowed to talk and pray with him without the presence of a gaoler until Wednesday 1 April when a gaoler was present and told them that they would not be permitted to come again on the next day. Sir John was much distressed by this order, for he earnestly desired to receive absolution from the two priests. He therefore asked them both if they would perform this office and hear his last prayers at the place of execution, a request with which both men complied.

Lady Parkyns was able to be with her husband until the last possible moment. Other friends and relatives came to bid him farewell during the first few days after the trial. On the Sunday before the day of the execution, according to a report in the *Postman,* 'Sir John Friend and Sir William Parkyns took leave of their friends and ordered that none but the ministers of their choice should come to them.'[2] One relative who was firmly denied access to Sir William was his nephew, Matthew Smith. Even now this unpleasant person hoped to make some profit from his unhappy uncle's plight by attempting to extract saleable information from him. On 30 March Smith applied for an order to see Sir William, 'by reason I thought it might be for the king's service'. He was told that there was a private order in being for relatives to visit the prisoner, but that he must first apply to Lady Parkyns. She must have known that Matthew was the last person her husband would wish to see, and put him off with the excuse that there was now an order that no one but herself might see Sir William during these last few days. Undeterred by this rebuff, Smith went over her head to the Duke of Shrewsbury and demanded the permit on the ground that thanks to their close relationship, he could induce Sir William to tell him the names of his confederates. To his credit, the duke refused the permit. Needless to say this refusal was interpreted by Smith as a manoeuvre to suppress information which might be compromising to Shrewsbury himself.[3]

Like Sir John, Sir William did not wish to be attended by the prison chaplain. He sent for Jeremy Collier, an eminent and learned non-juring divine, with whom he had been friendly in his more respectable past. Collier, who no doubt had heard and disapproved of Sir William's Jacobite activities, says that he had not seen him for the past four or five years. However, he at once obeyed the summons to Newgate 'as I thought myself obliged by my character'. For two days Collier and Sir William were allowed to talk and pray together undisturbed by the presence of a gaoler, but after that this privilege was withdrawn. On Wednesday 1 April Collier, like the other two priests, was refused admission to the prisoner and told that he must make no more visits. Sir William, as Collier says, 'being under an expectation of death from the time of his sentence, had given me the state of his conscience, and therefore desired the Absolution of the Church might be pronounced to him by me the last day'. As it was now impossible for Collier to perform this office in Newgate, Sir William sent a message asking him to come to the place of execution and pronounce the absolution there. Collier, no more than Cook and Snatt, could not refuse this request; it would be a betrayal of their priestly office to let a repentant Christian go to his death with all his sins upon him. Nor were they deterred by the probability that in performing this office so publicly they risked bringing down upon themselves and their Church the wrath of the Establishment. All three non-jurors, therefore, agreed without hesitation to be present at Tyburn and to give spiritual comfort and final absolution to the two men at the foot of the gallows.[4]

Suspicion was still rife that many traitors, some of them highly placed, were still at large, but so far all efforts to persuade the prisoners to name their associates had failed. The Whigs especially were out for blood and hoped to bring down bigger game than Sir William Parkyns and Sir John Friend. Moreover, very little information as to the numbers and names of the persons who were to compose the rebel troops had emerged at the trials. Right or wrong, the feeling that what had so far been uncovered was only the tip of the iceberg was firmly implanted in the minds of both public and parliament. Almost at the last moment the government decided to make a further effort to extract fuller confessions from the two prisoners awaiting execution in Newgate. On 31 March Sir Rowland Gwynne, the instigator of the Association in Defence of King William, wrote to Secretary Trumbull advising that they be reprieved, 'as their execution would relieve their party from fear of further confessions'. The order for a reprieve was issued from the Secretary of State's Office that same day. On the next day, 1 April, the Commons resolved that a committee be appointed to go to Newgate to examine Sir William Parkyns and Sir John Friend. The committee, headed by the Marquis of Winchester and composed of nine members of the Privy Council, was set up on the spot and instructed to repair forthwith to Newgate and interrogate the prisoners. They were to be offered their lives in exchange for the names of their accomplices.[5]

When the House assembled next morning, 2 April, a somewhat crestfallen Marquis of Winchester reported that the committee's mission had been a total failure. Quite unintimidated by the august assemblage that had so unexpectedly descended upon them, both prisoners had refused point-blank to betray their associates. Sir William had been interviewed first. Whatever his past faults and follies may have been, they were now redeemed by the steadfast courage in the face of what must have been severe temptation. He could have saved his own life: he would not do so at the expense of others. He could have abjured his loyalty to King James: he never wavered in his adherence. And having made up his mind to die, he had nothing to gain by concealing any longer his part in the plot or the beliefs and principles that had led him into it. His sincerity is apparent in his answer to the committee's questions:

An execution and its aftermath

Sir William Parkyns owned his being privy to the intended assassination; and of being in company when 'twas discoursed of at two or three meetings; and thinks 'twas a fault that he did approve of it. That he had received hints, several times, of king James his design of coming over, and particularly now; and was resolved to serve him, whenever he was, with himself and friends; thinking that he had wrong done him; and that it was his Duty to help him whenever he could: and that he consulted not with any but those that he could engage, and that he had influence upon. That he guessed he could have brought in to the number of a Troop; but that he would never redeem his own blood at the Expence of those he had drawn in. That since Christmas, he did see a Commission, which he understood to be king James's, directed to his loving subjects, to levy war against the Prince of Orange, and all his Adherents: he believes it was signed by king James. That it had a seal to it; and that he saw it in the hands of a Friend, which he desired not to name; but he believes he is not in England.[6]

The friend whom Sir William desired not to name can have been none other than Barkley, since no one else had seen the Commission.

Sir William's answer to the committee was clearly made of his own free will, and in full knowledge of the consequences; and there is no reason to suppose that any undue pressure was put upon him thus to endorse his own death sentence. His statement proves that the evidence produced by the crown at the trial was not fabricated in any particular, for he admits all the charges made against himself.

The interrogation of Sir John Friend was equally unrewarding, partly because he knew much less. He had been, as Burnet unkindly remarks, applied to and trusted only when the conspirators needed his money. He could tell the committee nothing that had not already emerged at the trials and, like Sir William, he refused to name any persons whom he might have involved. In view of the prisoners' intransigent attitude, the committee could do nothing more, and the law must take its course. The reprieve had only extended their lives by one day, for it was decreed that the execution would take place next morning, 3 April. Just and necessary though the punishment for his crime was almost universally held to be, there were some signs of sympathy for Sir William. Even the arch-Whig Burnet says of him that 'his tenderness in not accusing those he had drawn in, was so generous, that this alone served to create some regard for a man who had long been under a very bad character'.[7] Among the crowd who would flock to Tyburn on 3 April there would be some at least who would feel pity for the condemned men.

L'Hermitage, Agent of the Grand Pensionary of Holland, writing to his master on 3 April, remarked that no sight delighted the English so

227

much as a hanging, and that of all hangings within living memory none had excited so much interest as that of Sir William Parkyns and Sir John Friend. There had been no time to give official notice of the postponement of the execution, and so on 2 April an avidly expectant crowd filled the spectators' scaffolding around the gallows at Tyburn and packed the space in front of it. When it was announced that there would be no show that day the mob broke up in very angry humour and according to L'Hermitage, there was some fighting between those who had paid for their seats and those who refused to refund their money. As big a crowd gathered again the next day, and this time it was not disappointed.[8] As was customary on such occasions, short-hand writers accompanied the condemned men so that their last words could be recorded and published. A shortened version of the report of what passed is given here. It is grim reading, but Sir William and Sir John must be followed to the end.[9]

The courage, faith and composure with which so many persons went to Tyburn has always been a matter for wonder and admiration. Sir William and Sir John were not exceptional in this; it could truly be said of both that they died better than they lived. The conduct of the sheriffs and other attendant officials was also impeccable. In the not-so-distant past sheriffs had not scrupled to hustle a condemned man through his last prayers, or to attempt to bully him into a last-minute confession, sometimes at the very moment of execution.[10] Now they behaved with as much consideration, even kindness, as the circumstances allowed. Indeed, their attitude seemed to be that of persons carrying out a necessary operation on the bodies of the sufferers, rather than a punishment for a heinous crime.

The long winter of 1696 showed no signs of retreating, and Friday 3 April was a bitterly cold day; Evelyn records, 'excessive cold weather, no leaves on the trees'. The two prisoners were brought out of their cells into the prison yard. Their shackles were struck off and they were placed, unbound, in the waiting sledge. The procession with its mounted escort went at walking-pace through the streets lined with spectators; it is two miles from Newgate to Tyburn, a long last journey for the occupants of the sledge. A newspaper of the day records that:

They both had books in their hands the whole way, and Sir John seemed more penitent than Sir William. They prayed very heartily, being assisted by the non-jurant ministers, Mr Cook, Mr Collier and Mr Snatt . . . Sir William Parkyns was observed to smile several times in the sledge, and seemed to take much notice of the spectators . . . When they came to the Press Yard, Sir John said to Sir William 'We shall soon be in a glorious state.'[11]

An execution and its aftermath

When the procession arrived at Tyburn Sir William was the first to be released from the sledge; he climbed into the great cart or tumbril that waited under the gallows. The three ministers, who had walked beside the sledge all the way from Newgate, climbed up beside him. Almost at once the executioner approached to put the rope round his neck.

'May I not pray before it is put on?' Sir William asked.

'Yes, sir, if you please', the executioner answered, and he stood aside. Then Sir John mounted into the cart, and priests and prisoners knelt and prayed together. The account continues:

Then the ministers asked them, Whether they were in charity with all the world? and if they had offended any, whether they did ask them for forgiveness? And whether they did desire the absolution of the church? Upon their answer, that they did, they all laid their hands upon their heads, and Mr Cook pronounced the absolution, which ended in these words 'and by his authority committed to me, I absolve thee from all thy sins, in the name of the Father, etc.'

Their solemn office performed, the three priests got down from the cart. Sir William and Sir John were allowed to continue for some time in private prayer, the Sheriff assuring them several times that they would not be hurried: 'if you desire any more time, you shall have it, we will wait upon you with great willingness', he told them. When they had finished praying, Sir William handed the Sheriff a paper containing his last statement. Both he and Sir John were asked if they had anything to say, 'by way of confession or denial for the fact for which ye came here to suffer?' But Sir William said curtly that all he had to say was contained in his paper, while Sir John, holding up his paper, cried excitedly, 'Sir, here is a paper, I desire it may be printed. For I came here to die, and not to make a speech! . . . and I have no more say, but to beg of God to receive my soul!' 'The Lord have mercy on you!' the Sheriff said, and again offered them more time to pray. Sir John thanked him, and asked him not to let the cart be driven from under them until they had given a signal that they were ready. Their arms were bound and the ropes placed round their necks. Sir John cried out that he forgave all his enemies, as he hoped God would forgive him. The executioner put the black hoods on their heads, ready to be pulled down over their eyes at the last moment. As was the custom, he asked and received forgiveness from the men he was about to hang. Suddenly Sir John realised that the implements for the butcher's work to come were lying in the bottom of the cart.

'Will not the things lie in my way?' he asked.

'I will remove them', the executioner replied, and having done so he pulled the black hoods down over their eyes.

'The Lord receive my spirit', Sir William said quietly. Then he asked the executioner whether it would be better to stand or to hold up his legs when the cart went away. He was advised to stand, and was asked to give notice when he was ready for the cart to draw away. Sir John cried out once more 'Stretch forth thy arms, O Lord, and receive my soul and carry it to heaven! Executioner, when we knock, go away.' The account concludes: 'and after few ejaculations, they gave the sign and the cart drew away. They both of them gave money to the executioner; and having hung about half an hour, being a considerable time after they were dead, they were cut down and quartered according to the sentence.' On 10 April John Evelyn recorded in his diary: 'Now were the quarters of Sir: William Perkins and Mr [sic] Friend, lately executed on the Plot, set up with Perkins' head on Temple Barre, a dismal sight, which many pitied.'[12] Sir John's head was not included in this display; it was set up at the end of Aldgate, within sight of his brewery in the Minories.

There were others who took a very different point of view. For example, on 4 April Christopher Stockdale, in a newsletter to Viscount Irwin, wrote:

Yesterday Sir John Friend and Sir William Parkyns were executed, but died very obstinate and sullen, and have left the most impudent papers behind them that were ever known upon such occasions, especially in so bad a cause; but I hope we shall humble the rogues before we have done with them . . . the prisoners' papers are not yet printed because they are so malevolent that I suppose they must be punished with animadversions.[13]

The papers, when published, certainly caused indignation among the supporters of King William's government, for both were bold and impenitent assertions of the writers' loyalty to King James, and both men freely admitted the charges against them. It was commonly thought that his pastor, the Reverend Shadrach Cook, had composed Sir John's paper for him and this was probably so, for it reads more like a rallying call from a non-juror's pulpit than the production of a semi-literate brewer; it is beautifully written, the very cadences echoing the Anglican liturgy. Sir John (or Cook) begins by saying: 'the cause I am brought hither to suffer for, I do firmly believe to be the cause of God and true religion', and he asserts that it is both justifiable and a duty to assist his king in the recovery of his throne.

And I profess myself . . . a member of the Church of England . . . of that Church which suffers so much at present for a strict adherence to loyalty, the laws and Christian principles; for this I suffer, and for this I die . . . I must take this opportunity, and I do it for God's glory, to apply myself to you that are loyalists of that Church . . . and I beg you, for God's sake and for the love of your souls, to be very constant and serious in all religious offices, and holy duties . . . let no excuse, no dangers, prevent or hinder you . . . and be, I beseech you, very careful and circumspect in all your actions, behaviour and conversation, as I earnestly exhorted all who came to me.'

This last excellent piece of advice came too late to help the giver of it, and poor Sir John must bitterly have regretted that he had not himself been more 'careful and circumspect'. He was fated to be made use of. The conspirators had used his money, and now his last statement was used as a piece of propaganda for the non-juring Church. Not that Sir John would have objected to this; he was a devout man, and laid down his life 'in all cheerfulness and resignation' as much for his Church as for his king. The statement ends with a heartfelt prayer for the restoration of the exiled royal family, which must surely have been written by Cook, and finally there is a moving plea for divine mercy: 'And now thou art pleased to take me hence, take me into thy favour, and grant that my soul may be without spot presented unto thee, through the merits of thy most dearly beloved Son, Jesus Christ our Lord. Amen.'[14]

The hand of Cook was plain to read in Sir John's paper, but Sir William's could have been written by no one but himself. There can be no truth in the allegation made after its publication that it had been composed for him by Jeremy Collier, and indeed Collier himself refutes the accusation in a most convincing way:

It is well known that Sir William was a man of sense and bred to law and letters, and needed no help to assist him in writing a few lines. Besides, I was not permitted to come near him for more than two days before he suffered: neither was he allowed so much as a pen, ink and paper till the last morning. Then it was that he penned his speech, as I am told by those who were present.[15]

Sir William's statement, especially considering the circumstances under which it was composed, is so characteristic, and so clear a declaration of the principles under which he had acted, that it deserves to be quoted in full:

It hath not been my custom to use many words, and I shall not be long upon this occasion, having business of much greater consequence to employ my thoughts upon. I thank God I am now in a full disposition to charity; and therefore shall make no complaints, either of the hardships of my trial, or any other rigours put upon me. However, one circumstance I think myself obliged to mention. It was sworn against me by Mr. Porter, that I had owned to him that I had seen and read a commission from the king to levy war upon the person of the prince of Orange. Now, I must declare, that the tenour of the king's commission, which I saw, was general, and directed to all his loving subjects, to raise and levy war against the prince of Orange, and his adherents; and to sieze all forts, castles, etc. which I suppose may be a customary form of giving authority to make war; but I must confess that I am not much aquainted with matters of that nature: but as for any commission particularly levelled against the person of the prince of Orange, I niether saw nor heard of any such.

It is true I was privy to the design upon the prince, but was not to act in it; and am fully satisfied that very few, or none, knew of it but those who undertook to do it.

I freely acknowledge, and think it for my honour to say, that I was entirely in the interest of the king, being always firmly persuaded of the justice of his cause; and I looked upon it as my duty, both as a subject and an Englishman, to assist him in the recovery of his throne, which I believed him to be deprived of contrary to all right and justice; taking the laws and constitution of my country for my guide.

As to religion, I die in the communion of the Church of England, in which I was educated.

And as I freely forgive all the world, so whoever I may any ways have injured, I heartily ask their pardon.

WILLIAM PARKYNS[16]

Like the rest of the conspirators, Sir William knew only too well the damage that the allegation that James had sanctioned the assassination attempt was doing to the Jacobite cause and so, like King and Charnock, his first consideration was to refute it. This, as the only person besides Barkley who had actually seen the Commission, he was able to do with greater authority, and he must have hoped his evidence of James's innocence, together with his own clear statement of his belief in the justice of the cause for which he was about to die, would help to rally the stricken Jacobite party. It is small wonder that Sir William's uncompromising declaration was stigmatised as 'impudent' and 'malevolent' and that strenuous efforts were made by the government to nullify any effect that it might have on the more impressionable. Both papers were published in full shortly after the executions. The 'animadversions' followed at once, the press, particularly *The Remarker* and the *Weekly Intelligencer*, being especially censorious of the actions of the three clerics. The loyal public was scandalised enough by the spectacle of the laying on of hands, a popish practice obnoxious to every good protestant; even more shocking was the three priests' action in absolving the two traitors of *all* their sins. Bishop Burnet voices the general disapprobation:

A very unusual instance of the boldness of the Jacobites appeared on that occasion; these two had not changed their religion, but still called themselves protestants; so three of the non-juring clergymen waited on them at Tyburn ... and all the three, at the place of execution, joined to give them public absolution, with an imposition of hands, in the view of all the people; a strain of impudence, that was as new as it was wicked; since these persons died, owning the ill designs they had been engaged in, and expressing no sort of repentancy for them. So these clergymen, in this solemn absolution, made an open declaration of their allowing and justifying these persons, in all they had been concerned in.[17]

Cook and Snatt were shortly afterwards arrested and committed to Newgate to await trial for high misdemeanour. Collier at once went into hiding, and later escaped abroad. From his place of concealment, and by means of one of the secret presses, he published a paper entitled 'A Defence of the Absolution given to Sir William Parkyns at the Place of Execution, 3 April, 1696.'[18] In this paper Collier first justifies his giving of the absolution in public by explaining that, since he was denied access to Sir William in order to perform the office in private, he had no alternative but to go to Tyburn and perform it there; to have refused such a request from a man who was about to die would be to have failed in his Christian duty, both as a priest and a friend. As to the allegedly 'popish' practice of the laying-on of hands, this, he declares, was perfectly legitimate in the circumstances. The laying on of hands, he claims, was an ancient practice, sanctioned by the early Church and still used in certain ceremonies of the Church of England. When it came to the more serious accusation that by giving absolution to Sir William for *all* his sins he was thereby condoning the sin of murder and rebellion, for which Sir William had expressed no repentance, Collier was on less certain ground. It is true that Collier would never, for whatever reason, have condoned so great a sin as murder, and probably he had not fully considered the possibility that the established clergy would be quick to seize upon the implications of his action; but it cannot be denied that his defence, though vigorously expressed, was not altogether convincing. Sir William, Collier said, had been in a very proper state of repentance for the errors of his life, and greatly desired the forgiveness of the Church before he died; and these errors, Collier was careful to point out, did not include any mention of the intended assassination. And as to the paper in which

Sir William had owned to his involvement in the conspiracy without expressing any repentance therefor, Collier did not think that this in any way concerned him, since he had no knowledge of what the paper contained when he absolved Sir William, whose repentance had been in general terms, as was the absolution. Collier, therefore, maintained that he had done no more than his duty in acting according to the rites of his Church.

Collier's 'Defence' was published on 9 April. On 10 April there appeared a veritable broadside from the established Church, signed by both archbishops and no less then ten bishops, entitled 'A Declaration of the Sense of the Archbishops and Bishops now in and about London . . . concerning the irregular and scandalous proceedings of certain clergymen, at the Execution of Sir John Friend and Sir William Parkyns'.[19] In terms of thunderous disapproval their lordships censured both criminals and priests. First, they denounce as false and impious Sir John's claim that the non-juring Church was the only true Church of England. Sir William, too, was held to have made the same unfounded claim, by asserting in his paper that he died in 'the communion of the Church of England, in which I was educated'. This was an open affront to the Church as by law established. More reprehensible still was the conduct of Collier, Cook and Snatt in publicly absolving the sinners by the laying on of hands, a proceeding calculated to offend every good protestant, lay or clerical. More shocking still, in their lordships' view, were the implications of their action. For the criminals had been justly condemned by the law of the land for a most heinous offence, and neither of them had expressed remorse or penitence, and it was impossible to imagine that the three priests had been unaware of their unrepentant attitude. It followed that when they absolved Sir John and Sir William, either they did so knowing that they were unrepentant criminals, or they looked upon them as martyrs in a cause to which all of them were dedicated.

We are so charitable as to believe they would not absolve them under the former notion, for that had been in effect, sealing them to damnation: but if they held these men to be martyrs, then their absolving them in that manner was a justification of those grievous crimes for which these men suffered, and an open affront to both church and state.

Clearly, the situation had dangerous possibilities as martyrdom, in whatever cause, has a way of arousing sympathy. The schismatics must be denounced and the authority of the Church of England asserted at once and in no uncertain terms:

We do declare, that we disown and detest all such principles and practices, looking upon them as highly schismatical and seditious, dangerous to both church and state and contrary to the true doctrine and spirit of the Christian religion. And we also take this occasion to warn and exhort all the people committed to our charge, to beware of such seducers, and to avoid them.

Collier's reply, published a fortnight later, added little or nothing to the arguments put forward in his first 'Defence', and consisted mainly of innumerable quotations and precedents culled from his extensive knowledge of the writings of the early fathers, by which he hoped to justify himself and perhaps to overcome his clerical colleagues with the weight of his learning.[20]

Cook and Snatt were arraigned at the Old Bailey on 2 July 1696. The Church, however, was not minded to stir up public sympathy by making martyrs of them and so through the wise intercession of the Archbishop of Canterbury, they were released on bail and suffered no further punishment.[21] Collier too could have been put on bail but refused, as he considered that to do so would have been to acknowledge the government of King William. He fled abroad, and in his absence a sentence of outlawry was passed upon him. He continued under sentence of banishment until his death thirty years later, apart from occasional re-appearances in England to preach to the faithful in non-juring conventicles.

There can be no doubt that Collier, Cook and Snatt acted with the worthiest of motives, and that they did not fully foresee the consequences of that action, both to themselves and to their Church. They could not in any case have refused the last requests of Sir William and Sir John without betraying their office as priests and bringing down upon themselves the contempt of their own congregation. Furthermore, Sir John and Sir William, as well as the priests, may well have hoped that so public a demonstration of faith and loyalty would actually help their party; it might encourage the faithful and rally the discontented among the opposition. If this in fact had been in their minds it was, as might have been foreseen, a serious error of judgement, and one which was to cost their party dear. Thanks to the archbishops' and bishops' 'Declaration', together with a barrage of propaganda from the press, the idea took root in the mind of the loyal public that the non-jurors thought lightly of, even if they did not condone, so detestable and un-English a crime as assassination. Such an imputation was well calculated to antagonise many who had hitherto regarded the schismatics with tolerance, and even with a certain grudging repect. Thus the whole incident did grave damage to the reputation of the non-juring Church and it lost many adherents in consequence. Its decline was slow and gradual, for the non-juring

Church was to outlast the Jacobite movement in which it had its origins; but this decline, already under way by 1696, was accelerated by the events following the execution of Sir William Parkyns and Sir John Friend. Like so many other Jacobite demonstrations, this one did nothing but harm to the cause for which these two men died; hoisting themselves with their own petard was a political hazard to which the Jacobites seem to have been peculiarly liable.

15
The trials of Rookwood, Cranburne and Lowick

AMBROSE ROOKWOOD, Charles Cranburne and Robert Lowick were the next to be tried.[1] As this was the first trial held under the new treason law, a preliminary hearing on 15 April was deemed necessary to ensure that its provisions would be properly carried out; for although the Act laid down in general terms the way in which treason trials were from henceforth to be conducted, there were no precise rules for its implementation in court. This was a matter of primary importance for all concerned, for a precedent would now be set that would have to be followed in all future treason trials. Naturally, therefore, arguments about procedure took up a great part, both of the preliminary hearing and the subsequent ones, so much so that at times it seemed as if it were not the prisoners, but the Act itself that was on trial – as indeed to a great extent it was. The preliminary hearing was quite short, and was mainly concerned with ensuring that the new law would be correctly interpreted. Towards the end of it the three prisoners made a brief appearance at the Bar; the indictment, charging them jointly with conspiring to assassinate the king, was read; all three pleaded 'Not Guilty' and were remanded to Newgate for a further week. The court then decided that it would be best to deal with each case separately: Rookwood first, then Cranburne, then Lowick.

When the court re-opened at 8.00 a.m. on Friday 21 April, Rookwood was set to the Bar to face an imposing array of seven judges. Once again, the Old Bailey was crowded with eminent and interested persons. The attraction this time was probably not so much the trial itself, for Rookwood was a relatively obscure person who had not played a particularly important part in the plot, as in observing the new treason law in operation. The controversies that had for so long delayed the passing of the Act, and the fundamental nature of the principles of which it was an expression, were quite sufficient to arouse much public interest in the first treason trial in which the prisoner would have skilled counsel to defend him. In accordance with the spirit of the Act, which expressly states that persons accused of

237

high treason 'should not be debarred of all just and equal Means of Defence', the commission appointed Sir Bartholomew Shower, an eminent and able lawyer, to act as advocate for the prisoners. No more fitting choice could have been made, for Shower, as well as being a skilful pleader in court, was well known as one of the chief advocates of legal reform. His supporting counsel was Mr Phipps.

It was, as a modern historian says, 'an historic moment in the evolution of English criminal law, when for the first time Sir Bartholomew Shower took up the defense of Ambose Rookwood in open court'.[2] But Sir Bartholomew, although no doubt well aware of the historic importance of the occasion, was also perturbed by the novelty of the situation in which he and his colleague Phipps were placed. He would not have it thought that because they were defending persons accused of high treason they in any way condoned the crime for which the accused were to stand trial, and was at pains to make this clear at the outset:

My Lord, we are assigned as counsel, in pursuance of an act of parliament, and we hope that nothing we shall say in defense of our clients shall be imputed to ourselves . . . We come not here to countenance the practices for which the prisoner stands accused; for we know of none, either religious or civil, that can warrant or excuse them. But the act of parliament having warranted the appearing of a counsel for persons accused to make defense for them, we hope your lordship will give us leave to make what objections we can on their behalf.

Holt replied that the court must first hear what these objections were. Shower and Phipps then proceeded to raise objections to the way in which the Act had been interpreted, claiming that it was prejudicial to their client's case. Their argument occupies no less than nine closely printed pages of the report of the trial, and must have tried the patience of the court. But when Shower began to apologise for taking up the court's time with yet another objection, Holt cut him short:

Never make apologies, Sir Bartholomew, for it is lawful for you to be of counsel in this case, as it is in any other case where the law allows counsel. It is expected you should do your best for those you are assigned for, as it is expected in any other case that you do your duty for your client.

This reassurance clarified the position of the defence, and they proceeded with their argument, the main burden of it being that because insufficient time had been allowed for debating its provisions, their client had not had the full benefit of the new law. 'It is a new law, and has never yet received an opinion', Shower pointed out. The prosecution contended that the Act had been correctly interpreted and without prejudice to the accused at the preliminary hearing. Holt and the other judges listened patiently to the interminable debate, occasionally intervening to give an opinion, and even at one point deciding in favour of the defence. At last the court decreed that the objections could not be allowed, although it was admitted that there were grounds for upholding at least one of them. However, the precedent had been set, and must be adhered to; to alter it now would be most irregular, and tantamount to a bending of the law. This was too much for Holt, and he promptly settled the issue by declaring 'Well, for my part I will not commit any irregularity on any account whatsoever . . . Mr. Attorney, pray go on to open the evidence.'

The trial could now begin. Inevitably, the first of the two principal witnesses for the prosecution was George Porter. Shower, like the defendants in the previous trials, began by trying to prove that Porter could not legally give evidence, being himself a convicted felon, since he had been found guilty of the murder of Sir James Hacket in 1684. But Porter was able to prove that he had never been convicted of this crime; the charge had been reduced to manslaughter and he had been granted a royal pardon by King Charles. Moreover, he could show the court that he had never been burnt in the hand, the statutory punishment for manslaughter. This made him a legal witness, and he proceeded to give evidence in his usual smooth and practised manner. He told the court how Rookwood had been present at many meetings at which the plan to attack the king had been discussed, and how Sir George Barkley had appointed him as captain to one of the three parties that were to attack the royal coach at Turnham Green, adding several other incriminating details. Porter did at least say that Rookwood had had little relish for the enterprise, but went on to say that when Barkley, on hearing some objections from Rookwood, had told him that orders must be obeyed, the accused had shrugged his shoulders and said, 'there is an end of it', meaning, Porter implied, that he had no choice in the matter.

Harris, the betrayer of Rookwood and Bernardi, was the second crown witness. Shower made an unsuccessful attempt to get Harris disqualified on the grounds that he was too interested a party for his testimony to be credible. Harris, he pointed out, was an accomplice, and could only save himself by informing on his confederates. Moreover, since he had not been named in the first proclamation, he was entitled to claim the reward for the capture of Rookwood and Bernardi. But the court overruled the first objection, for the very good reason that the testimony of accomplices was often the only means of obtaining evidence, and disallowed the second; so Harris was declared to be a legal witness and was duly sworn. His testimony supported that of Porter and was equally damning, for he had been almost as closely involved in the conspiracy as Rookwood, to whom he had acted as A.D.C. Some grooms and tapsters then testified to the comings and goings of the accused at the relevant time and to the movements of the horses hired for him and his band. Their evidence completed the case for the prosecution.

The defence put up as good a fight for their client as circumstances would allow. Shower argued with some skill that there was no proof that Rookwood had agreed to take part in the expedition to Turnham Green. Clever use was made of Rookwood's remark, quoted by Porter, when ordered by Barkley to command one of the three troops that were to attack the coach. Rookwood had said, 'there is an end of it' and this, as the jury would realise, could just as easily be taken to mean that he would not take part in the attack. As to the accused's presence at the meetings, this was too well attested to be disputed but, Shower maintained, this amounted to no more than misprision of treason and could not in law be interpreted as an overt act. Unfortunately for the accused, the prosecution at once pointed out that there was plenty of evidence to show that, whatever the accused may have felt about it, he had taken an active part in the preparations for the attempt on the king's life.

Defeated on this point, the defence fell back on a fresh attempt to discredit the principal witness, Porter; Shower alleged that he was so wicked, and had committed so many crimes and misdemeanours, that no jury could possibly believe a word he said; with the court's permission, witnesses would be called to confirm this statement. Holt gave his assent to this, providing that Sir Bartholomew first specified what sort of offences the witnesses would testify to. Shower said:

Why then, my Lord, if robbery upon the highway, if clipping, if conversation with clippers, if fornication, if buggery, if any of these irregularities, will take off the credit of a man, I have instructions in my brief, of evidence of crimes of this nature . . . against Mr Porter . . . we hope that no jury that have any conscience will upon their oaths give any credit to the evidence of a person against whom such a testimony is given.

Shower could hardly have made these allegations unless he had some proof, but unhappily for the defence none of his witnesses were able to substantiate this impressive list of misdemeanours, probably because none of them was prepared to risk defaming so dangerous a man as Porter in open court. The first witness said he had never heard anything bad of him, while the worst the next could say was that 'he was sometimes lewd in his discourse'. Four more persons were called, but they had prudently absented themselves. The last of these witnesses was Porter's servant, Black Will. As the report quaintly puts it, 'He appeared, and was a Moor.' The court seemed a little startled by the Moor's appearance; 'Is he a Christian?' Holt asked. On being assured that he was, he directed that Black Will be sworn, while Phipps explained in a kindly way, 'You are sworn to tell the truth, sweetheart.' But Black Will was not to be drawn by endearments. He was clearly no simpleton and had seen what had happened to Porter's other servant, Keyes; he was not going to risk saying anything to damage his master's reputation and arouse his animosity. He may even have been speaking the truth when he said stolidly that Porter had been a very good master to him for nearly eight years and that he did not know him to be guilty of anything. With the testimony of Black Will the attempt by the defence to discredit Porter collapsed; as Holt remarked, these witnesses might just as well have been called for the crown, had they been needed.

Unlike the accused in the previous trials, most of whom had taken a leading part in the proceedings, Rookwood, except for a few short and non-committal answers to occasional questions, had maintained an enigmatic silence, apparently relying entirely on his lawyers to conduct his defence. Now he was asked by Holt what he had to say for himself, but even then all he said was, 'My Lord, Mr Porter does not say I was to command a party.' Since Rookwood seemed quite unable, or unwilling, to elaborate upon this bald statement Holt went on to sum up the evidence, after which the jury retired to consider their verdict. They returned in less than a quarter of an hour. The verdict was 'Guilty'.

Rookwood's trial, by seventeenth-century standards, had taken longer than usual, mainly owing to the protracted arguments about procedure. It was now two o'clock in the afternoon, and the court had been sitting since eight o'clock that morning, but judges and court officials in those days seem to have had remarkable stamina. There were no objections to Holt's proposal that they proceed without a break to the next trial, that of Cranburne. The prisoner was accordingly brought into the court and set to the Bar, still wearing his heavy fetters. This incensed Holt and with the concurrence of the rest of the bench, he at once ordered the keeper to release him, 'for they should stand at ease when they are tried'. The defence began by making a spirited attempt to quash the indictment on the grounds that it was inaccurate and misleading. Had they succeeded Cranburne would have gone free, for no one could be condemned on a false indictment. However, after much argument the court declared the indictment valid and the trial could proceed. As it was now past three o'clock, the court was adjourned until six o'clock that evening. It had been hoped to try all three prisoners on the same day, but this was now clearly impossible and before adjourning the court decreed that Lowick's trial would have to be postponed until the next morning. This was not very convenient as an entire new jury panel would have to be convened, but as Holt remarked, 'it was but a morning's work'.

When the court re-assembled it made short work of Cranburne. Porter, who seemed especially anxious to silence his former employees, compromised him as thoroughly as he had his other servant, Keyes. De La Rue, long-winded as usual, added little of importance to Porter's evidence, but the next witness, Captain Prendergrass, was more precise and more damaging; he made it quite clear to the court that Cranburne had taken an active part in the preparations for the attack on the king. The defence put up as good a fight as they could in view of the damning nature of the evidence. Shower, undiscouraged by his previous failure, made one more attempt to destroy Porter's credibility by calling more witnesses to testify to his wickedness. But only one of them, a Mrs Gerrard, ventured to appear and like Black Will frustrated the defence by saying that she knew nothing bad of Porter. Cranburne was of inferior social status to Rookwood and Lowick – the indictment describes him as a yeoman, while the other two were gentlemen – but he was not uneducated; he asked for pen, ink and paper and took a much more active part in his own defence than had Rookwood. In the face of the evidence, however, his rather lame denials of guilt failed to impress the jury. They took just a quarter of an hour to declare him 'Guilty'.

As Holt had predicted, Lowick's trial was no more than a morning's work, even though the defence spent some time trying once more to get the indictment quashed; but after much discussion it was pronounced fit to stand by the bench, and the trial proceeded. Porter for once did not appear, the first crown witness being George Harris, who was clearly out to save his own neck and gain the reward by implicating Lowick as far as he could. He made a particularly damaging statement to the effect that the accused, as well as Rookwood and Bernardi, had agreed albeit reluctantly to take part in the murder when they all met in Red Lion Fields on 14 February. Since there is no mention in Harris's original deposition of either Bernardi or Lowick being present on this occasion, or any other evidence that

Lowick knew of the real purpose of the conspiracy, Harris's statement was probably false. Certainly the allegation was strongly denied by the prisoner himself and by Thomas Bertram, the next witness, who was evidently torn between the need to save himself and a desire to exculpate his friend and benefactor if he could. All that Lowick had told him about the plan, said Bertram, was that 'they were to ride out very suddenly, and he believed the king was to be seized in his coach'. It was Charnock who told him, some time later, that they were to kill the king. More than that he could not say, since his wife had prevented him from taking any further part in the enterprise. He denied that the guinea given him by Lowick 'to buy necessaries' was for the purchase of boots or the hire of horses. He had been, 'never very plentiful of money of late', and Lowick had often helped him and his wife with small gifts of money or clothes. Asked by Shower to say what kind of man the prisoner was, Bertram said that he had known him for twenty years and had never known him do a rash or malicious thing: 'he has had the best character of all mankind . . . and was always ready to serve any man in his necessities'. Bertram was doing his best to save his friend, but his evasive answers to further cross-questioning soon made it apparent to the court that Lowick had in fact been quite deeply involved in the conspiracy, even though he was not a party to the proposed murder. The last witness was Captain Fisher, but since he had not seen the accused since 8 February when no mention had been made of an attack upon the king, Holt ruled out his evidence as immaterial.

The defence argued that there was not conclusive evidence of an overt act of treachery, since only Harris had said that the accused had known of, or intended to take part in, the attempted murder. Moreover, Shower maintained, it was surely inconceivable that a man of Lowick's exemplary life and peaceable disposition would participate in so wicked a scheme: he then produced two very voluble ladies to testify to his character. The first, Mrs Yorke, with whom Lowick had lodged for some years, concluded a long eulogy by saying that 'He was the most obliging man that ever lay in my house. He was so civil to all the lodgers, that they admired him for his goodness, and made them all in love with him.' The second lady, Mrs Mosely, spoke in equally enthusiastic terms, describing the prisoner as 'a peaceable, virtuous and honest man', while even Harris said that he was 'a man of honour'. But unfortunately for the prisoner these encomiums did nothing to prove his innocence. On the evidence of Harris, supported by the less certain testimony of Bertram, the jury found him guilty of high treason.

Ambrose Rookwood, Charles Cranburne and Robert Lowick were executed at Tyburn on 29 April 1696. The sentence was carried out in full. Cranburne left no written statement, or if he did it has been lost. Rookwood and Lowick both delivered their papers to the Sheriff immediately before they died. For the most part their last statements follow the same lines, and so it is not necessary to reproduce them in full. Both the condemned men begin by declaring their catholic faith and commending their souls to God. Next, they solemnly declare that they had never seen or heard of any commission from King James authorising the assassination and both are emphatic that no one who knew him would believe that he, 'the best of kings', would ever have sanctioned it. Rookwood adds that he knew for certain that James had often rejected such proposals in the past. Towards the end of the statements they assert their loyalty to the cause for which they are about to die: 'these twelve years', says Rookwood, 'have I served my true king and master, king James, and freely now lay down my life in his cause.' Lowick prays for the royal family: 'God preserve the king, queen, prince and princess, and all the royal blood of Stuarts; and may England never want one of that direct line to govern them, and make them once more happy!'

Where the statements differ is in the two men's attitude towards their sentences. Rookwood admits that he took part in the plot, but against his better judgement and only in obedience to orders. He claims that as a soldier he had no choice but to carry them out, and 'if it be a guilt to have complied with what I thought, and still think, to have been my duty, I am guilty. No other guilt do I own.' Finally, he forgives his judges and all who had a hand in condemning him, even the Prince of Orange, but thinks that as a soldier he 'ought to have considered of my case before he signed the warrant for my death'. Lowick, on the other hand, denies that he was ever 'concerned in any bloody affair', or that he ever went to any meetings where this was discussed. He could never, he says with every appearance of sincerity, have killed 'the meanest creature on earth', however much it might be to his own or his king's advantage to do so, 'because against the law of God'. He does, however, admit that he knew that James was coming and if he had had a horse he would have ridden to join him when he landed in England.

One cannot but feel that it was Lowick, rather than Rookwood, who was the more deserving of royal clemency, for the apparent sincerity of his denials and the comparatively thin evidence against him make it very doubtful that he was guilty to the same extent as Rookwood, if indeed he was guilty of anything except the intention to join King James if he could. It is significant that Lowick, alone among the condemned men, maintained to the end that he was innocent, and it is hard to believe that so devout and honourable a man would not have spoken the truth before he died. But given the current state of feeling against the Jacobites, it was surely inevitable that the unfortunate Lowick would suffer the greatest penalty for a lesser crime.

Rookwood's claim that William, 'as a soldier', should not have signed his death warrant seems a little unjustified. After all, he had on his own admission acted both against the rules of warfare and his own conscience; he could hardly complain if he were treated, not as a prisoner of war, but as a traitor to his country. But if his guilt is unquestionable, so too is Rookwood's courage and devotion to the cause for which he and Lowick died. With their deaths King James lost two of his most faithful servants.

It was in a way unfortunate for the advocates of legal reform that the outcome of these trials was no different from that of the preceding ones, and that skilled counsel could do no better for their clients than the defendants without their help had done for themselves. But in the prevailing climate of opinion there was in fact little chance of an acquittal, and the evidence, at least against Rookwood and Cranburne, was fairly well proven; to have given even Lowick the benefit of the doubt was in the circumstances too much to hope for from a seventeenth-century jury. Fear of invasion and anti-Jacobite fervour were still at fever pitch, and so there must inevitably have been some bias in the court against the prisoners. Even Sir John Holt, although as always he did his duty by the accused, was not immune to the general feelings of outrage and alarm aroused by their crimes. He gave rein to them when, before pronouncing sentence, he addressed the condemned men in what were for him unusually severe terms:

Your being engaged in such a horrid design against so precious a life . . . renders you worthy to undergo a greater and more severe punishment than by the law of England can be inflicted.

But those who framed that law, he went on,

never imagined that England could produce such degenerate wretches, as would by plots and contrivances endeavour to betray their country to a foreign yoke, and their fellow-subjects to the slavish dominion of strangers.

At the end of this diatribe, however, Holt's natural kindliness re-asserts itself:

yet I have that compassion for your persons, that I wish heartily you would make use of that opportunity that is now put into your hands to repent. And since you are adjudged by the law unworthy to live here, that you will make preparation to appear at another tribunal.

Clearly, neither Holt nor anyone else thought that this was a case where justice could, or should, be tempered with mercy.

Whether the involved legal arguments about the proper interpretation of the new Treasons Act put forward by the defence were sound is debatable, but certainly the bench heard them with patience and impartiality, and finally rejected them. A study of the trials of Rookwood, Cranburne and Lowick cannot fail to give the impression that Shower and Phipps fought hard for their clients, and that though they lost their case, defence and prosecution were for the first time fairly matched.

16
Final payments

Rookwood, CRANBURNE AND LOWICK were the last to pay with their lives for having taken part in the Assassination Plot. Two more men, Alexander Knightley and Peter Cook, were tried at the Old Bailey but neither of them ended at Tyburn. Knightley had been heavily involved in the conspiracy and was one of the three men sent out by Barkley to look for a suitable place to ambush King William's coach; he was also to have been one of the attacking party.

Knightley was brought to the Old Bailey for trial on 30 April.[1] Like many of the prisoners he had suffered in health during his confinement in Newgate. He told the court that he had been too ill to make any arrangements for his defence, and for this reason had hoped that his trial would be delayed until he had recovered. 'I did not expect, in this weak condition I am in, to be brought before the bar', he protested. But Holt, who had had a medical report on Knightley which declared him to be well enough to appear, ordered that the trial should proceed. The prisoner, after some more protests that he was too ill to be tried, pleaded 'Not Guilty'. However, it must have become apparent that he was not feigning sick and was really in no condition to stand trial for Holt, after some discussion with his fellow judges, considerately postponed the trial for a fortnight.

The delay, besides giving Knightley time to recover his health, also gave him time to reflect upon the hopelessness of his case. When he next appeared before the court on 20 May he had changed his plea to 'Guilty'. With fulsome expressions of repentance he read out a detailed confession and threw himself on the mercy of the king:

I expect to receive from your lordship the Sentence due upon conviction, from my own mouth, of a crime for which I cannot in modesty hope (for) . . . the king's most gracious pardon; yet the greatness of my offence does not rob me of all thoughts of mercy whilst I throw myself absolutely and entirely at his majesty's feet for it.

Knightley knew that the court would have to sentence him to death.

Holt was not over-encouraging about his hopes of a royal pardon, and evidently took a rather cynical view of the prisoner's assurances of repentance:

I wish out of charity to your person, it was as sincere as (I think it) was prudent in you . . . If your confession be a real effect of your repentance, you will reap the advantage of it in the next world; but what consequence it will have in this I cannot say, 'for the heart of a king is in the hands of the Almighty, which, as the rivers of water, he turneth whithersoever he will.' Live, therefore, in expectation of a speedy death, and prepare yourself to appear before another judgement seat.

After this grim homily Holt pronounced the sentence and Knightley was taken back to Newgate. Happily for him, the Almighty turned the heart of the king in the direction of mercy; William in any case was never vindictive and was far too wise to make a martyr out of this insignificant and apparently repentant sinner; Knightley in due course received a royal pardon.

Peter Cook was tried on 13 May.[2] He was a very minor conspirator and was not accused of having taken part in the Assassination Plot, but was charged with conspiring to assist the king's enemies at home and abroad. His importance to the authorities lay in his connections rather than in his having played a very active part in the conspiracy. Cook had been a hanger-on of Sir John Fenwick and other prominent Jacobites, and it was therefore suspected that he might have valuable information which would enable them to entrap far bigger game than this foolish young man. The only substantial charge against Cook was that he had been present at the two meetings at the 'King's Head' and Mrs Mountjoy's tavern in the summer of 1694, when he had joined with the rest of those present in sending Charnock to France with messages for King James; he had also, along with the rest, pledged himself to raise 2000 Horse to assist King James when he landed in England. There was little other evidence against him and indeed it is questionable whether he had much clear remembrance of those two meetings, especially the one at Mrs Mountjoy's. On that occasion, when the rest of the conspirators stood up to drink a solemn pledge to their enterprise it may be remembered that poor Peter was so drunk that he had to join in the toast kneeling on his chair with his elbows on the table. Apart from his general brainlessness, Cook would have been a dangerous recruit in so secret an affair; his father, Sir Miles Cook, Master in Chancery and a staunch Whig, might easily have got wind of his son's activities, and would have promptly informed the authorities. Cook was never mentioned as having been present at any of the later meetings.

Since his arrest in mid-March Peter Cook had been several times brought before the Privy Council for interrogation. He was no hero and as Ailesbury says, 'the poor creature was in such apprehension of dying that his weak head soon turned round, and he offered to discover whatever they desired, although in reality he knew nothing of moment'.[3] Repeated questioning of Cook both before and after his trial added little or nothing to the evidence already obtained from Porter and other witnesses. Porter and Goodman were the chief witnesses against him. He was found guilty and sentenced to death, but partly through the intercession of his father, who could not quite abandon him although he had already disowned him, he was reprieved and sent back to Newgate. A more important reason for the reprieve was that it was still hoped to get more information out of him. From the day of his trial until his final pardon in November 1696, the Privy Council played cat-and-mouse with this wretched young man.

On 5 June the Council directed that 'Peter Cook be acquainted that he must not expect a further reprieve unless he can make more satisfactory discoveries'.[4] Two days later Cook produced another repetitive and useless 'confession', but this was so unsatisfactory that the Privy Council ordered a Mr Baker to go and take a statement from the prisoner, 'that it may be seen whether he intends to deal sincerely, or will send anything that may be fit to lay before the king'.[5] Baker's report indicates that there was little sense to be got out of Cook, for his 'weak head' was by now turning round at an alarming rate:

I cannot say that he now deals disingenuously, for however he trifled at the beginning, he seems now so concerned for preserving himself as to cast off any considerations for anybody besides. He appears very defective in his judgement and can't well distinguish what is material and what is not. One may see he abounds with impertinences, which lying uppermost in his mind, crowd out first.[6]

After this interview Cook was granted a further reprieve until 1 July. On 30 July the Council even debated whether he should be pardoned, but instead reprieved him again until 6 November. On 15 September, however, Cook having expressed 'great willingness to serve the government', his pardon was again discussed but on 24 September, 'their excellencies did not think the pardon should proceed'.[7] At last, in mid-November, their excellencies decided that the sponge had been squeezed dry. Peter Cook received a royal pardon but was sentenced to perpetual banishment.

At first sight it is difficult to account for the Privy Council's persistence with this useless creature, but they had in fact very good reason for putting so much pressure upon him. They desperately needed evidence against Sir John Fenwick: that of Cook, had he known anything of moment, could have been crucial. The period between Cook's first reprieve and his final pardon coincides almost exactly with that between the arrest of Fenwick and his appearance at the Bar of the House of Commons. It was not therefore until the Privy Council were finally convinced that Cook would be useless as a witness against Fenwick that they finally let him go. Fenwick was never proved to have taken part in the Assassination Plot, and in fact was not seriously accused of having done so, but there is no doubt that he had taken part in the plans for the insurrection and it was of great importance to the government that he be brought to book. His trial is famous in the annals of British constitutional history, because he was the last man to be condemned to death by parliamentary Bill of Attainder. The proceedings which ended in his execution were immensely complex and protracted; a brief summary of them is given here as the interest and importance of Fenwick's trial are such that it cannot be omitted. It was also the last public appearance of one of the chief characters in this story, George Porter.

When the plot was discovered and the hue and cry went up for the conspirators Sir John went into hiding. From his place of concealment he followed the trials of those who had been arrested, and after the trial of Peter Cook he realised that if he were arrested the only two dangerous witnesses against himself would be George Porter and Cardell Goodman. If one of these two were eliminated he could not be brought to trial, for no one could be condemned on the testimony of one witness only. Goodman was still inaccessible in Newgate, but Porter had been enjoying full liberty for some time, so Fenwick's only hope was to try to get rid of Porter. Through the agency of his wife, Lady Mary Fenwick, he planned to bribe Porter to leave the country. The bribe would have to be a substantial one if it were to induce Porter to forgo the already considerable rewards he was reaping for his services to the government and the Fenwicks, though well-connected, were not rich. Since Lady Fenwick was unable to raise a sufficient sum herself she enlisted the help of the families of the Earl of Ailesbury and Viscount Montgomery. Ailesbury was by this time in the Tower and Montgomery was a fugitive, so both families had reason to fear the testimony of Porter, which had already brought eight men to their deaths. Help, then, was quickly forthcoming, each of the three parties putting up an equal share of the money. Porter was to be offered 300 guineas down, another 300 guineas on landing in France and an annuity of 300 guineas for life. In addition he was to be given a letter, purporting to be an amnesty from King James, which would protect him from the wrath of the Jacobites in France.

Lady Fenwick and her friends might have saved their money, for Porter predictably ran true to form. He knew in any case that no amnesty from King James would protect him from the vengeance of the Jacobites whose friends he had betrayed. With expressions of contrition for the part that he averred he had been forced to play in the trials, he pretended to accept the offer. A meeting was arranged with Lady Mary Fenwick's agent Clancy, a barber, at the Dog Tavern where Porter would be given his first instalment, the letter containing the amnesty, and his instructions for the journey to France. As soon as he knew the time and place of the meeting Porter informed the Secretary of State's office of what was afoot, and arranged for a posse of King's Messengers to be concealed in readiness at the 'Dog'. The meeting took place as arranged. At the appointed time Porter and Clancy repaired to an upper room in the tavern, where the unsuspecting barber counted out the money. First pocketing the guineas, Porter gave a pre-arranged signal, the Messengers rushed in, arrested the unfortunate Clancy and carried him off to Newgate. He was later tried and pilloried for his offence.[8] It should be added that Porter was not the only deceiver in this affair. When he took the letter purporting to contain King James's amnesty round to the Secretary of State's office it was opened and found to contain a blank sheet of paper.[9]

The failure of the attempt to bribe Porter left Sir John in a more dangerous position than ever. His name was in several of the proclamations offerings £1000 reward for the capture of the traitors and it was not possible that he could remain for ever in hiding. He decided that the time had come for him to fly the country and take refuge at Saint-Germain. Disguised in a black periwig and false eyebrows he made for the coast of Kent, hoping no doubt to cross the Channel with the aid of Hunt the smuggler. He got as far as New Romney, where a friend and sympathiser took him into his house for the night. But he had been detected in spite of his disguise by an informer, and was arrested in bed in his friend's house on the morning of 10 June;[10] he was escorted back to London by the Messengers and sent to join Ailesbury in the Tower.

Sir John Fenwick was generally reckoned to be 'a fearful [timorous] man', and so there was a strong possibility that he would try to save himself by informing on those of his associates as had so far escaped arrest. But Sir John, if not exactly heroic, was of a different stamp from George Porter. He would save himself if he could, but not at the expense of his friends and fellow-conspirators, particularly Ailesbury and Montgomery. He did indeed volunteer information, but to the disappointment and anger of the government none of it concerned his immediate associates in the conspiracy. Instead, after much procrastination and many promises of startling revelations to come, he made vague and unsubstantiated allegations of treachery on the part of a number of persons now high in King William's government. Prominent among these were Shrewsbury, Godolphin, Marlborough and Admiral Russell. Insofar as all these gentlemen had been in contact with Saint-Germain in 1692–3 there was enough truth in Fenwick's allegations to cause them all some disquiet, even though there was no evidence that they had had any dealings with King James since then. Shrewsbury especially was so much affected by anxiety that his always precarious health, made worse by a recent riding accident, broke down completely and he was unable for some time to carry out his duties as Secretary of State. However, since the persons named by Fenwick had been for some time trusted members of the government, his accusations did not stick and were contemptuously dismissed by King William as stratagems to delay the trial. And in this Fenwick was for some time successful, for it was September before a date could be fixed for it.

But now another and more serious obstacle arose to delay Sir John's trial. Goodman, after making a full confession of his own and Fenwick's part in the conspiracy, was released on bail on 10 June.[11] Shortly afterwards Lady Mary Fenwick and her agents approached him with the same offer they had made to Porter, and this time with more success. Goodman was not so double-dyed a villain as Porter and was besides probably in need of money, since the Duchess of Cleveland had at last dismissed him from her service. Moreover rumour had it that the proposition was made at the point of a knife, a form of persuasion that he would be unlikely to resist. Goodman accepted a handsome down-payment and a life pension, and was secretly conveyed to France. Fenwick's friends were determined that he should not have the chance to double-cross them by slipping back to England to give evidence; almost as soon as he arrived in France Goodman found himself imprisoned on a trumped-up charge; how long he remained a prisoner is not known, but he was reported in December 1698 to be incarcerated at 'Exilbe' (a possible mis-spelling of Aix-les-Bains).[12] He died of a fever in France in the following year.

The disappearance of Goodman put the government in a serious dilemma, for since there remained only Porter as witness for the prosecution Fenwick could not now be tried in the ordinary courts. Goodman, it is true, had left written depositions in Newgate, but under the terms of the Treasons Act these could not be used in evidence without the actual presence of the deponent. And it was essential that Sir John's accusations of treachery in high places be refuted without delay. The contents of his 'confessions' had not been made public, and consequently there was much anxious speculation and in some quarters eager anticipation as to who had been named in them. It was a dangerous situation, for if Sir John, in spite of William's professed disbelief, had been able to prove his allegations it could have meant the political ruin of some of the most prominent and able leaders of the government. And the undoubted fact that several of the persons thought to have been named had consciences not entirely clear of past dalliance with Saint-Germain naturally increased the atmosphere of tension and anxiety. Since an ordinary trial was now impossible, the only means of calling Sir John to account was by a parliamentary Bill of Attainder, that is, trial by both Houses of Parliament. In such trials the two-witness rule did not apply and written depositions could, in certain circumstances, be accepted as evidence.

The government's proposal to resort to this ancient procedure aroused much controversy. It was not primarily a party issue, although the Whigs were in the main in favour of it; but there were many among both parties who opposed it on grounds of principle. Those against the Bill protested at its injustice and doubtful legality. That same parliament, they pointed out, had only recently passed a law to ensure that treason trials were more fairly conducted. It was now proposing to evade that law, thereby setting a precedent that could threaten the life and liberty of every Englishman, and the protection from injustice so hardly won would be swept away 'as by a torrent, and no man would be safe'.[13] The main argument for the Bill was that when the safety of the whole realm was threatened parliament, and not the courts, must be paramount. Parliament made the laws for the protection of the country, and as the supreme legislator it had power to administer them if circumstances arose whereby the courts were unable to do so. Such circumstances had now arisen, and parliament would be failing in its duty if it did not use its powers to protect the nation from traitors.

Sir John's delaying tactics and the difficulties caused by the disappearance of Goodman had occupied much time, and it was not until 6 November that he made his first appearance at the Bar of the House of Commons.[14] This was a preliminary hearing to extract from him some factual confirmation of his previous statements. But Sir John was either unwilling or more probably unable to substantiate his charges, and the Commons after several such interrogations, voted them 'false and scandalous'. The fear of what might have become a major witch-hunt was thus removed, and the way was clear for the House to proceed to try the prisoner for high treason.

The trial proper began on 25 November. Sir Bartholomew Shower was chief counsel for the defence and Porter, inevitably, was the principal witness against the accused. Shower, on the grounds that Goodman was not a reliable witness, managed to get his written testimonies disallowed. Most of the evidence was concerned with the two fateful meetings of June 1694 and with Fenwick's part in the plans made at that time to bring back James with French help. There was no real evidence that he had taken part in the scheme to assassinate King William. The hearing of the evidence against Fenwick took up a very small proportion of the proceedings. The debates that followed were some of the longest and most heated of the century, and during them it became clear that the question of his guilt or innocence was of small importance to anyone except himself: the real point at issue was the legality of the Bill of Attainder. As one Member put it: 'Though Sir John is a great offender, yet I think his case is not so extraordinary. I do take his living or dying not to be of that consequence as this bill of attainder.'

So day after day, and often far into the night, the debate raged on over the head, in more senses than one, of the prisoner at the Bar. It was not until 25 November that the Commons finally passed the Bill by a small majority of thirty-three. The Lords, in spite of a well-organised and determined opposition, passed it by an even smaller majority of seven. The full sentence for high treason was pronounced, but in view of Sir John's social standing this was later commuted to beheading.

Sir John made a last futile effort to avert his fate by offering to make yet another 'confession', but this turned out to be only a repetition of his earlier vague statements, and it availed him nothing. William signed the death warrant on 11 January 1697, and on 28 January Sir John Fenwick was beheaded on Tower Hill. 'He died very composed', said Burnet, 'and in a much better temper than was to be expected, for his life had been very irregular.'[15] As was customary, he handed his last statement to the Sheriff before he died. In it he declared that he had 'ever endeavoured . . . to the uttermost of my power to support the crown of England, in the true and lineal descent without interruption'. He denied that he had gone to the two meetings in 1695 with any intention of helping to bring about King James's restoration, and claimed that he had never taken any part in that or any later conspiracy. He thanked all those who had voted against the Bill of Attainder, and concluded with a heartfelt prayer for the restoration of King James.

It is generally and usually rightly believed that men speak the truth when they are about to die. Nevertheless, Fenwick's denials are not entirely convincing. How far he was involved in the whole conspiracy will probably never be known. According to Goodman, he had accepted the leadership of the would-be rebels in 1694, but after the arrival of Barkley in London there is little mention of Fenwick in connection with plans for the rising in 1696 and nothing to show that he was to have had any part in the proposed attack on King William. On balance, it seems likely that he had taken part in subversive activities but perhaps not so much as his judges were led to believe. Fenwick had after all been an active opponent of William since the Revolution, and his personal animosity towards both William and Mary was well known. Some indication of his guilt comes from his own last statement, for if he was prepared to support James to 'the uttermost of his power' it is reasonable to suppose that he would do so when what appeared to be a favourable opportunity arose. And cleverer men than Fenwick had been deluded by over-optimistic estimates of the chances of success in 1696. In spite of his protestations of innocence, then, it is probable that he was not unjustly condemned, even if the means to bring him to justice were of doubtful legality.

Sir John Fenwick was the last man to be condemned to death by parliamentary Bill of Attainder. He was also the last man to be executed for his part in the conspiracy. Newgate was still full of persons who had been arrested on suspicion when news of the plot first broke out, but most of these had been discharged by May 1696. A further batch was set free when the Habeas Corpus Act came into force again in October 1696. After that only six men, all of them named in the proclamations, remained in Newgate. They were John Bernardi, who had been arrested with Rookwood; Blackburn, Counter, Cassells, Meldrum and Chambers.[16] All six applied under Habeas Corpus for their cases to be heard, or for release on bail. But the court had been severely castigated at Fenwick's trial for having prematurely released Goodman on bail, thereby making it possible for him to be spirited out of the country. The government was determined that this mistake should not be repeated. The court therefore adjourned the prisoners' hearing for two weeks, thus giving parliament time to pass an act confining them for a further twelve months. The Act was renewed each year until 1702, when several influential persons petitioned King William to suspend it and allow the prisoners' case to come to court. William was giving the matter favourable consideration, but died before the order could be signed. There were some stirrings in the Jacobite camp at the accession of Queen Anne, which was probably why the six prisoners were still kept under lock and key by means of yet another Act of Parliament. Queen Anne did, however, release Counter shortly afterwards, but petitions on behalf of the remaining five were ignored.

After the death of Queen Anne in 1714 fresh efforts were made to get the case heard, but probably because of the Jacobite rising of 1715, these met with no success. Yet another Act was passed confining the five men to Newgate during the pleasure of Anne's successor, George I. At some time during his reign, Meldrum and Chambers died, probably of old age, leaving as survivors Bernardi, Blackburn and Cassells. By the accession of George II in 1727 these three had been imprisoned in Newgate for thirty-one years without trial. They sent a pathetic petition to the new king asserting their innocence of the villainous crimes laid to their charge so long ago, and pointing out that they were now reduced to 'extreme miseries . . . in a melancholy, dismal and loathsome gaol, and by their great age, poverty and infirmity'. The government's response was to pass yet another Act continuing their imprisonment. Soon after this death released Blackburn and Cassells, leaving Bernardi as the solitary survivor of these forgotten men. Bernardi had long ago spent what money he had in trying to get himself and his fellows released. The friends who had helped him were all dead and he himself was poor, aged and ailing, and could not possibly have been thought a danger to the community. His long captivity, however, had some alleviations. He was not latterly confined in chains in a cell. He had chambers in the Press Yard, among the lesser prisoners, where he would have the freedom of the prison, such as it was; he could also occasionally go out under the supervision of a keeper. In 1712 Bernardi actually re-married in Newgate. His wife, Abigail, described by him as 'a true helpmeet', bore him no fewer than ten children. Surprisingly, if they were reared in the fetid atmosphere of Newgate, all these children survived to be both a blessing and a financial burden to their father.

In order to raise money to feed his family and to enlist some public sympathy for his plight, Bernardi in 1728 published a short autobiography. Much of this is concerned with a detailed account of the various efforts made over the years to set him free. It is a sad story, for poor Bernardi seemed fated throughout his long life to be dogged by misfortune. At the end of his book he laments the fact that he lived so long. 'Death, when all other friends fail, is most certainly a kind friend and deliverer.' He tells the reader that he has outlived all those who formerly contributed to the support of himself and his family, and that now they are almost at starvation point; and because he is a prisoner, there is no way in which he can make new friends to help him, 'unless this little book may perchance make him some friends among the good-natured, generous and charitable part of mankind'.[17] It is not recorded whether the charitable part of mankind were moved to help Bernardi. They were certainly not able to procure his release, in spite of a fresh and moving petition to Queen Adelaide from Mrs Abigail Bernardi. He died in Newgate in September 1736. He was eighty-one years old and had been a prisoner for more than forty years.

There could have been no real justification for denying these men the right to a trial and for keeping them for the rest of their lives in prison. It is true that during the period immediately following the discovery of the plot it would have been unwise to let them go; more evidence might have come to light against them, or they might have been needed as witnesses. But as time went on and monarch succeeded monarch in undisturbed occupation of the throne, the possibility that these ageing men might constitute a threat to public security became increasingly remote. Constant watchfulness was of course necessary as long as supporters of the Stuarts were capable of stirring up malcontents and threatening the peace of the realm. This necessity may have been one reason why the suspects were kept for so long under lock and key. But as age and infirmity crept upon the prisoners in Newgate, whatever capacity they might once have had for mischief diminished to vanishing point, and so too did the government's justification for keeping them in prison. Why then were they never released? One likely answer is that by the time the years of immediate danger were over there was nobody left to take up their cause. Without money or influence they had little hope of arousing interest in their plight. And since Jacobitism remained a live issue throughout their imprisonment it would not have been politically advantageous for anyone to do so, for to appear as the champion of Jacobites was to risk being tarred with the Jacobite brush. So no one was ever altruistic or interested enough to espouse so unrewarding a cause.

William III's successive parliaments brought in a number of overdue legal reforms, all tending to the better protection of the lives and liberties of his subjects. Of these the new Treason Act was perhaps the most effective. There was, particularly from the bench in 1696, a good deal of somewhat smug self-congratulation on the improvement of the administration of justice, and this was not altogether unjustified; trials for treason, by comparison with the past, were much fairer. But for all that the system was far from ideal and it was still too easy for the politicians to circumvent the excellent intentions of the legislators, as in the case of Sir John Fenwick. But at least injustice was seen here to have been done, and so shocked the national conscience that never again would a man be condemned to death by a Bill of Attainder. No such public furore was aroused by the injustice suffered by the helpless prisoners in Newgate. Denied both justice and mercy, their lot was in many ways the hardest of all.

The fate of Bernardi and his fellow-prisoners is a melancholy postscript to the story of the Assassination Plot. Those whose information had led to its discovery were duly rewarded by the government. Prendergrass, who had triggered off the unmasking of the whole conspiracy, received a grant of £2000 'as royal bounty . . . in consideration of good and faithful service in discovering the wicked conspiracy to assasinate [sic] our royal person'.[18] King William was so impressed with the integrity of Prendergrass that he later took him into his service, giving him a commission in the army. Prendergrass was killed at the battle of Malplaquet in 1709. A strange tale was afterwards told about his death. On the morning of the battle he told a fellow-officer that on the previous night he had dreamt of Sir John Friend, and was convinced that this dream portended his own death on that very day. But he was still alive at the end of the day and a friend who was standing beside him remarked that the dream must have been a false presage. No sooner had he spoken than one of the last shots in the battle laid Prendergrass dead at his feet.[19]

De La Rue and Harris both received a grant of £50, free lodgings in Whitehall and a pension.[20] The grant may well have fallen short of Harris's expectations, for besides being responsible for the arrest of Rookwood and Bernardi he had given much valuable information about the activities of Hunt the smuggler. It is possible that some of the Jacobites later attempted vengeance upon De La Rue, for Luttrell records that on the night of 29 December 1696 he was attacked, seriously wounded and left for dead; he eventually recovered.[21] He was not, however, to enjoy his weekly pension for much longer, for a Treasury minute dated 18 June 1700, states that 'It is the King's pleasure that the weekly sum which you now pay to M. De La Rue should now cease.'[22]

Porter, who had been of the greatest value to the government, received the highest reward. The king granted him a pension and a free house to the total value of £400 per annum. William also kept the other part of the bargain that Porter had made when he turned King's evidence and paid his debts, which amounted to over £1700.[23] Porter was thus freed from the fear of ending his days in a debtors' prison, but he lived as he had always done as an outcast from respectable society. His unsavoury reputation was enough to cause him to be ostracised, but it was his callous betrayal of his servant Keyes that was thought most shocking, as this piece of anonymous doggerel testifies:

> When God to punish Adam's sons inclined
> From fire and brimstone Judas saved Mankind:
> And P(orter) by a Pious treachery
> Preserv'd his King and set his Country free.
> Both did in a different sphere treppan,
> The one hang'd his Master, the other his Man.
> If for this deed P(orter)'s so highly priz'd,
> By God I'le have Iscariot Cannoniz'd.[24]

If Porter expected social as well as monetary reward for his services he was to be disappointed. One day in July 1696, at the fashionable Mary Bone bowling-green, he accosted Paul Foley, the one-time Speaker of the House of Commons:

Porter: 'Sir, I believe I once had the honour to bowl with you.'
Foley: 'Sir, I am glad it has not been of late.'[25]

No doubt Porter received a good many more snubs of this kind, but they appear to have had little effect on his thick skin. He remained in London for several years, living on the proceeds of his treachery; but it seems that his pension soon became inadequate to support his extravagance, for by January 1700 he was again heavily in debt and in daily fear of being apprehended by his creditors. He wrote a long begging-letter to Lord Jersey at that time, asking him to remind the king of his past services and of the royal promise that, if he served His Majesty faithfully, he would be 'taken care of'. Porter claimed that on this understanding he had been so zealous in the king's service that he had even sacrificed his only source of income, the small annuity that he had bought from Ailesbury, and this, he had the effrontery to say, was why he was now in such straits. The letter concludes:

Now I beg you will lay my circumstances before His Majesty, which are so bad that I expect daily to have my person and goods seized, and that except he order me some relief I shall be the miserablest man alive, for I must be a prisoner during life, and be the jest of those that are my enemies only because I have served the government. I beg you will move His Majesty to order me £1000, which will make the life he has given me easy.[26]

Porter had already been well rewarded for his services, as he admits himself. This is corroborated by a Treasury Account for the period 24 November 1696 to 29 September 1697, which shows that Porter, Harris, De La Rue and several others had been paid sums amounting to £1647 12s. 6d. for their pensions, household expenses and payment of their debts.[27] There is no record of any later payments to Porter, so it would appear that William had turned a deaf ear to his appeal for another £1000. At some time after this Porter went to France, probably to escape his creditors. He died there in 1724.

Apart from Sir John Friend, who was a childless widower, Sir William Parkyns was the only man among those executed at Tyburn who could be described as a man of property. His considerable estate was sequestered to the crown after his condemnation and this left his unfortunate widow and younger children entirely without means of support. In December 1696 Lady Parkyns appealed to the king:

setting forth that her husband by his ill usage forces her to levy fines on her own estate jointures, and she was always very well affected to his majesty and his government, and is left with severall small children without any provision for their support, and therefore prays ye small remainder of her husband's estate for the relief of her and her children.

William, perhaps influenced by Suzanna's claim that she had always been 'very well affected' towards him, responded kindly to this plea for help. A note attached to the petition records that 'His Majestie having been moved upon this petition is generously pleased to refer ye same to ye Right Honourable the Lords and Commissioners of his treasury, to consider thereof and report what may fitly be done for the petitioner's relief.'[28]

Acting on the advice of the Treasury, His Majesty granted Lady Parkyns the estate of Leicester Grange in Leicestershire, which had been one of her late husband's larger properties. She sold it to her son Blackwell in the following year,[29] and in March 1701 was again negotiating with the Treasury, this time for the return of the Bushey estate. This had been in the possession of the Blackwell family for several generations and had been Suzanna's own inheritance through her cousin Richard Blackwell. Although in law the estate had become the property of her husband on Suzanna's marriage she had, in equity, some claim to it. Possibly influenced by this consideration, and also by the fact that the Blackwell family had never been supporters of the Stuarts the Treasury, after prolonged deliberation, and on condition that she paid off certain debts and charges amounting to £700, granted Lady Parkyns the Bushey Manor estate in March 1701.[30]

Thus Sir William Parkyns's widow and her younger children were able to live in peace and relative posperity in their home at Bushey Manor. It is pleasant to record that the king did not visit the sins of a convicted traitor on his innocent family.

The conspirators who had escaped to France lay low for a while, but two years later they were back at Saint-Germain and, incredible as it may seem, were still in hopes of persuading Louis and the French to support another attempt to restore King James. The poet and diplomatist Matthew Prior, who in 1698 was Secretary to the English Embassy in Paris, reports that in April of that year:

Our friends at St. Germain are in great hopes (God knows upon what these hopes are founded) of seeing better days yet: they count upon a great many friends in England, and are satisfied that, our armies broke [disbanded], we shall not be in a condition of resisting such a body of men as they are sure the king of France will send them to land upon us. The Middletonians and the Melfordians, who are the Whigs and Tories, fall out every day . . . All the nest of rogues are here, Barkelay, Parker, Bryerly, Birkinhead, they threaten nothing but blood and slaughter.[31]

Prior was a great admirer of King William, and his account of life at Saint-Germain was no doubt biased. But even allowing for some distortion, there must have been a good deal of truth in it. It is a sorry picture of quarrels, frustration and dreams clung to in the face of impossibility. Barkley, Parker and their confederates were courageous and clever men who, had they not been dedicated to a hopeless cause, might have been successful and prosperous. Small wonder then that they compensated for failure and poverty with dreams of 'blood and slaughter'. They were the first of several generations of Jacobites, and they had had their day. By the time Jacobitism became once more a serious menace, the few surviving conspirators of 1696 were forgotten men.

The eddy that the Assassination Plot caused in the tide of history soon died away, and the King's Messengers went out in pursuit of other evil-doers. Some of these, inevitably, were Jacobites, for they were to be an intermittent threat to public order for the next half-century; but by the time of the next major Jacobite rising in 1715 the Assassination Plot had become a distant memory. None the less, it was not without its effect on the events of subsequent years. In the more immediate future, the plot affected the course of the war, which had not been going too well for the French. The enforced withdrawal of Admiral Rooke's fleet from the Mediterranean resulted in the Allies losing command of the sea in that area, while their armies were seriously weakened by the withdrawal of twenty battalions of English troops from Flanders, who had to be recalled to combat the threat of invasion and rebellion at home. Thus the Allies lost the initiative they had enjoyed since the capture of Namur, and the war dragged on for another eighteen months.

Political life was also affected by the plot. Had it not been for the sudden upsurge of loyalty to the crown which followed its discovery, the unrest and distress caused mainly by the coinage crisis might well have escalated under Jacobite leadership into tumults and serious riots. But this danger was averted when public attention was concentrated on what appeared to be a greater threat from across the Channel and the government, which had fast been losing popular support, suddenly found itself riding a high tide of popularity. In parliament the Tories lost what ground they still held, and William's attempt to keep a balance between the two parties received a set-back from which it never recovered. Godolphin, the last Tory member of the ruling junta, resigned at the time of Fenwick's trial, and the election of 1698 returned an overwhelming Whig majority. In provincial government too the purge of Lord-Lieutenants and other local officials who had refused to subscribe to the Association tipped the balance markedly in favour of the Whigs; many a Tory landowner was ousted from office and replaced by a rich Whig merchant after 1696. The Tories indeed were in eclipse for some time after the plot because in the popular view, assiduously fostered by the Whigs, Tory was synonymous with Jacobite, and the stigma of king-killing clung to them for some time. The non-juring Church also received a severe set-back after the arraignment of Collier, Cook and Snatt for what was taken to be their condonation of the crime of high treason. The Whig triumph was complete, and King William had an all-powerful Whig government for the rest of his life. For the king personally the plot resulted in an improved relationship with his English subjects that he never entirely lost, but it also caused him some inconvenience, for from then on his guard was doubled and his hunting expeditions were far more closely supervised; an irritating necessity for a man who prized quiet and privacy.

For James the consequences were more serious. The failure of the conspiracy marked the end of his attempts to regain his crown. The rumour, reinforced by Whig propaganda, that he had condoned if not sanctioned so vile a crime as the assassination of his supplanter lost him many a sympathiser and did much harm to his cause. James, however, had by this time accepted that it was not the will of God that he should regain his throne. Any faint hopes he may still have had were finally extinguished when the Treaty of Rijswijk, signed in October 1697, at last brought the War of the League of Augsberg to an end. Under the terms of the treaty Louis XIV was bound to recognise William III as King of England; although Louis continued to treat James with unfailing affection and generosity, there could be no question now of jeopardising for his sake the peace so hardly won. James's last few years were devoted to his religion and his family, and he seems to have lived quite detached from the belligerent schemers who surrounded him. His health, hitherto vigorous, began to fail in the spring of 1701 and in October he died after a short illness. Louis visited him on his deathbed and tearfully promised to recognise the thirteen-year-old Prince of Wales as the rightful heir to the throne of England. It was an unpopular and impolitic gesture but a generous one, prompted by the desire to comfort a dying man, whose misfortunes Louis considered unmerited and whose piety he revered.

By 1700 King William's life too was drawing to a close. His health had for some time past been giving cause for concern, and his condition had deteriorated further during the spring of 1701. In July, however, he was well enough to pay what was to be his last visit to Holland, but he was intermittently unwell during his stay there, although he continued to work and to hunt when his health permitted. He returned to England in October in a state of near collapse, but rest and quiet at Hampton Court brought about some improvement during the winter. On the morning of 21 February 1702, William was well enough to ride in Hampton Court Park on Sorrel, his favourite horse. Sorrel stumbled over a molehill and threw his rider, who broke his collar-bone. William was carried home and at first made light of the mishap, which for some days did not seem serious. But complications set in, and he died on 8 March.

The king's death was the occasion for much rejoicing in Jacobite circles; many a toast was drunk in the taverns to 'the little gentleman in black velvet', the mole that had caused Sorrel's fatal stumble. A story soon became current among the Jacobites that Sorrel had formerly belonged to Sir John Fenwick. There is no evidence for this but the story is feasible, since Sir John's property had been sequestered to the crown after his execution. But whatever the truth of it, the idea that Sir John, through his horse, had avenged himself on the usurper appealed greatly to the more rabid Jacobites, and they made the most of it. Sorrel was celebrated in claret and bad Latin verse; he was even apostrophised as 'the Saviour of our race' and was promised eternal freedom in this world and the next. But if many of the Jacobites, obsessed by blind loyalty to James, lost no opportunity to vilify the dead king whom they regarded as an usurping foreign tyrant, there were others among them who took a less prejudiced view of his character. There is no tribute so well worth having as that which comes from an adversary, and no doubt William himself would have appreciated the magnanimity of the Duke of Berwick's epitaph: 'Whatever reason I may have not to be fond of the memory of this Prince, I cannot deny him the character of a great man, or even of a great King, had he not been an usurper.'[32]

William III has been described as 'the least appreciated king England ever had'.[33] Certainly his English subjects, though they learned to respect him, never accorded him the affection given to far less able but more colourful monarchs. He was sincerely mourned by those close to him, but his passing does not seem to have been the occasion for much public expression of grief. His burial, at midnight as was customary for great persons, was a hugger-mugger affair; no sooner had the funeral torches been doused than the bells rang out for Queen Anne. Tumultuous rejoicings greeted her accession; once more England had a monarch who was both English and a Stuart. This enthusiasm for Anne reflects both the xenophobia of the English and their emotional attachment to a dynasty that on the whole had done far less to justify it than had the little Dutchman whom they had never really known or appreciated.

Over the next half-century uncounted lives were laid down, on the battlefield and on the gallows, for the Stuart cause. The Pretenders, Old and Young, came, saw, and failed to conquer the heart and mind of Hanoverian England. It was not until James II's grandson, Cardinal Henry York, died in Rome in 1807 that the last faint flickers of Jacobitism were extinguished. George III contributed towards the cost of a monument to Cardinal York, who styled himself King Henry IX of England 'By the Grace of God but not by the will of man'. He is commemorated in Rome by a simple stone obelisk that looks lost among the cavernous splendours of St Peter's. It has a forlorn and foreign air, as if left there to await removal to some more suitable site; it would have dominated a country churchyard in England. But the will of man has ordained that there should be no memorial to the last of the Stuarts in the country where his forbears had ruled by the Grace of God.

Appendix 1

MR CHARNOCK'S LETTER TO A FRIEND, WRITTEN SHORTLY BEFORE HIS EXECUTION*

'Tho' the soule of man after death be probably as litle sensible of the censures of this world as the body is that lyes in the grave, for their it stands before an other sort of a Judge who weighs our actions, not by the lying ballances of men, but by the never-varying standard of his owne Lawes, which are Justice itself, yet in regard that every dying Christian seemes bound, as farre as truth will permitt, to remove scandall and leave a good name behind him, I have thought it a duty incumbent upon me to give a plain and trew account before I dy both of the fact for which I am to suffer, and of the reasons and motives inducing me to that undertaking; which since it cannot well be done as it ought to be in that short paper I intend to deliver to the Sherif at my execution, for reasons too obvious to be mentioned, I have chosen this way of doing it, in confidence of your freindship to me, and of your discretion, that you will not divulge what I now write to you but in a proper season, when the minds of men, grown more calme, shall be more susceptible of reason, and when it may be done without drawing more persecution upon thos honest men, who ly under the jealosy and suspition of the present governement.

'As to the matter of fact for which I stand condemn'd, nobody can give a better account of it then Mr. Porter himself, who was the chief promoter and directer of that enterprise as now he is the cheif witnes against the partye therein concernd, and I must owne that in his evidence at my Tryall all that he sayd against me was trew, saving only which sayes I told him that Sir George Barclay broght over a Commission to levy war upon the person of the P. of Orange: An expression of which the impropriety shews the falsity. It could never come out of the mouth of a soldier, nor enter into any Commission, but smells of the gown or the green bagg, of hints given to mend an Evedence and bring it to whot they would be at, viz. to exasperat the minds of the people against their lawfull Soverain, so to keep up the spirite of Rebellion in the nation by the same arts which first serued to raise and introduce it. Besides, he passed over in silence some materiall circumstances well known to him, which thô·they made not much to the busines of the Court who minded only the condemnation of the Prisoners, and the setting forth the conspiracy in the

* *Magdalen College Register*, vol. IV, pp. 137–47.

265

blackest colours, yet would have served, had they been faithfully related, to give great light to the impartiall truth of that whole affaire. When I was sent (as he has it in his narrative) with a commission to St. Germans to fixe the time and number of men for the King's descent in England, thô the busines of attempting upon the person of the P. of O. had been often agitated before that time by him and some others, as appeares by the evidence given by him and taken, he could, had he so pleased, have given the reason why no proposall of that nature was putt into my instructions; for which indeed no other reason can be given but the trew one, viz. that such offers formerly made had allways been rejected by his majesty. And accordingly I now solemnly averre upon the word of a Christian, and of a dying man, that when I came to St. Germans with the proposalls I was commission'd to make about the King's landing, ther was not the least mention made ther, on any side, of an attempt upon the person of the P. of O.

'Mr. Porter could have allso told that he himself was a principall adviser to make use of Sir George Barclay's Commission which was in terms only to *levy war against the P. of O. and his Adherents,* as a warrant to attempt the seising on his person, supposing (with good reason), that nothing would more facilitate and secure the King's intended landing in order to the recovery of his Right. And I think t'is obvious to every understanding, that since Mr. Porter was allways a principall Manager in the designs of bringing back the King, had ther been ever any particular order or commission sent from St. Germans to attempt upon the person of the P. of O., he certainly must have seen or known it, and when he became an evidence he would as certainly have declared it to his new masters, from whom he expected his pardon and reward: since that would have pleased them better then all he could say besides. What I have hitherto sayd, is not with design to throw off any seeming guilt from myself, and to lay it upon others, but to sett matters of fact, as neer as I can, in their trew light.

'As to my owne particular, since I am to passe within few days, or rather houres, out of this transitory world into an other which will have no end, and wher I must stand or fall according to the state and condition of my soule (good or bad) at the time of that dreadfull passage, I shall be very carefull to be exact and sincere in the account I give you of the motives and reasons which prevailed upon me to engage in this undertaking. I can not say by way of excuse (as others perhaps may do) that I did it rashly or ignorantly; for it was after long thinking, and with a full conviction of my judgement, not only as to the lawfulnes, but allso as to the expediency, of the enterprise, that I joyn'd in it, I very well know that many things in themselves may be lawfull which in some circumstances are not fitt, and therfor ought not, to be done, wherfor to vindicate myself, I shall in the first place lay down the reasons which convinc'd me as to the lawfullnes of the action, and in the next place relate the motives which induc'd me to beleeve it in the present juncture no lesse expedient then lawfull to be undertaken. Nor shall I much concern myself for the censures of that sort of men who judge no otherwise of things then by their event, which alone determines them, without looking any farther, to cry Hosanna, or

Crucify, to applaud or condemn one and the same action. I only desire to justify myself to the reasonable part of mankind, who judge not of actions by Passion, Interest, or Successe, but by their conformity to the strict rules of Justice and Reason; and to their judgment I willingly submitt the reputation I shall leaue behind me.

'The P. of O. in reference to the King is to be considered under a double quallification, of an Enemy, and of an Usurper. Take him first under the single notion of an Enemy, and it must be allow'd, ther is no example in all history of any one so foule, so perfidious and so trecherous as he has been and still is torde his Majesty. When ther was no appearance but of a declar'd mutuall freindship, made inviòlable by all the tyes of Nature and Consanguinity, sound and sincere on his majestys part, tho' hollow and trecherous on the other, that Prince first corrupts and debauches the King's sworn subjects and servants (I am loth to say his very Children) by false suggestions and deluding promises; Next, without any collour of wrong done him, or injury received, he invades the kingdom of his uncle and father in law with armed force, drives him from his court at White-hall, clapps guards upon his person, and when his Majesty saved himself out of their hands, an assembly of profligate emissarys, proper tooles for such a worke, by a strange mixture of nonsense and treason, vote his withdrawing for the recovery of his Liberty to be an Abdication of the Crown.

'Thes were his steps when he first enterd into open hostillity against the King, since which time He with his janisarys, both of the sword and the gown, has continu'd an unhuman War without quarter to any of his Majestys loyall subjects by land or by sea that are found ingagd in his seruice. Now I desire to know, according to all the rules of Justice and Laws of nations, what measures ought to be kept with such an Enemy: shall it be lawfull for the P. of Orange, born a subject and a servant to the High and Mighty States, trecherously to invade the dominions of a lawfull King, and in conjunction with Rebells and Traitours to dispossesse not only him of the Crown but as much as in them lyes, to exclude for ever his rightfull heires from their Succession; to hang, draw and quarter all loyall subjects that appear for him and assert his Right; to waste and destroy the English Nation in favour of his country-men the Dutch, that they may be inrich'd and have a wider barriere for their security? And after all this, shall this Perkin Warbeck of a King be held sacred in his Person, not to be touched, but suffered with impunety to massacre and destroy all the honest part of mankind? Others may judge of this as they please; for my owne part I am convinced that, as Tertulliam says, *In hostes publicos omnis homo est miles,* and that t'is the duty of every loyall subject that has the courage and the opportunity to do it, to rid the world of a Publick Enemy, who has kindled a War all over Europe, and sacrificed more lives of men to his insatiable ambition and usurpation, then all your Marius and Syllas, Cesars and Pompys putt together. And to justify my owne undertaking I shall only borrow the words of that famous Roman Mutius Scevola, so much applauded by all Antiquity, who in a like attempt upon the Tyrant Porsenna sayd only for his vindication, *Hostis hostem occidere volui.* And yet I expect that many honest and loyall men who live under the lash of the Usurper, some out of fear, and some for want of penetration and discernment between just and unjust, will as loudly condemn me as the greatest sticklers for the Usurpation, and call the attempt Assassination, Murdration, and what not. But I desire to know of thos Gentlemen how they would have call'd it if it had succeeded, and that therupon the King had been restored? And 2ly, how they would have call'd it had it been performed by an army of 20,000 men? Faire War, no doubt. What if with ten, what if with five thousand, and so downwards? To conclude what is lawfull and just to be done by many is likewise so by few. If Jonathan only with his squire, when he sett upon the camp of the Philistians, had mett their Generall in his tent, what quarter do you think he would have given him? And had he kill'd him with the rest, would any body dare call it an Assasination? So that t'is not the number but the cause that makes the action just or unjust, faire or fowl. Nor can any body think that the King and the Prince of Orange are not in a state of War, still on foot ever since that time of the Invasion, and, how great so ever the unequality of their forces may be, the Right of war equally subsists with the justice of his Majestys claime, and cannot determine but by his owne consent. Lastly, lett the freinds and Partisans of the P. of Orange give me any tollerable reason why it should be lawfull for their master in the midle of a full peace and all outward marks of freindship, fraudulenly and trecherously to sett upon the King without any preceding quarell or complaint, and why it may not be lawfull for his Majesty after such agressiòn, and so many injurys and indignitys received, to take any occasion of attacking such an Enemy?

'Hitherto I have considered the P. of Orange under the single quallification of an Enemy, explaining only what sort of enemy he is, and what I thought might be lawfully attempted against an enemy of his sort. It now remaines to take a view of him in his particular character of an Usurper, which in its self without any other aggravating circumstances includes the highest injustice and greatest wrong that can be done by man to man. For since of all worldly goods a Crown and Scepter are beyond any proportion the most estimable, it follows that an unjust ravisher of them is by infinite degrees more criminall and more punishable then any other robber or malefactor whatsoever. And wheras nothing can be more plain and evident then that King James the 2d is the trew and lawfull King of England, both by an indisputable right of succession, and by an actuall possession of the Crown, and by a generall recognition of the whole Kingdom who had sworn alleigeance to him, so by necessary consequence t'is no lesse manifest that the Prince of Orange, notwithstanding any apellation or title given him by Rebells at home or by interested Potentates abroad, is a downright Usurper: for I suppose no body will beleeve that ther accrued any right to Oliver Cromwell intit'ling him to the supreme Government of England, because under the name of Protector he exercised Kingly power at home, and was recognised as such by all the Crowned heads of Europe, who sent their embassadors and stoop'd as low to him as any of them now can do to the Prince of Orange. Therfor what ever may lawfully be attempted against the worst of Theeves and Robbers, not only may, but ought to, be attempted against him. For if, when my Neigbours' house is assaulted and broke into by highwaymen, I am bound by the laws of human society, which oblige all the members therof to a mutuall defense of one another, to succor and assiste him, as farr as I am able, to drive out the Robbers, and to take them, or kill them if nothing els will do, with how much more reason then am I bound to aide and assiste my lawfull souvrain by any meanes whatsoever to drive out an Usurper, the greatest and worst of robbers, exceeding them in guilt as much as a Kingdome exceeds in vallue a private family. This is what all that are born within his Majestys dominions are obliged to do by vertue as well of their naturall as of their sworn allegeance, such oths being explanatory and declarative of a duty inherent in every Subject to defend his majestys person, crown and dignity, against all enemys whatsoever; and against whom if not against an Invader and an Usurper?

'To me it appeares to be an evident demonstration, that since Justice, both Human and Divine, requires that hainous and publick crimes should not remain unpunished, and since of all other crimes that of Usurpation is the most hainous in itself, and the most pernitious in the consequences of it, ther must be some ways and means allowed by God and man for the punishment of it. Now wheras an Usurper in possession is without the reach of the Law, and by force and violence controles, and makes impossible all regular forms of a juditiall proceeding against him, it must follow, that every loyall subject, thô a private person, is a warrantable minister of justice against him; or els you must grant, that the greater any crime is the greater would be its impunity, then which nothing can be more contrary to Justice, and to all Laws Human and Divine. And this I take to be the trew reason of the above mentioned maxime of Tertullian, *That against a Publick Enemy, &c. every man is a soldier,* and consequently impowred to assault him, without being listed upon a Muster Roll.

'And indeed t'is absolutly necessary for the common peace and safety of mankind that this should be so, for, otherwise such is the pride of human nature and inclination to superiority, that without such a generall license of destroying notorious Usurpers, every ambitious man would allways be mackinating and caballing to gett the reines of power into his owne hands, wherby all setled Government would be overthrown, and the world involvd in a perpetuall civile war. This convincingly proves how great the necessity is that men by all possible meanes should be deterr'd from the pernitious crime of Usurpation, and that Usurpers ought to be expos'd (as wolves and wild beasts) to be sett upon and to have justice done on them by any person whatsoever. And what can a common Usurper expect, when Julius Cesar himself for usurping upon the freedom of the Roman Commonwealth could not scape the poniards of Brutus and Cassius, and others the best men of that time, and some them (by him reputed) his intimat freinds?

'To this may be added the authority of the learned Grotius an Author equally famous for erudition and moderation, and therfor received by all Partys, who in his book *de Jure Belli* tells us that when any one by an unjust war contrary to the law of nations shall usurp the Supreme Power, he may be lawfully killd; *jure potest occidi*, are his words, *a quolibet privato*, by every private person that owes allegeance to him who has the Right. T'is trew, he afterwards gives a caution that is should not be done without authority deriv'd from the Legall Proprietor; but then this plainly shews, that if what the Enemy labours to have beleved be trew, viz. that the King has given a Commission which extends to the seising on the person of the P. of Orange, no action can be more just or honorable then that for which I now stand condemnd.

'I find this letter grows to a greater length then I first intended, and takes up more of my time in writing it then I can well spare in my present circumstance, but having formerly often meditated upon this subject, when once enterd upon it I can hardly stop my pen from giving my thoughts their full vent. I shall therfor conclude in as few words as I can, with telling you the reasons which moved me to think the attempt at this time to have been no lesse proper and seasonable then lawfull. In the first place, I was certainly informd that measures were taken for the King's landing in England about the latter end of February, which I suppose was afterwards disappointed by the contrary winds which kept the Toulon fleet so long from coming into thes seas; whereby the Enemy had notice and time given him to hasten out ships to prevent the design. I was allso told that the King was to land with a body only of ten thousand men, upon assurances given him of risings in England, and that he should be joyned at his landing with a body of two thousand horse. And wheras I was in my owne judgement perswaded that his Majesty would hazard his person too much by ventring into England with that number of men, that small reliance was to be made upon risings, so uncertain in themselves, and so easily dissipated by any regular troops, and that 2000 horse a e much more easily promised then brought together; upon all thes considerations I concluded that to make the King's landing safe and effectuall, ther was no better way then to seise and secure the person of the P. of Orange, which I thought the best peece of service that could be done to my King and Country in restoring the one to his Right, and the other to that Peace and plenty it injoyed in the time of his reign.

'Before I close this letter I must obviate an objection to which both you and others may perhaps think me liable in what I have allredy sayd. The question may be ask'd me, why I ingag'd in an attempt of this nature not only without any spetiall leave or order from the King, but after having been told how averse he formerly has been to propositions made him upon the same subject? To this I reply that, as to the doing it without an express leave, some actions ther are which carry with them their owne leave, as in the case above mentioned of robbers breaking in to my neighbour's house, I may help to drive them out without the previous cerimony of asking leave. And this holds much more strongly in our present case, wher the distance of place and other impediments made it unpracticable to send for leave and not loos the occasion. But then, as to the reluctancy which his Majesty has formerly shewn when such offers have been made him, thô it ought to be cheifly attributed to mildnes and goodnes of nature, which is more conspicuous in him then in any Prince or person living, yet regard allso must be had to the difference of times and circumstances; and it may reasonably be presumed that what in one juncture his Majesty had rejected he might in an other accept, when his owne and the Publick good necessarily required it. For I could not understand it in such a manner as if he had given a generall prohibition that at no time the person of the Prince of Orange should to touch'd, as David did in the case of his son Absalon, without which the action of Joab had certainly been the best service he ever did his master, whatever it may be reputed notwithstanding the prohibition.

'Lastly, as to the rightfulnes and legallity of the action in itself, no body that beleives his Majesty to be the lawfull King of England can doubt but that in vertue of his Commission to levy war against the P. of Orange and his adherents, the setting upon his person is justifyable as well by the Lawes of the land duely interpreted and executed, as by the Law of God.

'Thus I putt my justification into your hands, as my best freind, to be made use of in time and place according to your discretion, so as neither yourself nor any honest man may be harm'd by it.

'This is the last farewell of

Yr. &c.'

Appendix 2

SIR JOHN FRIEND'S PAPER*

Knowing that I must immediately give an account to God of all my actions, and that I ought to be specially careful of what I say in these last hours, I do solemnly profess, that what I here deliver is from my very soul, with all the heartiness and sincerity of a dying Christian.

The cause I am brought hither to suffer for, I do firmly believe to be the cause of God and true religion, and, to the best and utmost of my knowledge and information, agreeable to the laws of the land, which I have evermore heard do require a firm duty and allegiance to our sovereign; and that as no foreign, so neither any domestic power can alienate our allegiance. For it is altogether new and unintelligible to me, that the king's subjects can depose and dethrone him on any account, or constitute any that have not an immediate right in his place. We ought, I think, not to do this; and surely, when it is done, to assist him in the recovery of his right, is justifiable, and our duty. And however things may seem at present, I do believe, I am sure I heartily pray, that he shall be one day restored to his rightful throne and dominions.

As for any sudden descent of his majesty upon these his dominions, in order to the recovery of them, I declare I had no certain knowledge of it; nor can I tell what grounds there was to believe it, so little reason had I to be in a present preparation for it. I suppose it is not expected I should here endeavour to clear myself of the Assassination, which was not the thing alleged against me; however, it was mentioned, through what means I know not. As it was insinuated to my disadvantage, I forgive such as were therein instrumental; and I do also, from the very bottom of my soul, freely forgive, and beg of God to do so too, such as were any ways accessary towards the taking away my life, which I really look upon to be their misfortune more than mine.

I profess myself, and I thank God I am so, a member of the Church of England, though, God knows, a most unworthy and unprofitable part of it; of that church which suffers so much at present for a strict adherence to loyalty, the laws and Christian principles; for this I suffer, and for this I die.

Though I have a perfect charity for people of all professions, and do heartily wish well, and would endeavour to do so to all my fellow-subjects, of what persuasion soever. And indeed I have met with a great deal of uprightness and sincerity among some people of very different opinions in religious matters.

* ST, vol. xiii, pp. 136–8.

272

Appendix 2

And I hope and desire it may not be taken as an uncharitable censure, or undue reflection, that I objected to the legality of popish evidence, being advised so to do for my better security, upon the foundation of a statute-law.

Having owned myself a member of the Church of England, I must take this opportunity, and I do it for God's glory, to apply myself to you that are royalists of that church, and of the same faith and principles with myself: and I beg of you, for God's sake, and the love of your souls, to be very constant and serious in all religious offices, and holy duties, of divine worship and service, which I have too much neglected, as I own to my great sorrow: let no excuse, no dangers, prevent or hinder you in the most necessary and serious matters; and be, I beseech you, very careful and circumspect in all your actions, behaviour, and conversation, as I earnestly exhorted all that came to me.

I have, I thank God, a great deal of satisfaction in my present sufferings, and have found it so ever since I have been under them: And blessed be God it doth continually increase upon me. And I do now lay down my life with all cheerfulness and resignation, in sure and certain hope of a resurrection to eternal life, through our Lord Jesus Christ, through whose merits alone I hope for the pardon of my sins, and the salvation of my soul.

And so, O Lord! into thy hands I commend my spirit; for thou hast redeemed me, O Lord! thou God of truth!

And I do heartily and humbly beseech the Almighty God, and my most gracious Father, to forgive and bless this sinful nation; deliver it from the guilt of rebellion, blood, and perjury, that is now on all sides more than ever, and from all those other heinous sins which cry aloud. Preserve and bless this Church. Comfort our distressed king; restore him to his right, and his mis-led subjects to their allegiance: bless also his royal consort, our gracious queen Mary; his royal highness the prince of Wales, that he may grow in stature, and in favour with God and man; support and strengthen all those that suffer in any kind for a good cause; give them patience under all their afflictions, and a happy deliverance out of them. Forgive all mine enemies.

Pardon my former neglect and remissness in religious worship, and holy duties, and all the sins I have been guilty of to this very moment. Consider my contrition, accept my tears; and now thou art pleased to take me hence, take me into thy favour, and grant that my soul may be without spot presented unto thee, through the merits of thy most dearly beloved Son, Jesus Christ our Lord. Amen. JOHN FREIND.

Notes

Abbreviations

CJ   *Journal of the House of Commons*
CSPD   *Calendar of State Papers, Domestic*
CTB   *Calendar of Treasury Books*
HMC   *Historical Manuscripts Commission Reports*
LJ   *Journal of the House of Lords*
PwA   Portland Papers
PRO   Public Record Office
ST   *State Trials*

Note. Biographical details for minor sources and MSS. references are given in full. Others will be found in the Bibliography.

1. The genesis of Jacobitism

1 Bossy, p. 422; Kenyon, p. 28.
2 E. M. Thompson (ed.), *The Correspondence of the Family of* Hatton (Camden Society Publications, 1878), N.S., vol. I, p. 157.
3 Reresby, p. 586.

2. King James's men

1 E. Curtis, *History of Ireland*, 6th edn (London, 1964), p. 273.
2 *HMC* Finch, vol. V, pt 4, p. 204.
3 John D'Alton, *King James's Irish Army List (1689)*, 2nd edn (2 vols., Dublin, 1860), vol. I, pp. 246–7.
4 *CSPD*, 1694, p. 262.
5 Luttrell, vol. II. p. 95.
6 Porteus, p. 35.
7 *Ibid*, p. 33.
8 Prideaux, p. 151.
9 Luttrell, vol. II. p. 598.
10 Raparee: a short spear or pike used by Irish soldiers.
11 Macpherson, vol. I, p. 458.
12 Burnet, vol. II, p. 305.
13 *ST*, vol. XIII, p. 1320.

3. A quartet of conspirators

1   J. and J. A. Venn (compilers), *Alumni Cantabrigiensis* (Cambridge University Press, 1922), pt 1, vol. II, p. 235.
2   Cibber, vol. I, p. 56.
3   *Ibid.*
4   *ST*, vol. XIII, pp. 590–1; *HMC Lords*, vol. II, p. 280.
5   Cibber, vol. I, p. 99.
6   Theophilus Lucas, *Memoirs of the Lives of the Gamesters* (1714). Republished in C. H. Hartmann (ed.), *Games and Gamesters of the Restoration* (London, 1930), p. 260.
7   *CSPD*, 1684, p. 134.
8   *Ibid,* p. 180.
9   *Ibid,* p. 221.
10 *CSPD*, 1685, p. 362.
11 Cibber, vol. I, p. 57.
12 Anon. (London, 1707).
13 Ailesbury, vol. I, p. 352.
14 *Magdalen College Register*, N.S., vol. IV (Oxford University Press, 1904), ed. W. D. Macray, p. 135.
15 In the *Dictionary of National Biography* Charnock is said to have joined the catholic priesthood. This is incorrect; see *Magdalen College Register*, vol. IV, p. 136.
16 For a full account of James's attempt to convert Magdalen College, see Bloxam, *Magdalen College;* see also *ST*, vol. XII, pp. 1–111.
17 John D'Alton *King James's Irish Army List (1689)*, 2nd edn (2 vol., Dublin, 1860), vol. I, p. 246.
18 Ailesbury, vol. I, p. 353.
19 Trumbull Add. MS. 116, 6 March 1696, 9 March 1696, Berks. Co. Record Office.
20 Burnet, vol. IV, p. 298.
21 Ailesbury, vol. I, p. 368.
22 *ST*, vol. XIII, p. 782n.
23 Ailesbury, vol. I, p. 368.
24 *Ibid,* p. 369.
25 Charles Dalton, *English Army Lists and Commission Registers 1661–1714*, (6 vols., London, 1892–1904), vol. II, p. 185.
26 Luttrell, vol. II, p. 448–9.
27 *Warwickshire County Records,* vol. V, pp. xxv–vi; Thomas May, *The Visitation of the County of Warwick* (1682), ed. W. Harry Rylands (Harleian Society Publications, London, 1911), vol. LXII, pp. 82–3.
28 Bulkington Parish Register, War. Co. Record Office.
29 *Alumni Cantabrigiensis* (Cambridge University Press, 1922), pt 1, vol. III, p. 311.
30 *Calendar of the Inner Temple Records,* ed. F. A. Indewick (London, 1896), vol. VII, p. 37.
31 Fiennes, p. 307.
32 Evelyn, p. 1063.
33 Luttrell, vol. IV, p. 159.
34 Joseph L. Chester, *London Marriage Licences, 1521–1869*, ed. J. Foster (London, 1887), p. 1021.
35 Longman, p. 29.
36 Cat. 19, no. 37572, Herts. Co. Record Office.
37 May, *Visitation of the County of Warwick*, pp. 82–3.
38 PRO, E. 179. 6792. 15405.
39 Bushey Parish Register, Herts. Co. Record Office.
40 Burnet, vol. IV, p. 305.
41 Peter Le Neve, *Pedigree of Knights* (Harleian Soc. Publications, London, 1873), vol. VIII, p. 351.
42 Ailesbury, vol. I, p. 370.
43 *CTB*, 1679–80, 224–5.
44 T. D. Hardy (ed.), *Catalogue of the Lords Chancellors* (London, 1843), p. 113.

4. The secret armies

1 Beloff, p. 84.
2 *CSPD*, 1691–2, p. 500.
3 *ST*, vol. xii, p. 1320.
4 *Ibid*, p. 1321.
5 *Ibid*, p. 1334.
6 *Ibid*, p. 1315.
7 *Ibid*, p. 1348.
8 *Ibid*, p. 1352.
9 *Ibid*, p. 1321.
10 Macpherson, vol. i, p. 465.
11 *Ibid*, p. 487.
12 *Ibid*, p. 474.
13 Luttrell, vol. iii, p. 314.
14 PwA, no. 2486; HMC Buccleugh, vol. ii, pt 1, p. 321.
15 *ST*, vol. xii, p. 1332.
16 Luttrell, vol. ii, p. 450.
17 Ailesbury, vol. i, p. 273.
18 *ST*, vol. xii, p. 1334.
19 Ailesbury, vol. i, p. 273.
20 *Ibid*, p. 257.
21 A full account of the Lancashire Plot trials will be found in W. Beaumont (ed.), 'The Jacobite trials of Manchester', in *Proc. of the Chetham Soc.*, vol. xxviii, 1864.
22 *Trans. of the Hist. Soc. of Lancs and Ches.*, vol. cxv, pp. 91–106.
23 Smith, pp. 51–3.

5. 'If it be not now, yet it will come'

1 Burnet, vol. iv, p. 242.
2 *Ibid*, p. 243.
3 van de Zee, p. 476.
4 Burnet, *An Essay on the Memory of the Late Queen* (London, 1695), p. 86.
5 Evelyn, p. 990.
6 *LJ*, vol. xv, 31 December 1694.
7 Christopher Hill, p. 184.
8 Luttrell, vol. ii, p. 571.
9 *Ibid*, p. 610.
10 *ST*, vol. xii, p. 1332.
11 *Ibid*.
12 *Ibid*.
13 *Ibid*.
14 Kingston, pp. 165–8.
15 Clarke, vol. ii, p. 537.
16 *ST*, vol. xii, pp. 1291–8.
17 Ailesbury, vol. i, pp. 353–4.
18 *Ibid*.
19 *Ibid*.
20 *ST*, vol. xii, p. 1304.
21 *CSPD*, 1696, pp. 109–10.
22 *ST*, vol. xii, p. 1304.
23 Ailesbury, vol. i, p. 354.
24 *CSPD*, 1696, p. 110.
25 Macpherson, vol. i, p. 513.
26 *Ibid*.
27 *Ibid*, pp. 506–9.
28 *Ibid*, p. 516.
29 *ST*, vol. xii, p. 1305.
30 Turner, p. 459.
31 Clarke, vol. ii, p. 259.
32 Luttrell, vol. iii, p. 484.
33 *Ibid*, p. 512.
34 Ferguson, p. 115.
35 (MS) Locke, c. 17, fol. 37.
36 *ST*, vol. xii, pp. 1334–5.
37 *ST*, vol. xiii, pp. 98–9.
38 *ST*, vol. xii, pp. 1334–5.

6. 'King James is a coming'

1 Burnet, vol. iv, p. 289.
2 *Ibid*.
3 *ST*, vol. xii, p. 1332.
4 Clarke, vol. ii, p. 538.
5 *Ibid*, p. 539.
6 *Ibid*, pp. 541–2.
7 *CSPD*, 1696, p. 96.
8 Clarke, vol. ii, p. 546.

9 *ST*, vol. xii, p. 1328.
10 PwA, no. 1436.
11 *ST*, vol. xii, pp. 1336–9.
12 Ailesbury, vol. i, p. 318.
13 *Ibid.*
14 *Ibid*, p. 317.
15 *ST*, vol. xii, pp. 1323–4.
16 *Ibid*, p. 1325.
17 Macpherson, vol. i, p. 540.
18 Clarke, vol. ii, p. 547.
19 *Ibid*, p. 548.
20 *ST*, vol. xii, 1329.
21 Clarke, vol. ii, p. 547.
22 *Ibid*, p. 548.
23 *ST*, vol. xiii, p. 87.

24 *CSPD*, 1696, p. 112; *Magdalen College Register*, ed. W. D. Macray n.s., vol. iv (Oxford University Press, 1904), pp. 137–8.
25 Clarke, vol. ii, p. 548.
26 *Postman*, no. 128, 3–5, March 1696.
27 Berwick, vol. i, p. 132.
28 *Ibid*, p. 134.
29 *Ibid*, p. 135.
30 PwA, no. 2499.
31 *ST*, vol. xii, p. 1339.
32 *Postman*, no. 128, 5 March 1696.

7. 'A hunting we will go'

1 Smith, p. 54.
2 Luttrell, vol. ii, p. 189.
3 *ST*, vol. xii, p. 1335.
4 *ST*, vol. xiii, p. 93.
5 *ST*, vol. xii, p. 1341.
6 *Ibid*, p. 1335.
7 Luttrell, vol. ii, p. 437.
8 *ST*, vol. xii, p. 1357.
9 PwA, no. 2473.
10 *Ibid*, no. 2482.
11 *ST*, vol. xiii, p. 1357.
12 *Ibid*, p. 1301.
13 Clarke, vol. ii, pp. 549–50.
14 *ST*, vol. xii, p. 1303.
15 Clarke, vol. ii, p. 550.
16 *ST*, vol. xiii, p. 311.
17 *ST*, vol. xii, pp. 1313–14.
18 *Ibid*, p. 1308.
19 Abbadie, p. 143.
20 *ST*, vol. xii, p. 1330.
21 *Ibid*, p. 1306.
22 *Ibid*, p. 1307.

23 *Ibid*, p. 1326.
24 Clarke, vol. ii, p. 548.
25 *ST*, vol. xii, p. 1335.
26 Lerrying trumpet: perhaps a misprint for 'levying trumpet', presumably a bugle.
27 *ST*, vol. xii, p. 1411.
28 *Ibid*, p. 1422.
29 *Ibid*, p. 1329.
30 *ST*, vol. xiii, p. 310.
31 *ST*, vol. xii, p. 1317.
32 *HMC* Downshire, vol. i, pt 2, p. 623; PwA, no. 2506.
33 *HMC* Downshire, vol. i, pt 2, p. 623.
34 *ST*, vol. xiii, p. 96.
35 *ST*, vol. xii, p. 1312.
36 *ST*, vol. xiii, p. 353.
37 *ST*, vol. xii, p. 1326.
38 *Ibid*, p. 1308.
39 *Ibid*, p. 1310.

8. The betrayal

1 Taking physic: usually a strong purgative, which confined the taker to his house for twenty-four hours. This was a common practice. Seventeenth-century diet, surprisingly, seems to have been rather constipating.
2 *ST*, vol. xii, pp. 1335–6.
3 *Ibid*, p. 1314.
4 *Ibid*, p. 1343.

5 *Ibid.*
6 *ST*, vol. xiii, p. 101.
7 *ST*, vol. xii, p. 1319.
8 *ST*, vol. xiii, p. 88.
9 *ST*, vol. xii, p. 1313.

10 *Ibid*, p. 1425.
11 *Ibid*, p. 1425n.
12 *Ibid*, p. 1418.
13 *Ibid*, p. 1425n.
14 *CSPD*, 1696, p. 130.

9. 'Let them see how strictly we are united'

1 *CJ*, vol. xi, 24 February 1695.
2 *Ibid.*
3 *HMC* Hastings, vol ii, p. 259.
4 Burnet, vol. iv, p. 300.
5 *CJ*, vol. xi, 4 April 1696.
6 *CSP America and Indies*, 1696–7, p. 5.
7 *Ibid*, p. 492.
8 MS. Locke, c.17, fol. 37.
9 Evelyn, p. 1004.
10 *CJ*, vol. xi, 7 April 1696.
11 *Postman*, no. 127, 2 March 1696.
12 *CSPD*, 1696, p. 63.
13 *Ibid*, p. 53.
14 *Ibid*, p. 59.

15 *Ibid.*
16 *Ibid.*
17 *HMC* Downshire, vol. i, pt. 2, pp. 628–9.
18 *Postman*, no. 134, 19 March 1696.
19 *CSPD*, 1696, p. 53.
20 *Postman*, no. 125, 26–27 February 1696.
21 *HMC* Var. Coll., vol. viii, p. 81.
22 Evelyn, p. 1008.
23 *CJ*, vol. xi, 29 February 1696.
24 *Postman*, no. 128, 5 March 1696.
25 *HMC* Downshire, vol. i, pt 2, p. 624.
26 *Ibid*, p. 626.

10. The hunters hunted

1 Ailesbury, vol. i, p. 359.
2 *ST*, vol. xii, pp. 1336–41.
3 *CSPD*, 1696, p. 52.
4 Japikse (ed.), vol. 24, p. 669. The note is signed 'P' and is mistakenly attributed to Porter, but from the context can only be from Prendergrass.
5 *Postman*, no. 126, 27 Februa 1696; *CSPD*, 1696, p. 56.
6 *CTB*, 1695–6, p. 1345.
7 Japikse (ed.), vol. 23, p. 178.
8 *CSPD*, 1699–1700, p. 366.
9 *CTB*, 1695–6, p. 1362.
10 *Ibid*, p. 1345.
11 *HMC* Downshire, vol. i, pt 2, p. 627.
12 Brice Blair's depositions, *ST*, vol. xii, pp. 1317–23, 1346–58.
13 *Flying Post*, no. 129, 10–12 March 1696.

14 *ST*, vol. xiii, p. 130.
15 *Postman*, no. 128, 5 March 1696.
16 PRO E. 179.C. 15405.
17 *CSPD*, 1696, p. 72.
18 *Ibid*, p. 90.
19 *ST*, vol. xii, p. 1312.
20 'Rector Ibbetson's Journal'. Unpublished MS., p.5. Information from Grant Longman.
21 *Flying Post*, no. 129, 10–12 March 1696.
22 *CTB*, 1695–6, p. 1362.
23 Bernardi, Parts of autobiography reprinted in *ST*, vol. xiii.
24 *CSPD*, 1696, p. 67.
25 PwA, no. 2485.
26 Ailesbury, vol. i, pp. 287–8.
27 *CSPD*, 1699–1700, p. 366.
28 *ST*, vol. xii, pp. 1304–5.

11. 'The highest crime'

1 *ST*, vol. XII, pp. 1443–4.
2 *Report of all Cases Determined by Sir John Holt, Knt. from 1688 to 1710* (London, 1737), pp. 680–1.
3 The wording of the sentence was not changed until 1914.
4 Kenyon, p. 132.
5 *ST*, vol. X, p. 267.
6 *ST*, vol. XII, p. 664.
7 Trial of Treasons Act, 7 & 8 Will. III. Cap. 3. 1696.

8 *HMC* Downshire, vol. I, pt 2, p. 690.
9 *Ibid*, p. 625.
10 Burnet, IV, p. 302.
11 Macaulay, vol. III, p. 278.
12 *Tatler*, no. 14, 1710.
13 *Poems on Affairs of State, from 1620 to 1707.* Vol. IV (London, 1716), p. 327.
14 Edward Foss, vol. VII, p. 704.
15 *CSPD*, 1696, p. 73.
16 *Ibid*.
17 *ST*, vol. XII, p. 1385.

12. The trial of Charnock, King and Keyes

1 There is a full report of this trial, with the prisoners' last statements, in *ST*, vol. XII, pp. 1379–1464.
2 Ailesbury, vol. I, p. 352.
3 Burnet, vol. IV, p. 301.
4 Macaulay, vol. IV, p. 221.

5 Trumbull Add. MS. 116, 14–15 March 1696, Berks. Co. Record Office.
6 Macaulay, vol. IV, p. 224.
7 Evelyn, p. 1005.
8 *Flying Post*, no. 132, 17–19 March 1696.
9 Fiennes, p. 314.
10 *ST*, vol. XII, pp. 1462–4.

13. The trials of Sir John Friend and Sir William Parkyns

1 There is a full report of Sir John's trial in *ST*, vol. XIII, pp. 1–64.
2 *CSPD*, 1696, p. 92.
3 Macaulay, vol. IV, p. 226.
4 *CSPD*, 1696, p. 88. (Entry book no. 346, p. 280.)
5 Munteith, Monteith; a punch-bowl with a scalloped brim, also used for cooling and carrying glasses (*O.E.D.*).
6 *CSPD*, 1696, p. 109.

7 Sir Henry Chauncey, *The History and Antiquities of Hertfordshire* (London, 1826), vol. II, p. 460.
8 The last man to be condemned under the Statute of 25 Edward III was Roger Casement, executed 1916; but he was Irish.
9 There is a full report of Sir William Parkyns's trial and his execution with Sir John Friend in *ST*, vol. XIII, pp. 63–140.

14. An execution and its aftermath

1 *HMC* Downshire, vol. I, pt 2, p. 690.

2 *Postman*, no. 139, 28 March 1696.

3 Smith, p. 139.
4 *ST*, vol. XIII, pp. 408–9.
5 *CJ*, vol. XI, 1 April 1696.
6 *Ibid*, 2 April 1696.
7 Burnet, vol. IV, p. 306.
8 Macaulay, vol. IV, p. 225.
9 *ST*, vol. XIII, pp. 406–8.
10 See report of executions of Turner, Langhorn, Green *et al.* after the Popish Plot trials. *ST*, vol. VII.
11 James H. Wilson, *Temple Bar: the City's Golgotha* (London, 1853), p. 22.

12 Evelyn, p. 1005.
13 *HMC* Var. Coll., vol. VIII, p. 82.
14 Sir John Friend's statement is printed in full as appendix 2.
15 *ST*, vol. XIII, p. 410.
16 *Ibid*.
17 Burnet, vol. IV, p. 307.
18 *ST*, vol. XIII, pp. 408–11.
19 *Ibid*, pp. 411–13.
20 *Ibid*, pp. 413–20.
21 T. Lathbury, *History of the Non-Jurors* (London, 1845), p. 169; *ST*, vol. XIII, pp. 420–52.

15. The trials of Rookwood, Cranburne and Lowick

1 The preliminary hearing and the three trials are fully reported in

ST, vol. XIII, pp. 139–312.
2 Ryzneck, p. 23.

16. Final payments

1 Reported in full in *ST*, vol. XIII, pp. 397–406.
2 Reported in full in *ST*, vol. XIII, pp. 311–398.
3 Ailesbury, vol. I, p. 395.
4 *CSPD*, 1696, p. 218.
5 *Ibid*, p. 222.
6 PwA, no. 1456.
7 *CSPD*, 1696, p. 399.
8 *ST*, vol. XIII, p. 589–90.
9 Nicholson and Turberville, p. 109, n.1.
10 *CSPD*, 1696, p. 223.
11 *Ibid*, p. 218.
12 Carte MS. 208, fol. 178v, Bodleian Library, Oxford.
13 Burnet, vol. IV, p. 325.
14 Reported in full, in *ST*, vol. XIII, pp. 537–758.
15 Burnet, vol. IV, p. 327.
16 Reported in full in *ST*, vol. XIII, pp. 759–88.

17 Bernardi, pp. 133–4.
18 *CTB*, vol. XI, p. 134.
19 *ST*, vol. XII, p. 1421n.
20 *CTB*, vol. XI, pp. 113, 134.
21 Luttrell, vol. IV, p. 157.
22 *CTB*, vol. XV, p. 383.
23 *CSPD*, 1699–1700, p. 133.
24 Quoted in Wilson, p. 124.
25 *HMC* Hastings, vol. II, p. 272.
26 *CSPD*, 1699–1700, p. 366.
27 PRO, T.54. 17. 132. The account does not specify sums paid to each individual.
28 *CSPD*, 1696, p. 98.
29 John Nichols, *History and Antiquities of Leicestershire*, vol. V (London, 1795–1815), p. 469.
30 *CTB*, vol. XVI, p. 224.
31 *HMC* Bath, vol. III, p. 210.
32 Berwick, p. 156.
33 van der Zee, p. 482.

Select Bibliography

Primary sources

Abbadie, Jacques, *A History of the Late Conspiracy against the King*, London, 1697.

Ailesbury, Thomas Bruce, Earl of, *Memoirs*. 2 vols., Roxburghe Club, London, 1890.

Bernardi, John, *A Short History of the Life of Major John Bernardi*. London, 1729.

Berwick, James Fitzjames, Duke of, *Memoirs*. 2 vols., London, 1779.

Blackmore, Sir Richard, *A True and Impartial History of the Conspiracy . . . Against King William in the year 1695–6*. London, 1723.

Burnet, Gilbert, *A History of My Own Time*. 4 vols., London, 1823.

Calamy, Edmund, *An Historical Account of My Own Time*. London, 1830.

Cibber, Colley, *An Apology for the Life of Colley Cibber*. 2 vols., London, 1925.

Clarke, James Stanier, *Life of James II*. 2 vols., London, 1816.

Evelyn, John, *Diary*. Ed. E. S. De Beer, Oxford University Press, 1959.

Fiennes, Celia, *The Journeys of Celia Fiennes*. London, 1947.

Halifax, George Savile, Marquess of, *Complete Works*. Ed. J. P. Kenyon, Harmondsworth, 1969.

Japikse, N. (ed.), *Correspondentie van Willem III en van Hans Willem Bentinck*. R. G. P. Kleine Serie, vols. 23 and 24, The Hague, 1927–37.

Kingston, Richard, *A True History of the Several Designs and Conspiracies . . . 1688 to 1697*. London, 1698.

Luttrell, Narcissus, *A Brief Relation of State Affairs*. 6 vols., Oxford, 1857.

Macpherson, James, *Original Papers Containing the Secret History of Great Britain*. 2 vols., London, 1775.

North, Roger, *Examen*. London, 1740.

Prideaux, Humphrey, *Letters to John Ellis 1674–1722*. Ed. E. M. Thompson, Camden Society Publications, n.s., vol. xv, 1875.

Reresby, Sir John, *Memoirs*. Ed. A. Browning, Glasgow, 1936.

Smith, Matthew, *Memoirs of the Secret Service*. London, 1699.

281

Select Bibliography

Calendars, MSS. and other sources.
Calendar of State Papers, Domestic.
Calendar of Treasury Books and Papers.
Historical Manuscripts Commission Reports:
Bath, vol. III
Buccleugh, vol. II, pt 1
Downshire, vol. I, pt 2
Finch, vol. V, pt 4
Hastings, vol. II
Lords, vol. II
Var. Coll., vol. VII
Journal of the House of Commons.
Journal of the House of Lords.
Locke MSS. Bodleian Library, Oxford.
Newspapers: *Flying Post, Postman.* Burney Collection, British Library.
Portland Papers, Nottingham University Library.
State Trials, vols. X, XII, XIII. eds. Cobbett, W. and Howell, T. B., 34 vols.,
    London, 1809–28.
Warwickshire County Records, vols. V, VI, VII. War. County Records
    Committee, 9 vols., 1935–.

Secondary sources

Ashley, Maurice, *Charles II; the Man and the Statesman,* London, 1971.
Baxter, S. B., *William III.* Harlow, Essex, 1966.
Beloff, Max, *Public Order and Public Disturbance 1660–1740.* Oxford
    Historical Series, 1938.
Bloxam, J. R. (ed.), *Magdalen College and King James II, 1686–1688.* Oxford
    Historical Society, 1886.
Bossy, John, *The English Catholic Community.* London, 1975.
Cardigan, Earl of, *The Life and Loyalties of Thomas Bruce, Earl of Ailesbury.*
    London, 1951.
Every, George, *The High Church Party, 1689–1719.* London, 1956.
Ferguson, James, *Robert Ferguson the Plotter.* Edinburgh, 1887.
Foss, Edward, *The Judges of England.* 9 vols., London, 1848–64.
Furley, O. W., 'The pope-burning processions of the late seventeenth century'.
    History, XLIV (1959), 16–23.
Haswell, Jock, *James II.* London, 1972.
Head, F. W., *The Fallen Stuarts.* Cambridge Historical Essays, vol. XII,
    Cambridge University Press, 1901.
Hill, Christopher, *The Century of Revolution.* London, 1974.
Holdsworth, Sir William, *A History of English Law.* Vol. VI, 14 vols.,
    London, 1922–64.
Holmes, Geoffrey (ed.), *Britain After the Glorious Revolution.* London, 1969.
'Religion and party in late Stuart England'. *Historical Association Pamphlets,*
    General series, London, 1975.

282

Select Bibliography

Horwitz, Henry, *Parliament, Policy and Politics in the Reign of William III.* Manchester University Press, 1977.

Jones, G. H., *The Mainstream of Jacobitism.* Cambridge, Mass., 1954.

Jones, J. R., *Country and Court.* London, 1978

Kenyon, J. P., *The Popish Plot.* Harmondsworth, 1972.

Lathbury, T., *History of the Non-Jurors.* London, 1845.

Longman, Grant, *Bushey Then and Now.* Booklet no. 5, Watford, 1969.

Macaulay, Thomas Babington, Lord, *The History of England.* 4 vols., London, 1967.

Marks, A., *Tyburn Tree, its History and Annals.* London, 1908.

Middleton, Dorothy, *Life of Charles, 2nd. Earl of Middleton.* St Albans, 1957.

Miller, John, *Popery and Politics in England, 1660–1688.* Cambridge University Press, 1973.

James II. A Study in Kingship. Hove, 1978.

Nicholson, T. C. and Turberville, A. S., *Charles Talbot, Duke of Shrewsbury.* Cambridge University Press, 1930.

Ogg, David, *England in the Reign of James II and William III.* Oxford University Press, 1969.

Oman, Carola, *Mary of Modena.* London, 1962.

Overton, John H., *The Non-Jurors, their Lives, Principles and Writings.* London, 1902.

Petrie, Sir Charles, *The Jacobite Movement.* London, 1959.

Porteus, T. C., 'New Light on the Lancashire Jacobite Plot'. *Trans. Lancs and Ches. Antiquarian Soc.,* vol. 50, 1934–5, pp. 1–64.

Robertson, C. G. (ed.), *Select Statutes, Cases and Documents, 1660–1832.* London, 1904.

Rubini, Denis, *Court and Country, 1688–1702.* London, 1968.

Ryzneck, S., 'The Statute of 1696. A pioneer measure in the reform of judicial procedure in England'. *Journal of Modern History,* II, 1 (1930), pp. 5–26.

Straka, Gerald M. (ed.), *The Revolution of 1688.* Lexington, Mass., 1963.

Turner, F. C., *James II.* London, 1948.

Western, J. R., *Monarchy and Revolution.* Poole, 1972.

Wilson, John H., *Mr. Goodman the Player.* Pittsburg, Pa., 1964.

Zee, van der, Henri and Barbara, *William and Mary.* London, 1975.

Index

Note: **bold type** indicates biographical references

285

Index

186–99, 206–9, 213–22, 238–46, 247–8
Hough, Dr John, 29–30
Hunt, James, smuggler, 90, 91, 154, 251
Hyde, Anne, Duchess of York, 5

Ireland, rebellion in, 13–14
Irish Regiment, 14

Jacobites: origins of party, 6; factions among, 16–17; in Lancashire, 18–19, 44; support for, 40–2, 60; taverns, 41, 109; in East Anglia, 44–5; delay rising, 89, 98–100; measures against, 149–50, 151–2; in Nottinghamshire, 152–3, 261, 264
James Francis Edward, Prince of Wales: birth, 8; recognised as heir by Louis XIV, 263
James II: 2nd marriage and conversion, 5; succeeds to throne, 7; character of, 7–8, 15–16; flees to France, 9; in Ireland, 14; rejects Plot, 62, 95; refused loan of French army, 70; personality changes in, 70–2; lent French army, 86; briefs his officers, 92, 101; returns to Saint-Germain, 148; last years and death, 262–4
Jeffreys, George, Baron Wem, 8, 179
Johnson, Father (alias Harrison), 49, 106
judges: appointment of, 182–3; on Special Commission, 183–4

Keyes, Thomas, 166, 133; arrested, 155; tried, 186–200; executed, 201
King, Captain Edward, 109; reconnoitres for ambush, 111–13; arrested, 155; tried, 186–200; executed, 201; last statement, 202
King James's Commissions: to Parker, 22; for officers, 24–39 passim; to Barkely, 89; general, for war, 96
Knightley, Alexander, 96, 109, 114,

117; arrested, 157; trial and pardon of, 247–8

La Hogue, Battle of, 19, 20
Lancashire Plot, 51–3, 162
La Trappe: James II at, 72
Louis XIV: and Charles II, 4–5; helps James II, 9; declares war on Dutch, 13; attempts invasion (1692), 19; refuses help to James II, 21, 46 70; attitude to James II, 72–3, 146, 263; assists James II, 87; delays invasion, 98, 101; cancels it, 147–8
Louise Marie, Princess, 9
Lowick, Major Robert, 118; arrested, 158; tried, 242–3; execution and last statement, 244–5
Lunt, James, 51–3

Magdalen College, 28–51
Manchester, Jacobite trials at, 51-2
Marlborough, John Churchill, 1st Duke of: deserts James, 9; suspected disaffection of, 19, 57; accused by Fenwick, 252
Marshall, 14
Marston Jabbett, 35; arms concealed at, 53–4, 129–30, 160–2, 216
Mary Beatrice of Modena: marries James Duke of York, 5, 6; birth of son to, 8; flees to France, 9; at Saint-Germain, 72
Mary II: a protestant, 5; marries William of Orange, 10; crowned with William, 10; dies, 55; character of, 56
Meldrum, Robert, 169, 255–6
Melfort, John Drummond, 1st Earl of, 16, 18, 21, 53
Middleton, Charles, 2nd Earl of, 16–17
Monmouth, James Scott, Duke of, 7
Mongomery, Charles Herbert, Viscount, 21, 23, 63–7 passim
Mortimer, Mrs, 30
Mountjoy, Mrs, 67, 248

Namur, victory of, 74

287

Index

288